Performing Under Pressure

Performing Under Pressure

The Science of Doing Your Best When It Matters Most

Hendrie Weisinger

J. P. Pawliw-Fry

CROWN
BUSINESS
NEW YORK

Published in the United States by Crown Business, an imprint of the Crown Publishing Group, a division of Random House LLC, a Penguin Random House Company, New York.

www.crownpublishing.com

CROWN BUSINESS is a trademark and CROWN and the Rising Sun colophon are registered trademarks of Random House LLC.

Crown Business books are available at special discounts for bulk purchases for sales promotions or corporate use. Special editions, including personalized covers, excerpts of existing books, or books with corporate logos, can be created in large quantities for special needs. For more information, contact Premium Sales at (212) 572-2232 or e-mail specialmarkets@randomhouse.com.

Library of Congress Cataloging-in-Publication Data

Weisinger, Hendrie.
 Performing under pressure : the science of doing your best
 when it matters most / Hendrie Weisinger, J. P. Pawliw-Fry
 pages cm
 1. Success—Psychological aspects. 2. Stress management.
 3. Performance anxiety. I. Pawliw-Fry, J. P. II. Title.
 BF637.S8W358 2015
 155.9'042—dc23 2014031662

ISBN 978-0-8041-3672-3

eBook ISBN 978-0-8041-3673-0

Printed in the United States of America

Jacket design by Gabriel Levine

10 9 8 7 6 5 4 3 2 1

First Edition

Hank: To the memories of my parents—they make me feel confident, optimistic, tenacious, and enthusiastic every day!—I was lucky.

JP: To Brigitte, Grace, and Westley: my confident, optimistic, tenacious, and enthusiastic kids!

CONTENTS

Performing Under Pressure

When you are on the witness stand in a courtroom, everything you say is recorded, interpreted, challenged, and judged against the letter of the law. A distorted fact, a failure to remember, the truth told unconvincingly, a stutter or two can all influence a verdict that brings irrevocable, life-changing effects to you and to others.

It is not surprising that such high drama is center stage in Pulitzer Prize–winning novels, Academy Award–winning films, and television Emmy winners, as seen through such unforgettable characters as Captain Queeg, Atticus Finch, Daniel Webster, Perry Mason.

Bob Andreatta, however, is not a fictional character but a flesh-and-blood human being. In his late forties with thick, wavy black hair and dark-framed glasses, Andreatta, a partner at KPMG, was being subpoenaed by the Securities Exchange Commission to give testimony on charges of backdating stock options at Apple and Pixar.

When we first met him in San Francisco in 2013, the experience had been permanently etched in his mind. He didn't need a Hollywood writer to dramatize his telling of what he'd gone through five minutes before he took the stand: "My head was exploding, the pressure was so extreme. If I was indicted or found culpable in any way, my reputation would be ruined, my credentials taken away, my ability to work in a public company gone. I felt like I might end up living in a van down by the river. I was afraid to say the wrong thing. I felt this was it, I was on the line."

Bob Andreatta had faced a particularly harrowing high-pressure moment—the outcome was *important* to him, the outcome was

uncertain, and he would be *accountable* and judged on the results. If there had ever been a time that Mr. Andreatta's performance mattered, in his mind, that was it.

We all experience moments of extreme pressure in our lives, times in which we feel like Mr. Andreatta—when we *have to* deliver the goods or suffer dire consequences. For most of us, these moments create a sense of dread.

Over the last twenty years, the two of us, one as a psychologist, one as a high-performance coach, and both as researchers and consultants, have collected a great deal of information about how people experience pressure.

Our research has been conducted all over the world via workshops, seminars, business school presentations, clinical therapy, coaching sessions, and consulting activities with all sorts of organizations, including the US Navy and Army; the CIA; NASA; the Federal Reserve Banking System; the EPA; the FBI; the Department of Labor; the National Institutes of Health; the IRS; NBA and NFL teams, Olympic athletes, and other elite athletes; Fortune 500 companies such as Goldman Sachs, Chubb Insurance, IBM, Estée Lauder, Avon, Intel, Merrill Lynch, SAP, Morgan Stanley, Bank of America, Medtronic, Prudential, Nationwide, State Farm, Johnson & Johnson, IBM, TRW, Hughes Aircraft, Hyatt, Microsoft, Pfizer, KPMG, and Fidelity; the Institute for Management Studies; the Security Industry Association; and the Young Presidents' Organization.

We have also undertaken a multiyear study of individuals who are under pressure and asked this question: What is it about the top 10 percent of the twelve thousand people (the top twelve hundred) we studied that helps them handle pressure more effectively and receive the most promotions? This wasn't just anecdotal; we used cutting-edge "360" assessment to ascertain what these people did differently. This 360 or multi-rater assessment is a method of systematically collecting observations about an individual's behavior and performance from a wide range of sources including peers, direct reports, managers, customers, and even family and friends (see Appendix A). This allows us to understand how an individual deals with pressure from a number of different data points as opposed to just relying on the person's

self-perception. Each of the twelve thousand people we studied was assessed by anywhere from six to fourteen people, so in total we had more than one hundred thousand people assess the twelve thousand subjects. We identified the top 10 percent based on their manager's performance ratings from all who assessed them. In addition, each month, JP's organization, the Institute for Health and Human Potential (IHHP), sends out short questionnaires to more than ten thousand individuals around the world, asking such questions as "Do you feel you work better under pressure?" "Are you more concerned with failing in a pressure moment or more focused on succeeding in one?" Responses from tens of thousands of individuals have helped us identify the pressure patterns and pressure management interventions.

Hendrie Weisinger developed the Weisinger Pressure Assessment and Inventory, a clinical assessment tool that provides important insights into how people experience, respond to, and can manage pressure more effectively (see Appendix B for the full Pressure Inventory questionnaire).

Over the last fifteen years years, we've also sifted through vast amounts of research on every aspect of performing under pressure, drawing from social and cognitive psychology, sports psychology, neuroscience, and clinical psychology.

The bottom line—pressure is the enemy of success: It undermines performance and helps us fail. When under pressure, air traffic controllers, pilots, and oil rig chiefs make errors in judgment. NBA players, World Cup soccer players, and champion golfers frequently miss their usual shot under pressure. ER doctors and nurses can make inappropriate decisions and incorrect diagnoses. Actors forget their lines, politicians forget their talking points or otherwise stumble and fumble. Corporate executives, managers, and sales professionals make poor decisions, and parents have less patience with their children. Pressure is more than a nemesis; it is a villain in our lives. Here are just some of the findings we've assembled over the last five years that we'll elaborate on throughout this book:

Pressure adversely impacts our cognitive success. There are many tools that make us successful. But at the top of the list are our judgment, decision-making, memory, and attention. Whether we are

adding up numbers, identifying relevant data, analyzing information, listening to a client, or appraising a job applicant, pressure negatively impacts us. A financial advisor, a real estate agent, or an attorney under pressure to produce can do disservice to a client. Your son or daughter under pressure in the classroom may miss answers he or she "knows" on the midterm or final.

Pressure downgrades our behavioral skills. Divers, mountain climbers, basketball and baseball players, golfers, field goal kickers, chess players, quarterbacks and their receivers, concert pianists, mechanics, construction workers—all have their psychomotor performance skills compromised under pressure. If you are parallel parking and feel pressure from an impatient driver behind you who can't go around, you'll likely hit the curb or cut the wheel too sharply and have to start over, delaying the other driver further and embarrassing yourself.

In pressure moments, most people perform below their capability. Are you one of those people who are amazed by those who seem to thrive under pressure? Well, you may want to reconsider that amazement. Contrary to conventional wisdom, we discovered that more often than not, when people want to do their best, they don't. Pro athletes rarely do better than their average in pressure moments, and most—even the great ones—do worse! The fact is, people *frequently* perform far below their capability in pressure moments. Parents may not expect their C students to ace the SATs, but many parents are in for a shock when their A student scores a hundred points or more lower than expected. Thousands of college graduates, and even seasoned managers, exit job interviews thinking, *I should have said . . .*

Pressure is often camouflaged. The influence of pressure on derailing your performance is often disguised. We have found that many conventional tools, such as incentives or praising results, used to motivate ourselves and others, and improve organizational effectiveness, are actually pressure traps; these disrupt performance, stimulate cheating, encourage absenteeism, and, most noticeably, intensify our daily feelings of pressure.

Today we feel increased pressure in our lives. In today's fast-paced world, where we are connected to our jobs and to our work 24/7,

pressure is almost unavoidable. Take a look at the comments of some of the people who have taken our Pressure Inventory:

> *Every day at work, I feel the pressure, like I'm being squeezed like an orange.*
> *It sounds like a cliché, but I feel my office is a pressure cooker.*
> *Every client call is critical. The pressure is relentless.*
> *I feel my life is under a deadline.*
> *Every day is do or die. I call it pressure to produce . . . that's what I feel every day. I have nothing left when I get home.*

We live in a high-pressure time, where every day we feel we are *on the line*. More than ever before, working folks *feel the heat* . . . *that they have to produce, perform, get results or else* . . . And so we do. Every decision, meeting, presentation, negotiation, or pitch that we make feels as if it has a major impact on our career. A single misworded or hasty e-mail can spell disaster. In an age where many of us can lose our jobs at any time, a single ill-considered utterance can derail years of hard work; think of Mitt Romney's now famous "47 percent" line in the 2012 presidential campaign.

Many factors have increased the perceived pressure in our lives: the recent economic meltdown, the fierce competition for jobs, the advent of the global economy, the erosion of job stability, the intensified competition to get into top colleges, universities, and graduate programs.

A manager of a prestigious Fifth Avenue store in New York City told us, "Every morning I wonder if I can meet our sales goals. The butterflies *start* right away." A financial advisor told us, "I worry about whether I can keep making my condo payments." We call this feeling *pressure anxiety*—the perpetual feeling of uncertainty, fear, even dread about whether or not you can produce, whether or not you have what it takes to make the grade, knowing that if you can't or don't, you might be "weeded out" or, at the very least, have your career or professional goals stymied.

There is a clear and present danger to pressure anxiety: It often becomes generalized to other aspects of our lives. The perpetual feeling that you have to perform, and the underlying doubts as to whether or

not you can continue to produce, lead to stressed conversations and relationships at home. Who wants to talk about a vacation or home improvement or grapple with medical or dental bills when all we experience is the pressure to finance them? Under pressure, parents often unleash their distress on their kids—making more demands, expressed with a shorter temper. Often the feelings become so unmanageable that emotional conflict is experienced regularly. All of a sudden, we feel as if we are under siege from every front. Considering the demographics that show that people are working longer hours, and that the working world is becoming more competitive, pressure anxiety is apt to become a contemporary plague.

Our Mission

A finding that continually intrigues us is that most of the thousands of individuals who've participated in our research take a *haphazard approach to managing pressure* in their lives. Very few think about how to handle pressure moments better—until it's too late. Few have strategies grounded in the latest science of the brain or in psychology. Like many of the Olympic athletes and businesspeople we have worked with, they simply model what they have observed from others and hope it works. Sometimes these strategies are helpful. But many times they are not. Our mission in this book is twofold:

First, to provide an easy-to-use playbook of *pressure solutions*—accessible strategies and techniques that individuals can use immediately to *depressurize* a situation—to immunize themselves against the sabotaging effects of pressure, so they can perform their best in those critical moments—a presentation, an interview, a test, a crucial negotiation, a sales call. Pressure solutions are short-term strategies for overcoming pressure.

There is an important caveat here which we will reiterate throughout the book. Managing the pressure of the moment *does not* necessarily equate to success. *The best you can do is your best*—which in truth might not be good enough. An athlete can make a Herculean effort and not have it be good enough. Your son or daughter can ace the SATs but still be denied admission to his or her first-choice school.

Our point is that managing the pressure of the moment will allow you to perform closer to your *capability*, which increases your likelihood of being successful. Managing pressure puts you in a position to succeed because it lets your experience and skills do the talking.

The second part of our mission is supported by our research into the twelve thousand subjects described above and the plentiful research of other psychologists. It strongly suggests that helping people manage pressure in their lives is an *untapped strategy* for unleashing their creative and intellectual potential. This strategy allows them to *consistently* perform up to the level of their capabilities, rather than having their capabilities dismantled or compromised by pressure.

Accordingly, we provide the nuts and bolts for building the attributes that allow individuals to consistently do their best when they are in pressure moments. These attributes include confidence, optimism, tenacity, and enthusiasm, which we collectively refer to as COTE. Metaphorically, these attributes offer users a COTE of Armor. Instilling them in yourself offers a long-term strategy for consistently defeating pressure and doing your best when it counts the most.

Overview

Performance Under Pressure is organized into three sections.

Part 1 provides readers with an understanding of the nature and science of pressure. Among the points we emphasize are these:

+ The crucial differences between pressure and stress, and how those differences impact us
+ *Why* we *feel* the heat in a pressure moment
+ *How* we inadvertently put pressure on ourselves—and others
+ *Common* pressure traps and how they make us "choke"
+ *What* pressure does to our brains—and how it affects our thinking

We've found that the more familiar you are with the impact of pressure in your life, the more adept you become at successfully coping

with it. In this way we want to challenge you to become a student of human behavior, starting with your own.

Part 2 provides readers with twenty-two powerful, often counterintuitive pressure solutions, strategies to use when you are in the midst of a pressure moment—or about to encounter one. You will find pressure solutions for all sorts of pressure moments, both at work and in your personal life. These solutions can be applied instantly. So if you are currently in the midst of a high-pressure situation that you feel ill-equipped to handle, peruse this section *now* for a quick fix.

Part 3 offers long-term strategies to help you build a *COTE of Armor*, a metaphorical suit you can wear daily. The emotional blending of confidence, optimism, tenacity, and enthusiasm makes up the fabric of that coat. With these attributes, you can immunize yourself against pressure so that your capability isn't diminished or compromised by it, giving yourself your best chance to succeed. We've found this strategy, *pressure management,* to be lacking in many organizations and that it is a powerful strategy for success because it allows individuals to maximize their creative and intellectual resources rather than have them diminished.

All of the individuals in the organizations we've worked with, from US Navy officers to CEOs and NBA coaches, are like you—they all experience acute pressure on a regular basis and yet have to deliver, time and again, in the face of it. With our help, over time they have come to understand that while mastering technical knowledge or expertise in their field provides them with a leg up, their true ticket to success often comes from being able to respond well under pressure. The information contained in this book has helped to give them specific strategies, as well as a long-term program, to handle pressure situations better. And it will help you, too—not just in the high-pressure, intense moments you experience at work, but in situations that matter in every facet of your life.

So if you find yourself in a situation like Bob Andreatta—whose head was "exploding" five minutes prior to testifying before the SEC— the morning of an important presentation, interview, sales call, difficult conversation, or audition, this book is for you. You will be taking more control over your performance. You'll be better able to respond

to the pressure, and in the process you'll feel more confident and optimistic. You will be using the cutting-edge results from what the neurocognitive and psychological sciences have to offer. Under pressure, you will experience less distorted and distracted thinking, less indecision, and abundantly more creativity. We believe that when you walk into pressure situations, you will see them more as challenges than as crises, and you will walk away feeling confident that you performed in a way closer to what you are capable of, not less.

Our first matter of business: understanding the power of pressure so that you know exactly what you are up against, and why pressure is *always* the villain.

PART 1

THE POWER OF PRESSURE

Have you ever thought about how you handle pressure in your marriage? You would be wise to. Of all the things that make marriages difficult, the inability to manage pressure tops the list.

The "Love Lab" sits near Yesler Terrace in Central Seattle, Washington, between Seattle University and Swedish Cherry Hill Medical Center, on East Jefferson Street. Officially, it is known as the Relationship Research Institute, and the nondescript white brick building is home to two of the leading experts on relationships in the world: Dr. John Gottman and Dr. Julie Gottman. The institute's nickname suggests a bohemian enterprise, but it is anything but that.

A professor emeritus at the University of Washington, John Gottman has spent a lifetime studying more than three thousand couples in research and four thousand more couples in intervention and treatment. He is the author of 190 published academic articles and author or coauthor of 40 books, including the *New York Times* bestseller *The Seven Principles for Making Marriage Work*. As a team, the Drs. Gottman have worked with approximately eight thousand couples in workshop and therapy settings.

Of their many empirical findings, none is more amazing than this one statistic: They can predict, with 93.6 percent accuracy, which couples will divorce. To put that number in context, the odds of making a chance prediction with 90 percent accuracy are 1 to .0000000000000000001.

How do they do it? Armed with decades of clinical research and data, Dr. John Gottman examines how couples interact when under

pressure. That single element—*pressure*—whether managed or succumbed to in a difficult conversation, is a more accurate predictor than financial and social compatibility, "chemistry," or any number of other commonly held relationship keystones. It's all about pressure.

In his research, the psychologist recognized that many variables thought to be important for a successful marital relationship are not in fact predictive of whether couples stay together. What he looked at instead was how couples interact when they feel the heat or experience the pressure that comes with discussing a contentious issue. He found that couples who can't navigate their way through the pressure experience crack and divorce.

John Gottman's scientific methodology is rigorous. Couples are hooked up to state-of-the-art apparatuses so physiological responses—heart rate, galvanic skin conductance—can be measured and connected to how the couple is acting and how they're responding to each other. Are they relaxed? Psychologically aroused? On edge? At the same time, trained observers record and code their behavior or body language, facial expressions, voice inflection—all of which is later connected to their dialogue and physical reactions. "Do the partners look at each other when speaking to each other, smile, or frown? . . . Do they lean into each other or lean away? Are they open and expansive or closed and contracted? How long does it take for their voices to sound angry?" It is a lot of data and it is analyzed meticulously.

Dr. Gottman's data-heavy approach has been incorporated into the work of thousands of therapists, and has changed the course of countless relationships. He has challenged traditional marriage counseling techniques. He has suggested that some of the techniques that therapists routinely use simply do not make much of a difference in a marriage, and may even be counterproductive. For instance, the idea of "active listening," where partners are encouraged to use "I statements" and play back what their partner is feeling in a conversation. For many years this has been the bedrock of marriage counseling. Yet according to Gottman's data, it makes virtually no difference in the success of a relationship or in therapy.

According to Gottman, "If your partner is saying, 'You're terrible,' according to active listening, you are supposed to be able to empathize

and be understanding. We found in our research that hardly anybody does that, even in great marriages. When somebody attacks them, they attack right back."

Gottman says, "Well, it kind of makes sense. Let's say my wife is really angry with me because I repeatedly haven't balanced the checkbook and the checks bounce. I keep saying: 'I'm sorry, and I'll try not to do it again.' So finally she gets angry and confronts me in a therapy session. What would it accomplish if I say: 'I hear what you're saying, you're really angry with me, and I can understand why you're angry with me because I'm not balancing the checkbook.' That's not going to make her feel any better; I still haven't balanced the damned checkbook!"

His lab identified negative behavior patterns that can take couples down the path to divorce. One is *negative criticism*, stating your complaints as a defect in your partner's personality: "You always talk about yourself. You are so selfish." Another negative behavior is *contempt*: statements that come from a relative position of superiority. Contempt is the greatest single predictor of divorce. For example, telling your partner, "You're an idiot." A third is *defensiveness*: making excuses for one's behavior or accusing your partner—"You always blame me, I am always the bad guy." Defensiveness is used to ward off a perceived attack. The last is *stonewalling* and *emotional withdrawal,* such as when the listener intentionally ignores the speaker, fails to provide the usual nonverbal signals that the listener is "tracking" the speaker, or simply doesn't respond to what the speaker is communicating.

What Dr. Gottman was able to determine is that success is less about the "chemistry" that exists between a couple and has more to do with how they manage their own internal chemistry as they interact under the pressure of threatening conversations.

The more a couple/individual cannot handle pressure, the more "physiologically aroused, mentally rigid, and impulsive they become during a conflict. This state of affairs increases the likelihood they will engage in destructive communication patterns that inevitably decrease marital satisfaction and increase marital dissatisfaction." Dr. Gottman found that happily married couples handle the pressure of conflict more effectively and are able to make conversational repair attempts even in the middle of an argument.

At heart, what the Love Lab has found is that if you want your marriage to be long and enjoyable, you need to *learn to handle pressure*—and hope your partner can handle it too.

Truths About Pressure

There are three basic and powerful truths about pressure. They are powerful because they influence our life every day, often in ways that we are not aware of, and almost always to our detriment.

The first is that pressure disrupts what we value most: our relationships, our careers, our parenting effectiveness, and our core ethical and moral decision-making. The consequences of pressure can break a marriage, derail a career, and cause children to pull away from their parents or feel the need to cheat to meet their parents' expectations. And it can compromise our very integrity.

The second truth is that people who handle pressure better than others do not "rise to the occasion" or perform statistically better than they do in non-pressure situations. If you are a sports fan, you've been fed a myth by the media that some athletes are "clutch" performers who do better under pressure. Or maybe you've heard that some people at work do more creative work, are more productive, work better as a team, or add more value to a client under pressure. But it's not true. Moreover, perpetuating this fiction only exacerbates poor performance under pressure.

The third truth, confirmed by our study of more than twelve thousand people and conducted over a ten-year period, is that you simply need to leverage the *natural pressure management tools* each of us already possesses to counteract pressure's injurious effects. When it comes to handling pressure, most individuals fail to leverage these tools, and thus handicap themselves.

These insights regarding pressure have specific applications in organizations of all kinds because individuals and teams react to pressure in predictable ways. Being aware of these truths in your daily activities will help you achieve your *best possible* performance when you need it the most. More important, it will allow you to remove the damaging effects that pressure creates for you. Let's look at a few examples of

people under pressure both within organizations and outside of organizations to see why they react as they do, and to better understand the circumstances that amplify the negative effects of pressure.

The Sabotaging Force of Pressure

Heidi K. Gardner is an assistant professor of Business Administration in the Organizational Behavior Unit at Harvard, where she studies how pressure impacts team dynamics. Professor Gardner's research suggests that teams like to think they do their best work when the stakes are highest—when the company's future or their own future rests on the outcome. But that is not what happens. In extensive studies of teams at professional service firms, Professor Gardner saw the same pattern repeat itself: Teams become increasingly caught up with the risks of failure, rather than with the requirements of excellence. As a result, they revert to safe, standard approaches, instead of offering original solutions tailored to clients' needs.

She found that when teams face significant *performance pressure,* they tend to defer to high-status members, at the expense of using expert team members. This would be analogous to a team of physicians ignoring the expertise of the best surgeon in the group and deferring to another doctor who is not a specialist in the field but he or she is senior on the staff.

Gardner labels this phenomenon the *performance pressure paradox.* Here's how it develops: As pressure mounts, team members drive toward consensus in ways that shut out vital information. Without realizing it, they give more weight to shared knowledge and dismiss specialized expertise, such as insights into the client's technologies, culture, and aspirations. The more generically inclined the team becomes, the more mediocre the solutions they offer.

The effects of pressure show up not just in our marriages and work; they also influence the choices we make, at all ages.

Vinay Mayar was the 2010 valedictorian of Stuyvesant High School, widely regarded as the best of the nine elite New York City public high schools that select students based on a highly competitive Specialized High Schools Admissions Test (SHSAT). The school is

a regular feeder to the most prestigious colleges and universities in America.

In his valedictorian commencement speech, Mayar, who now attends MIT, talked about the pressure at school. He referred to his classmates as "a volatile mix of strong-minded people armed in opposition against one another." He listed what his friends said epitomized the Stuyvesant experience: "copying homework in the hallway while walking to class"; "sneaking in and out of school during free periods"; and "widespread Facebook cheating." Only a few months earlier, Stuyvesant had been the scene of one of the most notorious acts of cheating to take place at a high school; it involved more than one hundred "excellent" students in a ring of deception. But Stuyvesant is not alone. Cheating scandals are hardly rare at elite, pressure-cooker high schools and colleges.

Just months from graduation from Leland High School, an acclaimed public school in San Jose, California, nine seniors were accused of taking part in a cheating ring. One student was said to have broken into at least two classrooms to steal test information before winter exams. A top-notch junior from Panther Creek High School in Cary, North Carolina, was busted for distributing a test to four classmates. Some twenty students from Great Neck, Roslyn, and other Long Island Gold Coast towns were arrested in an SAT cheating ring. In 2012, more than a hundred students were caught cheating in the same Harvard class in US Government.

Why do smart kids cheat? On the surface, it doesn't make sense. They are bright enough to get ahead honestly. We now understand enough about brain science to lay some of the blame on biology. Current research shows that the parts of the brain responsible for impulse control (measured in the lateral prefrontal cortex) may not completely develop until early adulthood, while the parts that boost sensation-seeking (the ventral striatum and the orbitofrontal cortex) start growing just after puberty begins. Teenagers may cheat (or do drugs or drive too fast) partly because their sense of the thrill outweighs their sense of the risk.

The phenomenon is magnified when peers—friends—are present, which may help explain why teens often cheat in groups. A 2010

Temple University study found that when playing a driving video game, teenagers were more likely to take big risks and even crash when their friends were watching than they were when playing the game alone.

But a more plausible explanation put forth by educators and psychologists (and Vinay Mayar, the Stuyvesant valedictorian) is that cheating is caused by pressure. Sally Rubenstone, a Massachusetts-based senior advisor with College Confidential, puts it this way: "The pressure these kids feel to do well on the tests makes kids feel cheating is necessary." Gabe Kaplan, principal of Great Neck North High School, concurs: "With intensity to do well on tests comes pressure to cheat."

Every day, kids are susceptible to peer pressure, which often makes our children engage in activities that later come back to haunt them. Drug use is one, bullying another. One can also add irresponsible adolescent sexual activity, and the most tragic consequence of teen pressure: suicide. The message is clear: Our kids might be smart, but pressure can cause them to use bad judgment and do foolish things.

Most of us think of pressure as situation-specific: the bottom of the ninth, taking the SATs, or giving a presentation in front of management. Yet the reality is that pressure is a daily force that infiltrates our everyday activities and builds up to the moment when everything is on the line.

Nancy Medoff, a senior director of Global Sales for Marriott International, describes what we mean. She calls it *The Challenge*:

"Technology increases the expectation that we need to be on 24/7, everyone expects a response NOW, and we are all moving at the speed of light. This creates a constant feeling that I am *falling behind*. Then there are 'pressure spikes' where something new gets added to your plate. For example, this year Marriott added a well-known Caribbean resort to its Autograph collection. It's an amazing property, so almost overnight, customers were calling wanting to know more about it, availability for groups—and we need to be the experts and handle the new workload on top of what we are already doing.

"When the pressure spikes like this, I start feeling like I'm not getting enough done and I feel overwhelmed. If I am not managing

the pressure, then I start responding to e-mails right away, being more reactive, and I can have an impact on people I don't want to have. It affects my leadership and the performance of my team.

"And it's not just in business—it's in my personal life, too. If a friend texts me and I don't get back to them in ten minutes, I get another text saying 'Is everything okay?' At this point I feel like I am going to implode and now I start impacting my key personal relationships, too."

It is the everyday pressure of "having" to succeed that causes a trader to ignore and violate trading regulations and causes the student to cheat. It isn't just the pressure of the presentation before the CEO or the senior team; it is the constant pressure to "make plan," to achieve the year's sales or revenue goals, and to get the annual bonus that causes managers to contemplate doing something unethical.

This is where pressure can be most nefarious—it can bend our character. Almost all of us believe we have good intent toward others, especially those who need our help. Testing this belief was the premise of the final episode of the most successful and best written comedy television show (as voted by the Academy of Television Arts & Sciences) in history: *Seinfeld*.

If you weren't one of the 100 million individuals who saw the last episode, the show's characters Jerry, George, Elaine, and Kramer are in a small town, where they witness a helpless individual being robbed. Instead of helping, the four of them enjoy the spectacle, making jokes at the victim's expense. But before they can exit the crime scene, they are arrested for violating the town's new "Good Samaritan Law," which requires them to aid the individual. Part of the humor lies in the fact that their actions are so morally reprehensible that we cannot take them seriously—we can only laugh at such absurd, repulsive behavior. And we are certain: "We would never act like that. We would be good Samaritans!" But is that true? A classic experiment by psychologists John Darley and C. Daniel Batson suggests otherwise.

Students at Princeton Theological Seminary unknowingly were part of the experiment. One morning, the students, presumed to be an ethical bunch given their field of study, were told they would be speaking across campus. Some of them, Group 1, would be giving a lecture

about job options in the seminary, while others, Group 2, would be giving a sermon. Those assigned to give a sermon learned they would be speaking on the topic of the New Testament parable of the good Samaritan, the man who helps a stranger on the road while others, including a merchant, a Levite, and a priest, pass the beaten and robbed man by and leave him for dead.

What the students did not know was this: There was no appointment across campus. The researchers were interested in seeing who would stop and help a needy student on their way. They wondered if in a contemporary setting, people predisposed to ethical behavior and bearing a message of compassion would be more or less inclined to offer assistance.

To test their hypothesis they planted a man slumped in a doorway, coughing and groaning and in distress, on the path the students would travel. It would be very obvious to the students passing by that this man needed help. Half of each group were told that they were running late for their lecture or sermon, the other half that they were on time. In other words, the experimenters put half the students in a pressure situation: choosing between their own self-interest and helping someone in need. Previous studies have demonstrated that self-interest takes precedence over the interest of others. The question here was whether *morality* was a strong enough force to cause people to put another's interest above their own.

The results were disheartening, although predictable. Those seminary students thinking about their sermon on the Good Samaritan did not stop any more frequently than those giving a lecture on seminary vocations.

The variable that made the biggest difference was feeling the pressure to get to their appointments on time. Of those students who were on time, who did not feel under time pressure, 63 percent stopped to help the man in distress. Of the group who were told they were running behind schedule, only 10 percent stopped to help. Some frazzled students literally stepped over the victim on their way to the next building! Many of the subjects who did not stop appeared disturbed and anxious when they arrived, perhaps because they were in conflict between helping the victim and their appointment.

In other words, pressure has the potential to alter our behavior in ways we may not be aware of, whether we are working on a team, performing in a classroom, or having a difficult conversation with a spouse or partner. If unmanaged, pressure will sabotage our best intentions.

The Roy Hobbs Myth

Most of us share the perception that there are folks out there who are particularly gifted at exhibiting grace under pressure, people who always rise to the occasion, who hit the money shot. These are the people we think have nerves of steel and are oblivious to pressure.

Nowhere is this thought more prevalent than in the minds of sports fans who idolize their heroes/players and consider them to be pressure-proof. Fans, as well as the media, refer to players who perform well under pressure as clutch players. The perception is that these athletes play—and excel—not in spite of high pressure, *but because of it:* the basketball player who makes the game-winning basket as the clock runs out in the NBA finals, the baseball player who hits the ninth-inning home run in the World Series, the soccer player who scores the goal in overtime at the World Cup, and the golfer who sinks the putt in a sudden-death hole of the US Open golf tournament. They are superheroes, and in comparison, we are, well, not very super at all.

Pressure makes sports great entertainment, and the film business has cashed in on those high-stakes moments with many films in which the culmination of the film is a heroic clutch performance. These films inadvertently perpetuate the myth of pressure.

A perfect case in point is the film *The Natural*, starring Robert Redford and hailed as one of the most beloved sports films of all time. Honored by critics and the Academy Awards, the story follows Roy Hobbs, a baseball prodigy whose career is sidetracked and who then attempts to return to baseball later in life, when he plays for the fictional baseball team the New York Knights, accomplishing his feats at the plate with his legendary bat, "Wonder Boy." The climactic moment in the film occurs when Hobbs comes to bat with two outs in the bottom of the ninth and the pennant on the line.

After fouling off a few pitches, and with blood starting to ooze

and how one team, the Oakland Athletics, out of necessity, tries a new statistics-based approach. David was interested in the truth behind the idea of the "clutch hitter," the individual who could deliver when the chips were down, when the game was on the line.

To analyze clutch hitting, over the course of 245 player seasons Grabiner studied batters who had at least 250 at bats in the late innings of games in which the scores were close. Were there hitters in baseball who hit better under pressure than they did when they were under less pressure? He wanted to see if there were players who were consistently, for more than one year, high-pressure hitters. Or did they just happen to have a "fluke" year where their average was better in high-pressure moments than in low-pressure moments. In other words, if a player truly performed better under pressure, he should be able to do it for more than one season. Otherwise, his performance would be considered a statistical outlier and not reproducible. Grabiner decided to ignore some memorable at bats in baseball history and to let the current data set speak for itself. Were there hitters in baseball who hit better under high pressure than when they were under less pressure?

His answer? No. "The correlation between past and current clutch performance is .03, with a standard deviation of .06. In other words, there isn't a significant ability in clutch hitting; if there were, the same players would be good clutch hitters every year."

In fact, Grabiner could not find any data to back up the "clutch" label. He conclusively found that there is no such thing as a batter who consistently hits better in the higher-pressure moments of the game. It is a myth. According to David, even Reggie Jackson, "Mr. October," never hit better in the play-offs than he did in the regular season. Grabiner looked over the data and found that Jackson's best play-off appearance only equaled his fifth-best regular season.

Grabiner's work has been validated by any number of statisticians. James Click, a former *Baseball Prospectus* writer and now the head of the Tampa Bay Rays' analytics department, describes it this way: "Clutch hits exist, clutch hitters do not." In other words, while some hitters are better than others, and now and then someone is going to get a big hit when the pressure is on, no one will do it consistently. That is, a player does not become a better player just because of the

from an old wound and soak through his uniform, Roy blasts a majestic home run that shatters the stadium lights, which cinematically are transformed into fireworks as Roy trots around the bases. Viewers and critics alike loved the emotional ending. We left the theater thinking Roy Hobbs was the best who had ever played. He came through in the clutch. That was what a sports hero looked like.

David Grabiner, however, probably walked out of the theater thinking, *Bull!* In fact, he was right—literally. In the original novel *The Natural*, written by Bernard Malamud in 1952, when the game is on the line, Roy Hobbs strikes out and the pennant is lost.

David is a math whiz. He is a past winner of the William Lowell Putnam Mathematical Competition or, as it is better known to its competitors, "the Putnam." This is an annual contest for college students established in 1938 in memory of its namesake, William Lowell Putnam, who was an advocate of intercollegiate intellectual competition, and it is considered by many to be the most prestigious university-level mathematics examination in the world. Over the years, many winners of the Putnam competition have become distinguished mathematicians. A number of them have gone on to receive the Fields Medal, the top prize in math worldwide; several have gone on to win the Nobel Prize in physics.

To win this award once is a big deal. To win it more than once confers almost legendary status. David Grabiner won this award three times, in 1986, 1987, and 1988, as an undergraduate student at Princeton. He went on to earn his PhD at Harvard. During this five-year period at Cambridge, he became a very devoted Boston Red Sox fan. Naturally, he combined his love of baseball and his love of math. We interviewed him about what he found in his research on baseball and pressure, specifically about "clutch" hitting, like that of the fictional Roy Hobbs, or any number of real-life baseball heroes.

To David, statistics had the power to provide deeper insight about performance than could be found simply by watching a game. This was the principle behind the bestselling book and acclaimed movie *Moneyball*, in which curmudgeonly traditional baseball scouts make decisions based on how a player looks and the number of tools he possesses—hitting, throwing, speed—rather than on critical statistics,

pressure he faces. The phrase "thriving under pressure" is a falsehood. According to Click, "There is no statistical evidence to support the idea that some hitters consistently perform better in situations defined as 'clutch' as compared to normal situations."

The same holds true in basketball. In a seminal study published in the April 2009 issue of the *International Journal of Creativity and Problem Solving*, researchers examined the performance of NBA basketball players using free throw shooting. The free throw is a particularly salient example to study in terms of pressure in sports because the variables are easy to measure. The distance from the basket never changes, the shot is always "free" from defense, and most notably, the time in the game when the shot is taken (i.e., late or early in the game, when there is more or less pressure) is measured.

The researchers for the study collected their data from game transcripts for every NBA game played between 2003 and 2006, including play-offs. They identified every free throw taken in the last minute of a game when the teams were within five points of each other and the outcome was still uncertain. The smaller the point differential, the greater the pressure. So the highest-pressure situation is when a player's team is down by one point, because making the free throw will tie the game.

The researchers compared the percentage of free throws made for each point difference between teams to the average percentage of the free throws made by those players across the whole season. If the shooters shot *below* their season average, then they were performing worse under pressure. If the shooters shot *above* their season average, then they were excelling under pressure.

The season average for free shots made successfully was 76 percent. In the highest-pressure situation, however, the results showed that players only made about 69 percent of their free throws. In other words, they shot significantly worse when their team was down by one point than they did overall. This difference was statistically reliable. From this data the authors concluded that all NBA players perform statistically worse under pressure. And that includes even the legendary Michael Jordan, one of the greatest players in the history of the sport.

With Game 6 of the 1998 NBA Finals on the line, everyone in the Delta Center in Salt Lake City, Utah—Utah Jazz coaches, players,

and fans included—knew the ball would end up in Jordan's hands. He was the player who time and again had been able to rise to the occasion. With Jordan's team, the Chicago Bulls, down 86–85 with sixteen seconds left to play, with the game *on the line*, Jordan indeed got the ball. Jordan dribbled to his right, crossed back over to his left, and shot a jumper with 5.2 seconds left. Swish—nothing but net. The ball went directly through the basket without hitting the rim and Jordan's Bulls won the championship. That image of spectacular success is burned into our collective brains. Jordan, we came to believe, was the rare player who became superhuman when it mattered most. It was indisputably a great moment. But it was an uncharacteristic moment, too. And that's worth exploring in the context of pressure and the expectation to—as the title of the 2002 movie said—"be like Mike."

It is not a diminishment of Michael Jordan's career to clarify facts. Jordan did not shoot better in the pressure moments he faced. Of course, that's not what basketball fans remember. We remember last-second shots more than the rest of the shots a player took because of the significance of them: They are more "available" to our brains so we are more likely to assign meaning to them. Psychologists call that the "availability bias." When you look at the statistics, you can see that Jordan was *not* a better shooter at the end of the game over the course of his career. He shot below his career average when the game was on the line. And on that night? In his final game as a Chicago Bull and in the most memorable night for the franchise—a true pressure situation—he had a *lousy night*, connecting on just fifteen of thirty-five shots.

Nonetheless, the idea, unsupported by statistical evidence, that some people, like Michael Jordan, perform better under pressure, and come through in the clutch when the game is on the line, affects how we all think we should perform when it really matters. Jordon himself acknowledges his clutch mythology. He candidly said, "I've missed more than nine hundred shots in my career. I've lost almost three hundred games. Twenty-six times, I've been trusted to take the game-winning shot and missed. I've failed over and over and over again in my life."

In business, similar myths exists around pressure and performance. Most people we have studied in our assessment center or have worked

with in organizations around the world believe they perform *better* under pressure—better at problem solving, better at creative thinking, better at delivering higher-quality work, and more effective in general when they are under pressure. In one study we conducted over a five-month period of 7,123 individuals from more than sixty countries, we found that 67 percent of people agreed or strongly agreed that they do their "best under pressure." Perhaps you feel the same. But is it true?

Harvard Business School professor Teresa Amabile is in the midst of a ten-year study looking at, among other things, how time pressure in a corporate setting affects employee creativity. She is the Edsel Bryant Ford professor of Business Administration and director of research at the Harvard Business School and one of the world experts in creativity, and she has written numerous influential articles and books about the topic.

In her groundbreaking research into creativity in the workplace, she has done what few researchers have ever attempted: observed creativity as it was happening within teams who were supposed to be doing creative work.

"We believed that the best way to get real-time information on these individuals, the teams, and their work, in a relatively unobtrusive way, was to have the participants fill out an electronic 'Daily Questionnaire' (DQ) for us. So every workday, Monday through Friday, the HBS computer emailed the DQ to everyone participating in the study; we asked participants to fill it out and send it back by the end of the day. Each team did this through their entire project (or project phase) that we were studying (anywhere from five weeks up to nine months)."

Getting research of this magnitude—twelve thousand daily questionnaires answered by so many employees in so many companies—is an unprecedented opportunity to see the effect of pressure on performance—in this case, on creativity.

"Over the course of my twenty-five-year career in research and teaching," Amabile said, "I've been fascinated by the complex effects that time pressure (and other forms of pressure) had on my own creativity and productivity. And, in working with many companies, I've noticed an interesting phenomenon: Most managers—and employees—hold strong beliefs about how time pressure affects creativity." "Creativity"

refers to *how* people approach problems and solutions—their capacity to put existing ideas together in new combinations.

"Perhaps the most surprising finding from the time pressure study is that time pressure really does seem to have an important impact on creativity, even though our intuitions are contradictory. I was very surprised to learn that, while our participants were giving evidence of *less* creative thinking on time-pressured days, they reported feeling *more* creative on those days. This helps me gain a bit of insight into those contradictory intuitions.

"In our diary study, people often thought they were most creative when they were working under severe deadline pressure. But the 12,000 aggregate days that we studied showed just the opposite: People were the least creative when they were fighting the clock. In fact, we found a kind of time-pressure hangover—when people were working under great pressure, their creativity went down not only on that day but *the next two days as well*. Time pressure stifles creativity because people can't deeply engage with the problem."

Amabile's research found that people get confused about time pressure and the difference between *getting stuff done* and *doing good work* (in the psychological literature, this is termed *skilled versus effort-based performance*). Yes, time pressure can stop us from procrastinating, get us off our rear ends, and help us actually get more things done. Yet, as Amabile and her colleagues pointed out, time (and other) pressure might *make you feel* more creative, but it does not help you do higher-quality work. In fact, it does just the opposite, usually with consequences to the project that is being worked on. According to Amabile, "When creativity is under the gun of time pressure, the project that group was working on usually ends up getting killed: it does not get supported by the company and it loses funding. Time pressure may drive people to get more done, but it causes them to think *less creatively*." This same effect can be seen in teams.

Married couples in the Love Lab, students who cheat in high school, well-intentioned seminary students at Princeton, professional athletes, and businesspeople trying to create the next great product or trying to work effectively as part of a team have to accept that pressure

has negative effects on them. Roy Hobbs is a myth, a fiction. And that's the truth.

Pressure and the Top 10 Percent

If there is a simple direction for performing to your capability in a pressure moment, it is to *minimize* the injurious effects of pressure.

Since it is impossible to live a life without pressure, the key is to negotiate your reactions to it—to gain insight into how pressure affects you and puts you at risk, and then to learn techniques of pressure management. As Al Doddington, a highly successful senior executive at CIBC, one of North America's largest and most profitable banks and a client of ours, put it: "We can't change how much pressure people are going to feel, but we can change how they deal with that pressure by providing them with learning on how to be more effective under pressure."

In our multiyear study of individuals under pressure who were able to perform in the top 10 percent of the twelve thousand people we studied, and who statistically received more promotions that *advanced* their careers, we found that each of them was doing the same thing as basketball star LeBron James or New England Patriots quarterback Tom Brady: *allowing themselves to be affected less* by pressure than those around them. This simple fact is the impetus for the key *pressure mind shift* that allows you to minimize your travels on the mean streets of pressure and that has been one of the most stunning findings in our studies of pressure management.

Pressure has a powerfully negative effect on people. What this group of 1,200 (the top 10 percent) were able to do was manage pressure *better than the other 10,800 people we studied.* They still experienced pressure. They still were negatively affected by pressure. But, just like the most successful athletes and students, they were able to manage it and themselves more effectively than those around them who were under the same pressure.

In other words, they did *not* rise to the occasion, or generate a mythic superhero performance (even though it might have appeared

that way to people on the outside)—trying to do so, counterintuitively, is a losing strategy, even if it is our most frequent attempted response to an anticipated pressure moment.

Take the pressure of starting a new job. We tend to think, *I have to show I am worthy. I have to prove myself.* In sports, this leads to the athlete "pressing," or trying too hard. In psychology, this is called a *re-investment strategy*—the individual attempts to cope with the situation by increasing his or her effort, which numerous studies show has little effect and, in fact, intensifies anxiety and stress, which can lead you to do worse.

You are not going to generate superhuman performance when you are under pressure. The best you can do is your best—you can't do magically better than you have before. And because of the ubiquitous negative effects of pressure, it is more realistic to think that the best you will be able to do under the circumstances is approximate your true capabilities. As sports statistics indicate, pressure reduces optimal performance. But it does so less for some than for others.

A C student is not going to rise to the occasion with a stellar college admissions SAT score (unless he or she has been underachieving and unmotivated during the school year and earning marks below his or her potential). And a star in the shot put event in track and field who throws one distance in practice should not go into the Olympics with the expectation of throwing a personal best (unless juiced by steroids).

In order to perform closer to their best under pressure, what these individuals need to do is let go of the myth that in order to be success-ful they need to perform better than their best under pressure. They don't. And neither do you. The exemplars in our studies certainly did not. Believing this performance-under-pressure myth only creates an unrealistic expectation that does nothing but erode your performance. By holding on strongly to this fairy tale, you come to believe that you, *too*, should be able to rise to the occasion and come through in the clutch. When you don't, distressful feelings such as embarrassment, shame, and dejection often follow, and these feelings make your next encounter with pressure even more difficult.

Taken to an extreme, if you believe that the only way to be suc-cessful in a pressure situation is to perform better than you ever have

performed before—that is, to be perfect—you stop trusting your capabilities, and worse, you start doing things that do not help you succeed. You start moving away from the strategies and mind-sets that got you in the first place to the position that made you successful. You stop trusting others on your team and, in fact, are more apt to blame them and create conflicts.

Individuals who falter less under pressure than others have a different road map for handling pressure than those who try unsuccessfully to be Roy Hobbs: They use the *natural tools* within themselves to perform to the best of their capability.

Your natural tools are your *thoughts, physiological responses, body movements, voice*, and *senses*. They determine how you handle pressure, regardless of your level of expertise, abilities, or good intentions. People who are less susceptible to pressure's negative effects use these inherent tools much more effectively than those who are overwhelmed by pressure. In a pressure moment, they use them to counteract pressure's negative effects.

For instance, with the assessment tool we used in the study, one of the differentiators of the top 10 percent performers in the twelve thousand people we studied was an ability under pressure to *not become defensive when criticized*. Under the pressure of being questioned or given tough feedback, they were able to stay open to the information and not take the feedback or questioning personally and get defensive.

In effect, they were able to use their cognitive processes to create an inner dialogue, or "reframing" of the situation, that helped them stay focused and increased their "observational awareness," an awareness of how their actions lead to specific results. Individuals who can perform under pressure appraise the criticism as information that can help them. In the Love Lab, couples likely to divorce interpret the same criticism as "attacking and insulting."

We have found that individuals who handle pressure well are also sensitive to their physiological arousal "shifts," which allows them to regulate their arousal by, for example, breathing slower, which enables them to process information more effectively and prevent themselves from becoming mentally rigid, thus preventing counterproductive, impulsive, defensive comments, products of unmanaged physical arousal.

Regulating arousal is crucial if you are going to manage emotions such as anxiety and fear that usually accompany pressure and make you do worse. Couples in the Love Lab, on the other hand, tend to be insensitive to their arousal levels, so their anxiety and anger easily get out of control, especially in a pressured conversation.

Learning to use the natural tools each of us has can help you to manage the external expectations and demands that pressure puts on you. Practicing your presentation and knowing it cold is a given for giving a stellar presentation. Developing and practicing your tennis serve so that you can hit the ball effortlessly, without much conscious thought, may be essential to your game. However, in the moment of truth, it is your natural tools that provide the avenues that allow you to utilize your knowledge or show off your skills. One of the things *Performing Under Pressure* will do is to show you how to leverage natural "pressure management" tools each of us already has.

Nevertheless, all of these natural tools are negatively affected in pressure moments. The power of pressure can throw us off our thoughts, make our heartbeat zoom, and disrupt our actions. So let's examine the *nature* of pressure and how it differs from the other stresses in your life.

THE STRESS OF PRESSURE

"What's the difference between stress and pressure?" is frequently the first question we are asked in our seminars and workshops on performing and leading under pressure.

It's easy to see why the question is a popular one. After all, stress and pressure share a lot of similarities. Most of us, for example, find both stress and pressure to be undesirable. We rarely ask our partner or family to provide us with more stress, and in all our consulting experiences, no one has ever told us they want to be under more pressure at work.

A second similarity is that each provokes behavior that is detrimental to ourselves and to others: mismanaged emotions, criticism of others (as well as destructive self-criticism), compromised ethics.

And the ability to handle both stress and pressure effectively is a desirable trait we seek in others and aspire to achieve for ourselves. We want to work for a boss who is a good manager of stress; we want a staff that can deliver on our goals when it matters most. And each of us wants to be able to perform well under pressure.

So it is easy to see why so many of us think of stress and pressure as one and the same. Even in the academic literature, the terms are often incorrectly used interchangeably, sometimes in the same paragraph.

Yet there are crucial differences between stress and pressure. Think about a Wimbledon match point, a World Cup Soccer shoot-out, or when it's two outs in the bottom of the ninth of the World Series with the potential tying run in scoring position. You've rarely heard the

announcer exclaim, "The stress is increasing." But "the pressure is on" is a familiar cliché of such moments.

While everybody feels stress and everybody experiences pressure, we've discovered that understanding the differences between stress and pressure is a requisite for learning how to do your best when it matters the most.

We can start to differentiate them by thinking of pressure moments as *stressful moments in which the consequences or results matter*. In other words, pressure moments or situations might *feel* like stress in our bodies and in our thinking, but they are different because, in a pressure moment, your success or your survival is truly on the line. For prehistoric man, those moments were related to immediate survival. And for some of us, that is still true.

Standing about six-foot-four, with sandy blond hair, John Ruggles looks like an athlete. He is the owner of J. Randolph Restorations, whose services include painting, power washing, carpentry, decks and fencing, plumbing, electrical repairs, tile and roofing. In a chance encounter with Dr. Weisinger at Dunkin' Donuts in Westport, Connecticut, John described a pressure moment that is a frequent occurrence in his business:

"Crawling around on the edge of a roof that's fifty feet high, installing high-voltage electrical equipment, and having to paint around this stuff. Especially when it's windy. You screw up and you're dead. Literally." Ruggles uses what he calls "relaxed focus" to help him do his best when his life depends on the outcome. "I remind myself to relax, to breathe deeply. I like to smell the air. Then, I do what I do automatically." (John is a Connecticut State golfing champion, and he uses the same pressure protocol when he's on the greens.)

In contrast, while stressful moments might feel important in the moment and have some of the same physiological signs and symptoms, a closer look reveals that they do not matter nearly as much as pressure moments to your success or survival.

When you increase your awareness of this difference, it allows you to react *more proportionally* to the kind of situation you are facing, and not waste your emotional resources by, for example, worrying about things that you don't need to worry about, or continually being in a

state of "readiness arousal," always on edge. These reactions inevitably drain you, distract you, and derail you from doing your best. A situation John O'Donnell faced many years ago highlights the point.

We met John O'Donnell one year after he had become president and CEO of Allstate Canada. John, an athletic, good-looking man, held a variety of interesting and high-pressure jobs at Goldman Sachs and the Walt Disney Company before starting at Allstate. He is confident yet self-effacing, optimistic yet realistic, enthusiastic yet measured. More than any other quality, John displays the ability to be clearheaded in the midst of chaos. An ability that Vietnamese monk Thich Nhat Hanh terms being "the calm person in the boat."

Thich Nhat Hanh, a peace activist who grew up in Vietnam and now lives in France, draws his metaphor from his country's history. His compatriots found themselves in horrendous conditions and decided to flee Vietnam; pandemonium ruled. Here is how Hanh described those he called the boat people: "In Vietnam, there are many people, called boat people, who leave the country in small boats. Often the boats are caught in rough seas or storms, the people may panic, and boats may sink. But if even one person aboard can remain calm, lucid, knowing what to do and what not to do, he or she can help the boat survive. His or her expression—face, voice—communicates clarity and calmness, and people have trust in that person. They will listen to what he or she says. One such person can save the lives of many."

Being the calm person in the boat is a quality that O'Donnell has needed many times in his career and in his life. When his wife was genetically identified as having a significant risk of being diagnosed with breast cancer, the couple faced a difficult decision—should she have a double mastectomy and reconstruction in the hope of preventing the disease that had killed her mother and her grandmother? Their decision was complicated by the fact that John had just started commuting to his new job with Allstate Canada and his family was in the middle of moving to Toronto from Atlanta.

John went on to tell us a story that we think is helpful in differentiating between stress and pressure. O'Donnell used to be a flight instructor in the Marine Corps. Fifteen years before we met, in Camp Pendleton, California, he was training new pilots on the Cobra

helicopter, a two-bladed, twin-engine attack helicopter. One after-noon, John was working with a beginning student, demonstrating a "sliding landing," a maneuver used to simulate the loss of an engine. As he was bringing the copter down, he heard a scraping noise—not a sound you want to hear when you are about to land.

O'Donnell pulled his helicopter back to a hover and asked another pilot to observe his landing gear. Due to what was later identified as a preexisting crack, he had lost his skids, the two flat pieces of metal that lie below the body of the Cobra and are critical in landing. Without skids, a helicopter like the narrow attack Cobra would tip on its sides. This might not be a problem if the rotors were not moving, but if they were engaged, the result would be catastrophic.

As John's rotors were very much in motion while he hovered in the air, ground control declared an emergency. Over the next forty-six minutes—the amount of fuel remaining—John and the personnel on the ground had to craft a plan to land safely.

That is what we call pressure.

Because tuning into the difference between stress and pressure is our first step in learning how to better manage the pressure moments we encounter, elaborating on a few more stress-pressure differences will serve us well.

Stress and Pressure: The Response Difference

The term "stress" started its popular usage in 1936 when Hans Selye coined and defined it as "the nonspecific response of the body to any *demand* for change." Seyle's definition was steeped in biological sciences and was the building block for the more psychologically oriented defi-nitions that promote the well-researched, validated, and accepted view that we experience *feelings* of stress when the demands (stressors) of the environment in which we are working outweigh our ability or perceived ability to respond to them. Think about all the demands made on you in the course of a day, from paying the mortgage, to doing well at work, to parenting, etc. Stress refers to the situation of too many demands and not enough resources—time, money, energy—to meet them. A day in which you are picking a friend up at the airport, taking your kids to

their soccer game, shopping for ingredients for dinner, retrieving your dry-cleaning, getting to the post office before it closes, cleaning your house before guests arise is a stressful day. The same kind of schedule at work can lead to similar feelings of stress—two project deadlines to meet, back-to-back meetings, and a difficult client you need to respond to. You feel stressed, you feel overwhelmed.

John O'Donnell could identify with feeling overloaded. During the time of his emergency, he was preparing for a squadron deployment, taking business classes at night, planning his wedding, and applying to the top business schools in the country. On that day, John's life was already filled with a high level of tension. Or, in our vernacular, he was stressed.

But John's day highlights a further difference between stress and pressure. What makes the activities leading up to that emergency flight different from pressure is that if he didn't complete preparations for the squadron deployment or attend night school, he wasn't jeopardizing his career or his life.

Those who study pressure and its effects describe pressure as a *situation in which you perceive that something at stake is dependent on the outcome of your performance*. Typically, the outcome either advances your chances of success or sets you back. For our earliest ancestors, these moments were related to survival. Often their lives were dependent on the outcome of their performance. Success would allow them to live another day. Today, a stellar presentation to your boss is apt to advance you; mismanaging a mission-critical project can set you back.

While in a stressful situation there are (nonspecific to the task) *multiple ways to respond* that can help you manage stress better, in a pressure situation there is only *one* response requirement: that you get the job done correctly—whether that means safely landing a helicopter, delivering a persuasive presentation, or, in basketball, making a game-winning free throw. In other words, while there are multiple ways to manage pressure, the end game is always task-specific; you are trying to successfully do something to meet the demands of the situation. In a *stressful* situation, reduction is the goal. In a *pressure* moment, success is the goal. Thinking that you have to be successful all the time means you are under pressure all the time.

John's day illustrates this distinction. Having to manage the many moving parts of his morning, including securing ordnance and firing ranges for the upcoming deployment while also completing the next day's flight schedule, might be stressful, but if he doesn't deliver the exact response required, he will not face a significant consequence to his success or survival. The situation becomes a pressure moment when what he is facing demands a specific effective response. Failure to perform a successful landing of his Cobra helicopter means there is a good chance that John and his copilot trainee will die. That's pressure. What John faced, while an extreme example, illustrates a key differentiator of a pressure moment: While it feels stressful, high-pressure moments *matter more* because an effective response typically advances you and an ineffective response often sets you back and may, in fact, "weed you out." John had to respond effectively, or he might have been *weeded out* permanently. While stress is feeling overwhelmed, pressure is feeling "I have to succeed or else."

In a *stressful* situation, practicing a relaxation technique might help us feel less overwhelmed and help us regain our perspective and composure. In a *pressure* moment, relaxing might help us, but we also have to deliver on the required behavior or we don't advance. John might have stayed calm, but if he was unable to land the helicopter, he would not have been considered to have performed under pressure.

Stress and Pressure: The Function Difference

There is a specific evolutionary function for stress and one for pressure. Since the beginning of time, human beings have had demands placed on them by their environment. Meeting these survival demands—fleeing and fighting predators, gathering food, seeking shelter, tending a fire, taking care of progeny, engaging in rituals to the gods, and so on—required effort and time, so a stress response evolved that would set off a chemical cascade in the body to get it ready to get things done. It arouses and alerts the body that there are demands being made upon it, and thus it helped us. This was true for our ancestors and it is true for us today, until we reach the point that we have so many demands placed on us that we can't respond to all of them—then we feel stressed and

negative consequences begin to appear. Up to that time, though, stress can be useful, a point that has been research-validated hundreds of times.

Pressure functions differently. Pressure evolved as a *selection mechanism* to decide who would advance in life and who would not. Having a disagreement with your wife about how to discipline your firstborn child is stressful. Escaping a predator chasing you is more than just stress; it's pressure—either you find a way to escape or fend off the predator, or you potentially will die. With pressure, something critical is on the line.

For prehistoric man, his life was on the line—failure to make a leap across a path would be instant death. For him, "I have to succeed or else" was a realistic appraisal of the situation, but today, it is best described as a primal pressure thought that will derail you in your pressure moments.

Today, in most high-pressure situations, your life is not literally on the line, except for those who operate in high-risk environments— Navy SEALS, police officers, mountain climbers, air traffic controllers, emergency room medical staff. But on a primal level, the feelings and thoughts of pressure are similar: If you don't perform, you or others could be negatively affected, and you will be held back, you will not succeed.

Pressure's Function in Action

One of the most noticeable arenas in which pressure plays out its evolutionary function of weeding out is the college admission process, which becomes more and more competitive each year for high school graduates, especially those trying to get into the more select schools. And gaining admittance to the college of their choice acts as a significant gateway and boost for young people in terms of their future success.

Erinn Andrews knows something about this competition. Not only did she successfully apply to and earn undergraduate and graduate degrees at Stanford University; later, she spent seven years reading applications of prospective students as one of Stanford's admission

officers. We caught up with Andrews at her home in Northern California, not far from the Stanford campus.

According to Erinn, the competition to get into competitive colleges has increased to unbelievable levels. At some schools, the odds of being admitted are so long that acceptance is almost like winning the lottery. In 2014, Yale had a 7 percent acceptance rate, Harvard a 6 percent acceptance rate, and Stanford had a 5 percent acceptance rate, the lowest in the nation. Students with virtually perfect test scores and high school grades are routinely denied entrance. "The amount of pressure that high school students feel is unbelievable," she says. The application process is a complex one. Students don't compete with every applicant to the school; they compete only with other students who come from their "pool," meaning those who share the same geographic background or athletic skill or some other unique attribute.

In other words, if you are a student who went to a private school in the Bay Area and you have good marks and you are applying to Stanford, you're not alone. Andrews told us that Stanford would sometimes get fifty kids applying from the same elite Bay Area school. Imagine the pressure that these kids feel in trying to get into Stanford. Stanford will receive in the vicinity of 42,000 applications for 2,200 spots.

"We knew we had a lot of power," says Andrews, referring to the admissions process. "Nobody, and I mean no one, took this job lightly. We did our absolute best. We were trying to uphold what the university wants in terms of the type of students they are looking for and also trying to spot the authenticity of those qualities in these applications. In some ways, you felt . . . like you are determining their fate. I wasn't alone in feeling overwhelmed."

In the admissions process, officers read a number of applications in a batch and then advocate for the applicants they think deserve to get in, first with a larger selection team and, depending on the school, then with the dean. "Sometimes as an officer, you are pushing for the students whom you really like, but they don't get in. These can be crushing days—when you don't get someone in who you really feel could make a great contribution to the university. Or maybe they are the first person in their family to go to college," Andrews said.

The proliferation of online chat rooms like Classroom Confidential

has only increased the pressure of the application process. Students go to these sites to get a handle on what's going on at various schools and find, among other things, students comparing their grade point averages and standardized test scores. According to Andrews: "This comparison only adds more pressure and anxiety. They only see a small bit of information—an anonymous person's marks and scores (are they even honest about their scores?) and not the full sense of the person, and so they don't have an actual comparison. It is like the blind leading the blind."

The student who manages to achieve consistently high marks, and nails the standardized tests, and writes a great personal essay may get in. But the unlucky losers are "weeded out," and can sometimes feel devastated and think their life is over—a primal pressure response.

If you take a larger perspective, you can see how pressure associated with the admissions process shows its environmental, evolutionary utility. For the organization/environment, the stringent selection criteria ensure that students admitted can handle pressure, as seen by their consistently high marks, performance on standardized tests, and achievement of honors in sports and creative endeavors. These select few students exude confidence, optimism, tenacity, and enthusiasm, and thus perpetuate the intellectual, innovative, creative, challenging environment that characterizes Stanford and other elite colleges and universities.

Confusing Stress and Pressure

Our inability to distinguish pressure from stress inevitably has dire consequences. Every stressful situation—a longer meeting than you expected, a colleague letting you down on deliverables—can start to feel like a pressure situation when, in fact, it is a mild inconvenience that has no impact on the success of your day. You start to feel that you are always "under the gun," that you always have to produce. You start to develop pressure anxiety.

At work, everything becomes super-important, which needlessly intensifies and elicits distressful feelings of pressure.

When we confuse daily stressful situations for pressure moments,

we react physically, mentally, and behaviorally in ways that are out of proportion to the circumstances. The danger lies in the fact that continually confusing stress for pressure habituates, and we lose the ability to think clearly. Misdiagnosing stress as pressure reduces our abilities needlessly.

Here is an example. A client of ours was in charge of the sales organization of a large division of a pharmaceutical company. After a series of decent but not great quarters and much change in the organization, the sales group was facing an important year in the business. The sales head said to us, "Tomorrow [the kickoff event for the year] will be the most important day of my career." The most important day of his career? A career that might span forty-five years? We suggested that he "slow down his thinking," a technique that helps people keep perspective and thwart counterproductive self-statements. Doing so enabled him to look a bit deeper and to accurately appraise the situation to see what was truly on the line.

It became clear to our client that he was confusing stress for pressure. He might have been feeling as if it was a pressure moment—but in reality, this was far from the most important day of his career. Yes, it was stressful. But his career and the survival of his company *were not* on the line. And he came to see that his reaction to this kickoff was having a negative impact on the people around him, needlessly infecting them with anxiety and diminishing their performance.

It is hard enough to perform under pressure, but confusing stress for pressure makes it even more difficult, because we end up wasting physical, emotional, and psychic energy on things that, ultimately, don't matter. It also leaves you with fewer resources to deal with real pressure situations when they happen and makes it more difficult to tune into the pressures others are experiencing, a pressure reducer for them and a relationship builder for you. For example, at the height of the financial meltdown at the end of 2008, Rick Waddell, the CEO of Northern Trust Corporation in Chicago, was in a high-pressure situation. Rick was in a recording studio being interviewed about how his company was responding to the financial crisis and significant news about a competitor that had broken that morning, trying to assure investors, clients, and employees that they were not in the same situation.

Needless to say, Rick had a lot on his mind when he ran into Andrew Stevens in the hallway after the interview. Andrew was the VP for talent management at Northern Trust, and his reporting structure was actually three levels below Rick, so he wasn't sure how well Rick would remember him. He saw Rick coming from the interview and stopped to say hello.

Rick began to answer, "Hi, Andrew. Have you heard this morning's news . . . ," when suddenly he stopped, looked at Andrew, and said, "but none of that's important. . . . How are you doing?" To Andrew's amazement, Rick not only knew that his goddaughter had passed away two weeks prior, but he had the presence of mind despite all that he had going on to ask Andrew how he was doing. They had a short conversation, and Andrew thanked Rick for asking. Six years later, Andrew remembers that moment like it happened yesterday. "I don't know how he had the wherewithal, given the incredible pressure he was under, to remember in that moment to ask me how I was doing. I will always remember that and have told the story to many others."

We've helped many individuals limit their inappropriate pressure responses with this simple pressure reduction strategy: Whenever you feel pressure, ask yourself: Does the situation really call for the reaction I am having? Or am I wearing myself out by overreacting when I don't need to? Can my performance in this situation actually threaten my success? Your answers will help you gauge whether you are really in a pressure moment or are merely feeling stress.

Using the above strategy will inevitably help you reduce your inappropriate pressure reactions—distorted thinking, spiked arousal, impulsive hostile comments—as well as help you reduce your feelings of stress. You'll end up with more resources and will be better prepared to perform closer to your best in a true pressure situation. This is no small matter. In our work with individuals in organizations, we have found that by confusing stress for pressure, employees get so worn-out over time that it becomes a major contributor to their careers derailing or their relationships falling apart at home.

John O'Donnell wasn't sure how he would get his Cobra helicopter safely on the ground. When he discovered that he had lost his skids and had only forty-six minutes of fuel left, he and his student faced an

uncertain outcome. He needed to nail a difficult landing against long odds. What John was able to do was use a few key pressure strategies and solutions to think creatively, work with those on the ground, and come up with an innovative solution to land safely.

That is exactly what we must do at times in business and in life. When our generally stressful lives cross the line into something more dire, we need the tools to overcome the innate challenges of performance under pressure.

O'Donnell, working together with the ground staff, devised a makeshift platform out of various materials to land on. He told us, with a small smile, it was like "landing on a needle." Did John feel under pressure? Of course. Was his performance perfect? Certainly not. But in most pressure situations in life, you don't need to be perfect. You just need to deliver the task or behavior required of you in the situation. You have a better chance of doing that when you manage pressure and get as close to your full capability as possible. And when you do so, you'll usually live to fly another day.

THE NATURE OF PRESSURE

Early on October 29, 2012, Superstorm Sandy, the largest Atlantic storm on record, as measured by diameter, with winds spanning eleven hundred miles, moved ashore near the New Jersey coast, just to the northeast of Atlantic City. The storm became the second-costliest storm in United States history. As of June 2013, estimates assessed the damage at more than $68 billion, a total surpassed only by Hurricane Katrina. At least 286 people were killed along the path of the storm, in seven countries.

On November 13, 2012, New York governor Andrew M. Cuomo established a commission under the Moreland Act to investigate the response, preparation, and management of New York's power utility companies to several major storms impacting the state, including Superstorm Sandy and Hurricane Irene the year before.

Months into the investigation, on a rainy Saturday night in June, Julie Howard, chief executive officer and a member of the board of directors of Navigant Consulting, received a call alerting her that there was going to be an article in the newspaper the next day mentioning her company and its connection to the Moreland Commission investigation. Navigant was a public company consulting firm that specialized in helping organizations manage critical business risks in energy, health care, construction, and financial services. The Long Island Power Authority (LIPA) was one of those organizations. Navigant had provided services to LIPA for years.

What Julie was told in that telephone call shocked her: The article was going to state that the Moreland Commission's report raises, among

other things, questions about some of Navigant's work for LIPA. And that the commission is referring these questions to federal prosecutors in Brooklyn to determine if criminal charges are warranted against officials of LIPA or against Navigant. You can imagine how concerned Julie felt when she hung up the phone. She was absolutely certain that Navigant had not engaged in any wrongdoing and was confident that her company would ultimately be vindicated. But the damage to Navigant's reputation in the interim could be significant.

As is consistent with many of the leaders we work with, Julie felt immediate pressure to plan, to respond, and to perform in the face of great uncertainty and limited information. This pressure was in addition to the pressure that Julie and other leaders routinely experience. First and foremost is the feeling that she needed to be *on* all the time. "When you are the CEO, there isn't a meeting where there isn't an expectation that you will lead the discussion, contribute in a more intellectually significant way, or be the final decision maker in situations of uncertainty. Whether you like it or not that is the expectation that seems to come with this job."

As a leader, she also felt pressure from the amount of public speaking that she does. "There is always the spotlight—I feel like I need to say something witty or motivational at all events."

Then there was the constant pressure to perform and meet expectations. As a public company CEO, Julie and leaders like her live this pressure on a daily basis. But in this instance, the pressure became exacerbated given the potential "unknown" impact the Moreland Commission report could have on her business. It was by far the most acute pressure she had felt in her career.

What Julie was experiencing was a classic high-pressure situation. While the specifics of high-pressure situations vary, they all share three common attributes that stimulate our anxiety and fear, and these are major determinants for why we underperform under pressure:

+ The outcome is important to you.
+ The outcome is uncertain.
+ You feel *you* are responsible for, and are being judged on, the outcome.

The more important the outcome is to you, the more uncertain the outcome, and the more responsible you feel for the results (and the more judged you feel), the more *intense* the pressure situation and the *more likely* you are to underperform.

The Outcome Is Important to You

Because our brains are hardwired to attend to important tasks first, and because importance intensifies pressure, encountering pressure moments is inevitable, as we all have important tasks we have to perform. And ever since early man faced a predator and either performed effectively or perished, pressure moments seem to have evolved into being almost always all-or-nothing situations. A field goal kicker either makes or misses the goal. Style points don't matter—if the ball just misses hitting the uprights or hits them and gets a lucky bounce is of no consequence—the successful execution is what matters. Likewise, a business presentation to convince an audience that a new marketing plan is needed either is persuasive or it's not. There is rarely a middle ground. Pressure moments are like that: They have a tough performance appraisal; you either succeed or you fail.

Today, most of us are not physically facing a predator, but psychologically, pressure moments often feel that way, most likely because we become ego-invested in our important tasks. Accordingly, it is easy to see why we often feel our self-esteem is dependent on whether we succeed or fail. We want to succeed in the tasks that we deem important, or at the very least to avoid failure. In essence, there is pressure to succeed, and pressure not to fail.

The Outcome Is Uncertain

Pressure-packed sporting events are anxiety-provoking because we don't know the outcome. The stock-in-trade of reality television shows like *The Amazing Race* is the uncertainty of their outcome. You never know who is going to win and who is going to lose. While uncertainty might be entertaining to us when we experience it as observers, it is not much fun when you are in the middle of it.

Uncertainty, for Julie, came in three forms: first, what the press was going to say or imply about the conclusions of the Moreland Commission; second, how quickly Navigant was going to be able to demonstrate to the US Attorney's office to conclude its review; and third, how this situation would affect her firm's reputation and consequently their business. Uncertainty has a particularly powerful effect on the brain; it is part of what causes us to feel the heat in a pressure moment.

An interesting study by John Hennessey and Seymour Levine provides some clues about what uncertainty does to the brain and body. They conducted a series of studies that by measuring cortisol levels looked at animals' reactions to mild shocks given to their paws. Cortisol is a steroid hormone produced in the adrenal glands in response to stress and pressure. It is primarily responsible for activating the body's "fight or flight or freeze" response.

In these experiments, the researchers found that the biggest cortisol reaction was elicited not by increasing the magnitude of the shocks but by changing the *variability* of them. The more random the shocks, the more uncertainty that the animals experienced, the greater the cortisol reaction.

You can observe the particularly powerful effect of uncertainty on the brain and body from the patterns of stomach ulcers recorded in London residents during the Second World War. In general, higher cortisol levels deplete a stomach's mucosal lining, which, in turn, leads to an increased frequency of ulcers. During the war, central London was bombed relentlessly every night by Germany; in the suburbs, the Germans bombed in a more sporadic, unpredictable fashion. Interestingly, it was in the suburbs, not central London, where doctors found a higher incidence of stomach ulcers. It wasn't the magnitude of the bombings, but the uncertainty of them, that had a greater effect on the brain and body.

John Coates of Cambridge University studies the effect of uncertainty and cortisol on behavior. John spent a decade on Wall Street, first trading independently and later managing derivative trading desks at Goldman Sachs and Deutsche Bank in the 2000s. After a decade in the financial world, John decided to leave finance to study neuroscience at Cambridge University.

John and his team hypothesized that the physiological arousal that

traders experienced when facing uncertainty and pressure had a profound effect on their trading decisions, particularly in market bubbles and crashes.

He believed that their physiology systematically changed traders' risk preferences. In other words, they were taking too much risk in bull markets (when the market was going up) and not enough risk in bear markets (when the market was going down). So the Cambridge team set up a series of experiments in The City, London's equivalent to Wall Street, to test their hypothesis, collecting a range of traders' biological markers over the course of their day and in various markets.

They found that in bear or down markets, traders' cortisol levels went up to such an extent that it led to *risk aversion* and an irrational focus on negative information in their environment.

Cortisol is an important hormone when it comes to how we react under pressure. Principal among them is its effect on our ability to think and to retrieve memory. Along with another chemical, corticotropin-releasing hormone (CRH), produced by the amygdala, cortisol incites anxiety, commonly called "anticipatory anxiety," and suppresses the production of testosterone. Testosterone acts to invigorate behavior. In the absence of testosterone, approach-based behavior diminishes and our attention becomes selectively focused on the negative aspects of a situation. Called attentional bias, it causes us to *see all the stimuli in our environment as threatening*. We become more paranoid. We amplify the negative. In effect, Coates found that the uncertainty that traders faced sharply increased their cortisol, and caused feelings of anxiety and fear.

For early man, it was advantageous to see his environment as threatening, because, in a very real way, it was. Threatening perceptions helped early humans be cautious, an early version of *playing it safe*. Today, though, the reaction is less advantageous and often disadvantageous.

For example, the traders shifted to a selective attention to negative information, which made them take fewer risks, and consequently, they missed buying opportunities. When a sports team becomes more risk averse, the team plays conservatively; the mind-set becomes overly self-focused—"don't do anything wrong"—and focus is taken away from what the team has been doing that helps them win. Consequently, they do worse.

As John Coates wrote in his book *The Hour Between Dog and Wolf*, prolonged exposure to cortisol also does longer-term damage to two structures of the brain that proportionally have more cortisol receptors: the amygdala and the hippocampus. The amygdala is where the *emotional* content of memories is stored, and the hippocampus is where *factual* memory of an event is stored. The amygdala records how you *felt* as you faced a pressure moment from the past; the hippocampus stores the facts: what happened, who was involved, how it was resolved, and what was learned.

While the receptors of the hippocampus (where factual information is stored) *shrink* under the influence of excessive cortisol, receptors in the amygdala undergo a significant growth in number of branches when immersed in cortisol. This is why, over time, our thinking can become more emotional and less factual.

As cortisol levels rise, and exposure to the hormone becomes chronic, we increasingly recall events that were stored when under its influence—mainly difficult moments we had in the past, when things didn't turn out well.

In other words, an individual's memories can be overly influenced by what happens in a high-pressure moment.

The amount of uncertainty Julie was experiencing in dealing with the Moreland Commission findings had the potential to release a significant amount of cortisol into her system. She needed to be extra careful that she didn't "amplify the negative" of the situation and let her thinking become more emotional and less factual.

Julie described it this way: "I felt like I was in the 'eye of a tornado,' watching. You feel like everything is swirling around you. You can see all the debris. If you react, you will get sucked into that."

You Feel You Are Responsible For, and Are Being Judged On, the Outcome

In high-pressure situations, success or failure lies in your hands. You're the one negotiating with the client, you're the one speaking for the team, you're the one at bat.

Knowing that her actions would determine the outcome for her company heightened Julie's sense of responsibility for the success or failure of her response to the investigation. That sense of responsibility leads us to become preoccupied with thoughts of failure and thoughts of social embarrassment, which can cause us to lose our ability to focus on the task at hand.

A big part of the pressure Julie felt came from juggling the expectations of the board, the investors, the employees, the clients, and her own family and friends. While she felt supported by the board, she also felt like she was in a bit of a fishbowl and didn't want to let any of these people down. The "weight" of pressure in such a situation doesn't just come from feeling responsible to deliver—that's the conventional thought. We've found it also comes from how we think *people watching us will judge us.*

We each have a deep-seated need to be loved, to be respected, and to belong. When we feel judged or criticized, or when we perceive that we will be judged, in a high-pressure situation, it can evoke feelings of inadequacy (are we good enough?) or embarrassment (am I doing it right?) or humiliation (will I look stupid?).

When we feel judged and rejected, it stimulates feelings of *social pain,* the pain we experience when social relationships are damaged or lost. This pain is very real. Pioneering research by Matthew Lieberman at UCLA using neuroimaging studies shows that social pain and physical pain share the same underlying processing system in the brain. When you break an arm, you experience the same type of pain, neurologically, as when you feel the loss of a loved one.

According to Lieberman, "Different cultures have different beliefs about how important social connection and interdependence are to our lives. In the West, we like to think of ourselves as relatively immune to the sway of those around us while we each pursue our personal destiny. But I think this is a story we like to tell ourselves rather than what really happens. Across many studies of mammals, from the smallest rodents all the way to us humans, the data suggests that we are profoundly shaped by our social environment and that we suffer greatly when our social bonds are threatened or severed."

This is part of what makes us feel the heat when we are on the line in a high-pressure situation. According to Lieberman: "The things that cause us to feel pain are things that are evolutionarily recognized as threats to our survival, and the existence of social pain is a sign that evolution has treated social connection like a necessity, not a luxury. It also alters our motivational landscape. We tend to assume that people's behavior is narrowly self-interested, focused on getting more material benefits for themselves and avoiding physical threats and the exertion of effort. But because of how social pain and pleasure are wired into our operating system, these are motivational ends in and of themselves. We don't focus on being connected solely in order to extract money and other resources from people—being connected needs no ulterior motive."

Certainly Jon Theuerkauf found his "motivational landscape" altered at a key meeting in 1992. Jon was working with MCI Telecom in Chicago. Having been successful in a number of roles, he was transferred to Atlanta to work on a special project that focused on improving customer service. At the time, MCI was going through huge growth and its customer service was not keeping up. It was starting to impact the company's reputation with its customers.

So Jon was brought in to help devise a solution. He had spent only one week in Atlanta when his boss asked to speak with him about his approach. After so short a time looking into the problem, Jon didn't really have a good sense yet of what was going on. But he agreed to the briefing.

In the early 1990s, creating slides from software like today's PowerPoint was fairly new. The only software like that at the time had been created by IBM and Jon had not been trained in it. So he showed up at the briefing with his ideas on a yellow pad of paper.

At the appointed time, Jon's boss walked in with his own boss, MCI's chief administrative officer (CAO). They asked Jon to present to them, in slides, what his thoughts were. Jon was completely flustered. He did not have his ideas prepared on slides. Nor was he sure yet what the fix for customer service should be. Jon used transparencies to hurriedly throw out some ideas for the two men.

As you can imagine, it all went horribly wrong.

Not only did Jon lack insight into what the problem was and what the fix might be, but using transparencies at the best of times looks

sloppy and unorganized. Jon felt the pressure of the situation and was frozen—he found he could not think straight or answer in a thoughtful way even the simplest questions that were put to him. "My mind was in complete overload. . . . They wanted a full concept, not just a conversation. I knew five minutes in I was dead."

Jon's boss and the CAO thought Jon's presentation was dreadful, and they lost confidence that Jon was up to the task. He was immediately relieved of his new position. It was a crushing blow to him. His demotion kept him up at night for weeks, ruminating about what went wrong.

Recollecting the story years later, Jon realizes his mistake. He was not ready for the meeting, but did not say so. He did not stop the meeting five minutes in when it was clear to him that it would be a waste of time. Looking back, Jon realizes why. He was thirty-one years old at the time, and this was his first foray into the "C" suite, the seniormost level of the organization. He felt like he would be harshly judged if he said he was not ready. He felt like he would be letting his boss down in front of his boss's boss. What Jon was feeling was the heat of social pressure that Lieberman's research described.

"I felt like I needed to say yes but should have said no. Wrong, wrong, wrong. I was a young senior manager, and I did not realize I could say that I was not ready. Or, even, to have the wherewithal to ask to use the time instead to ask the executives what *they* thought the big issues were. I didn't. The pressure of being worried about what they thought about me was overwhelming."

Step back and see the neurological and psychological dynamics of a pressure situation: The attributes of a pressure moment—importance, uncertainty, responsibility to others, and feeling judged—are all factors that have the potential to stimulate *feelings of fear, anxiety, failure, embarrassment, and stress.* These are powerful psychological and physiological forces that can be helpful in the right context, *but not in a pressure situation.* While they were often helpful to your ancestors in pressure moments when the threats were more physical in nature, today these "primal pressure reactions," if unskillfully managed, have the potential to prevent you from doing your best by limiting your brain's capacity to effectively respond.

What did Julie do when she received that phone call about the

Moreland Commission that rainy June night? She excused herself from an evening at the theater with her family to talk to the chairman of the board of Navigant and craft a plan of action. The news called for an extraordinarily fast and thoughtful response, which Julie was capable of, as long as she could successfully manage the pressure of the situation.

Fortunately, Julie was able to regulate her feelings of anxiety and fear by using a number of pressure strategies that we describe in more detail later in the book, such as slowing things down by stepping back and "going still," as she calls it, in order to make sure she was focusing on the right things. "If you aren't careful, you could focus on the wrong things—the 'car flying by' that might not be that important in the big picture." As she puts it, you have to feel "confident that you've taken the time to evaluate the situation and made the best decision you could, and then, *don't second-guess yourself.*"

Taking responsibility for a problem is one of Julie's strengths. "Some CEOs would call the board immediately and ask for help. Instead, what I did was just call the board chairman and tell him that I was going to evaluate the situation, obtain counsel, and come up with a plan to present to the board." She wanted to make sure she had something to say to the board that would ease their concerns, understanding that they would be affected by the pressure of the situation as much as anyone.

Outcome

When she was ready, Julie went to the board with a plan, which they approved. They decided to immediately approach the US Attorney's office to offer full cooperation and assistance to enable the office to conduct and conclude its review as swiftly as possible. They told the investigators that they would share whatever was needed, and asked them to let the company know what the specific concerns were so they could address them. The investigators at the US Attorney's office appreciated the direct and transparent approach and, after a thorough review, closed its investigation without any indication of wrongdoing. Navigant achieved the favorable outcome Julie expected from the outset and was able to effectively manage the concerns of its shareholders, clients, and employees through clear and direct communication throughout the process.

Your High-Pressure Moments

Envision a high-pressure moment in your life. The anxiety of meeting a new client? The fear of giving a presentation? Embarrassment over a social gaffe with your boss? Make a list of your likely high-pressure situations; reflect on the feelings and thoughts you associate with each. Why is a presentation or meeting so important? What is making you unsure about the upcoming meeting with your boss? What is the realistic consequence if you fail in a pressure moment? Who do you feel responsible to, and are these expectations realistic for your performance? We have discovered in working with Olympic athletes, or with clients like Julie Howard of Navigant, that if you can bring some insight to how high-pressure situations make you feel, and reflect on the thoughts that are generating these feelings, you will have a better chance of not allowing your emotions to sabotage your performance and decision-making.

Once you have deeper insight into your thinking and behavior in such moments, turn to Part 2 of this book and learn *specific pressure solutions* that will help you inhibit your primal pressure reactions; that is, minimize your feelings of anxiety, stress, fear, and embarrassment in such situations. Keep in mind, however, that these are short-term strategies, to help you get through a high-pressure situation that you are experiencing today, or in the near future. In Part 3 of the book, we offer a longer-term strategy—strengthening the attributes that will help to immunize you against the debilitating effects of pressure.

THE ANATOMY OF CHOKING

The scenarios are so familiar they are clichés:

+ A well-practiced presentation goes astray.
+ An actor flubs the lines that he has said ten thousand times before.
+ A student blanks on a math formula on her SAT day.

It's one thing to be adversely impacted by pressure—we all are. But to deliver significantly worse than your typical performance, to perform substantially below your capability when you want to do your best, that is another matter. In sports parlance and in educational vernacular, too, that's a *choke*, and we've found that understanding how choking happens will help you reduce its occurrence so you can do your best when it matters the most.

In order to learn how to stop ourselves from underperforming, we have to understand how the brain's memory systems react to pressure; or, in other words, how we choke.

A Performer's Nightmare

By 1950, the modern usage of the term "choking" was so commonly associated with negative connotations in sports that when the great Jackie Robinson grabbed at his throat in a game between St. Louis and the Dodgers to signify that he (Robinson) thought that umpire Bill Stewart missed a call, Stewart threw him out of the game. Choking became a

common term for "blowing it" in the 1964 sports world when the Phila-
delphia Phillies "choked" by blowing a six-and-a-half-game lead over the
St. Louis Cardinals with just twelve games left in the regular season by
going on a ten-game losing streak and losing the pennant.

We all know a choke when we see one. In sports, it is the failure
of an athlete or an athletic team to win a game or tournament when
the player or team was strongly favored to win, or the squandering of a
large lead in the late stages of an event. Competition—in sports, busi-
ness, school, fine arts, etc.—has winners and losers. Choking, though,
has more to say about expectations than merely success or failure. For
instance, you can lose a competition and *not* choke, just like you can
give a great presentation and not get the job. Choking has more to do
with the effects of pressure on performance than on the outcome.

A teenager taking a driving test is not competing with her friends,
nor does she have to "win" to get her license. She simply needs to
demonstrate that she is competent to drive. If she has demonstrated
countless times that she can parallel park and then, with the driving
inspector sitting next to her, cannot fit the car into the allotted park-
ing space, this would be considered a choke. If this happens a second
time, her friends will be quick to urge her on her third attempt, "Don't
choke," which of course only increases the pressure she experiences.
The same is true for the student who has to stand up to give a speech
to the class. He knew the speech perfectly the night before, but with
all eyes in the class on him, he forgets his lines and speaks much too
quickly and nervously. He feels himself choking.

We have all experienced this. You have a great idea to pitch your
boss, and he or she gives you ten minutes to present it. Ten minutes
later, you walk out thinking, *I screwed up; I should have said* . . . In these
moments, when you *want* to do your best, you suffer an *occurrence of
suboptimal performance under pressure conditions.*

Note the operative word "want." Choking occurs only when the
individual *wants* to perform well in that situation. A basketball team
might blow a twelve-point lead to an inferior in the last three min-
utes. But if they have already clinched their division championship and
there is little motivation to win, their less-than-stellar performance is
likely because of a lack of motivation, not because they choked. The

same is true for a second-semester senior already accepted to the college of his or her choice who doesn't do well on a chemistry test. The student didn't choke—he or she just stopped studying as rigorously because the outcome no longer mattered.

Furthermore, we can only be thought of as choking if we have already established that we are capable of successfully and consistently performing the task. If you're a weekend golfer who misses a three-foot putt when dinner is on the line, you are not choking unless you can typically make that three-foot putt. In contrast, Tiger Woods, Phil Mickelson, and Rory McIlroy can make a three-foot putt ninety-eight times out of a hundred, so when they miss a three-footer with the match on the line, we can assume it's because they choked. In Chapter 1, we described how players in the NBA demonstrated they can make foul shots at a *higher percentage in non-pressure* situations. In other words, in pressure situations, their performance, when they want to do their best, is suboptimal to their capabilities and is, by definition, a choke.

How Pressure Chokes You

A complex interaction of three factors is the heart of the human performance system: (1) physical arousal, (2) thoughts, and (3) behavior. These factors operate as a system, and each of them influences the others; a change in one stimulates a change in the others. Think about a recent time that provoked strong emotions in you—and you will recall how quickly the physiological effects showed up in your body and the impact they had on your behavior and decision-making.

In order to perform effectively under pressure, you need to be able to leverage these factors to your advantage. That is, you need to be able to regulate your physical arousal, think clearly, and execute the appropriate response to your capability.

The way pressure upsets performance is straightforward: One way or another, it disrupts your performance system. In a pressure moment, if your heart rate starts to zoom, your thinking is apt to become rigid and distorted. Similarly, if you perceive that your survival depends on the outcome of the pressure moment, you are apt to stimulate anxiety and fear arousal that, in turn, make the moment even more

threatening. The end result: You lose control of your physical arousal, thinking ability, and capability to execute the behaviors you need.

While there are many factors that can cause and perpetuate a disturbance in your performance system, one of the most cited reasons for choking is that your memory systems malfunction and either cause you to forget information you need in the moment, or prevent you from executing a task that you have successfully performed numerous times, be it a musical recital, golf putt, or presentation.

One memory system, referred to as "working memory," helps you perform tasks that involve judgment, analyzing data, recalling crucial information, and decision-making. In pressure moments, your working memory stores the information you need. On test day, you want your son's working memory to be filled only with test-taking information.

The other memory system, termed "procedural memory," is responsible for how you perform tasks that you have already mastered, such as a tennis swing, starting your car and pulling out of your driveway, or giving a well-rehearsed presentation. In pressure moments, your procedural memory helps you perform these tasks effortlessly and automatically.

Although these memory systems are different in function and brain location, their shared point is that if either one malfunctions in a pressure moment, the result for you is the same—a choke.

Swimming with the Sharks

An entrepreneur, Kim Adams Nelson, appeared on the current hit television program *Shark Tank*, seeking money to enlarge her baking company. We later interviewed her in order to understand what she was feeling in this high-pressure situation.

In *Shark Tank*, entrepreneurs pitch their businesses in front of a panel of investors ("Sharks") in the hope that one of the five investors on the panel will invest in their business in exchange for equity in the company. In the space of two or three minutes, they need to successfully communicate the value of their business, and its future prospects, as well as to connect with the Sharks in a way that encourages them to invest their own money in the business. It is a frightening situation for

most entrepreneurs, and a great example of a high-pressure moment. Many of the entrepreneurs come to the show at a crossroads: If the business receives an infusion of money (and media exposure), it will survive; if not, it may fail and disappear. This intense pressure, and the emotions it generates within the entrepreneurs (and within viewers), is one of the reasons that the program has become the number one show on Friday night television.

Kim was a fifty-year-old baker from South Carolina. She had never heard of *Shark Tank* until a friend urged her to submit an application and a five-minute video about her business.

One can imagine why appearing on television would be a high-pressure moment for Kim. The outcome was *important* to her: If she was to get funded and the television audience liked her pitch, she would receive a big cash infusion and a significant marketing push for her product. The outcome was obviously *uncertain*: She was not sure how the show would go; she had never been on television. Would she make a good impression, and more important, would she get funded? Finally, she would be *responsible* for and *judged* on how she performed—she would get the investment and the opportunity it afforded or she wouldn't. Her family, friends, and employees as well as the general public and potential clients were watching the show, and she didn't want to disappoint them or humiliate herself.

When we talked to Kim from her home and cooking facility in Spartanburg, South Carolina, it was obvious why she had been given a chance to appear on a competitive show like *Shark Tank*: She has an endearing, positive personality and is clearly enthusiastic about her product and company. She comes across as sincere and authentic. When we met her, she was wearing the same Daisy Cakes black T-shirt that she made famous on the show.

Kim grew in up in South Carolina. The mother of three, she has been around cakes and cooking all her life. Her two grandmothers, Miss Nellie and Miss Nervilee, and her great aunt Daisy taught her to bake when she was very young. The secrets to their cakes: farm-fresh eggs, carefully sifted flour, and sweet cream frosting. Similarly, Kim does not use artificial flavors or preservatives in her cakes; everything

is made from scratch. She sold her first one—a yellow cake with chocolate frosting—when she was just ten years old.

She went on to manage two restaurants and conduct cooking classes. In 2009 she decided to start up her own business, naming it after her aunt Daisy. That first year, she, her mother, and an assistant sold $27,000 worth of cakes directly to consumers, mainly through holiday gift shows and Junior Leagues in Louisiana, South Carolina, and Texas. The cakes were a hit; the next year they sold more than two thousand cakes, increasing revenue to around $85,000.

In the summer of 2010, a friend from college called and told Kim about *Shark Tank*, which was completing its first season. Her friend told her that she absolutely had to be on it. Kim decided to take a chance and via ABC's website fill out an application to get on the show. She received a call from the casting coordinator the next day to say they wanted to talk to her about the show, though not yet apply more formally. She wasn't sure what to make of this opportunity, but she went along with it. She worked with two producers, Bill and Laura—whom she came to adore—over the summer, honing her pitch, first to a presentation three minutes long and then to a two-minute-long version, in hopes of being asked to move forward in the process. On Labor Day weekend, she found out that she had made the cut and was asked to put together an official application. She filled out a twenty-seven-page application and put together a five-minute video, and waited.

Finally, on a beautiful Carolina fall day, Kim received a call from her producers alerting her that she would be getting an opportunity to pitch to the Sharks. This was no assurance that her segment would be picked to be shown on an episode in the second season, but she was one step closer.

She flew to Los Angeles the next day, to pitch the day after, on the 31st of October. At the hotel that evening, she met fifteen to twenty other entrepreneurs who also would be pitching the Sharks for an investment. In all, eighty entrepreneurs made pitches, of which fifteen would make it into an episode and actually be shown on television. Even if Kim were successful in receiving and accepting an offer from the Sharks, she might not necessarily appear on the show when it aired.

As she walked out onto the stage to make her pitch, her brain and body set off a small neuroendocrine cascade of body chemicals (norepinephrine and epinephrine at first; cortisol later) to get her body "ready" and physiologically aroused.

Choking Apparatus: Working Memory and Procedural Memory

In recent years, cognitive and neuroscientists have put forth new explanations of choking that take into account the two types of memory housed in different parts of the brain—*working memory* and *procedural memory*. Each type of memory influences choking. But how and why they do is *dependent on the type of task you are attempting to perform*. Although interrelated, they are typically treated as being distinct entities.

The term "working memory capacity," or WMC, was coined by cognitive psychologist George Miller and neurosurgeon Karl Pribram, and was used in the 1960s in the context of theories that likened the mind to a computer—that our brains have a specific amount of space that can hold a limited amount of data. For this reason, we liken WMC to a "mental scratch pad" that facilitates the manipulation of information held in consciousness. Obviously, those individuals who have the most space on their mental scratch pad, like a computer with more storage space, have an advantage—they have more cognitive horsepower.

When your WMC is disturbed, so is your performance, especially if the task you are performing is dependent on deliberate thinking, such as solving a difficult math problem, writing an essay, remembering a phone number, or studying data you need to explain to your client. Pribram's animal lesion research and functional imaging upon humans tell us that WMC is located in the brain's prefrontal cortex.

In contrast, your procedural memory is located in your cerebellum and is responsible for coordinating the lightning-fast motor activation needed to perform complex actions—the actions that were of first importance to early man's survival.

The two memories are interrelated in that many complex tasks—for example, playing a piano or guitar—are first learned by the WMC system. But with more and more regimented practice, the complexity

of the task becomes automatic, and because of this, the memory of the operation is transferred to the cerebellum. Now it's part of your procedural memory—you perform it without deliberate consciousness; you are able to operate on "autopilot." When you watch musicians flawlessly play a complex piano piece, they are using their procedural memory—it seems automatic. But it becomes automatic only after their WMC has helped them learn the music they are playing so adeptly that it becomes a simple procedure. Another common example: Your working memory helped you learn how to drive. As a beginner, you went through your checklist for pulling out of the driveway. Now you perform your checklist "without thinking."

Both memory systems factor into choking. One scenario is that you perform a task—maybe presenting some ideas to a client. The information you need to explain a complex solution to a complex problem is in your work, but halfway through, you start to wonder what your client is thinking and if he or she is approving or disapproving of what you are saying. You start to become preoccupied with this concern, and a few seconds later, you blank on a crucial point that you knew cold.

Thinking about your client's reaction takes up valuable space on your mental scratch pad that you needed to store crucial information. These competing thoughts about your client *delete space* on your scratch pad that you were using to store presentation information. That space has evaporated and, with it, the information. The result: You can't remember the crucial information you knew perfectly well the night before—you choked by letting your concerns use up the space in your working memory system that was storing the information you needed.

Interestingly, individuals are not always aware of this process when it is occurring. But after the fact, they quickly realize, "I should have said . . ." In reality, they couldn't have given their client the information because their working memory was compromised.

Now let's switch tasks and settings. In the 1995 NBA Finals, the Orlando Magic, an organization JP started working with in 2002, was protecting a slim three-point lead in the final moments of Game 1 against the Houston Rockets. Nick Anderson of the Orlando Magic stepped to the free-throw line with the chance to put his team up by five—and likely clinch the game.

But he missed both shots. Amazingly, he got the rebound from his second shot and was fouled *again*. He headed back to the free-throw line, determined to seek redemption. Taking his time, Anderson shot again, and he missed both attempts. The Rockets went on to tie the game and force an overtime, eventually winning in the extra period and the championship.

This type of choke involves your other memory system, your procedural or implicit memory. It is what guides the skills an athlete like Anderson has perfected and seems to use unconsciously. Ironically, however, when athletes try to use it "consciously," they often choke.

Imagine a school music recital; your daughter's performing for the first time. She's practiced her solo for weeks and can play and sing it perfectly—"automatically," you could say. She's all alone when the curtain goes up, and as it does she reminds herself to stand up straight, to smile, and to project her voice and play her guitar gently. She starts to focus on her finger movement, and for the first time in weeks, she plucks the wrong string and sings the wrong note. She begins to choke.

In this scenario, the choking culprit is that the task had been incorporated into her "procedural memory." When she *consciously* focuses on the "automatics" of the well-coordinated skill (mainly because she wants so badly to do well), her musical process is slowed down and becomes out of sync; the well-rehearsed performance becomes downgraded. When a sportscaster comments, "He's thinking too much," it is a reference to the slowing down of the athlete's procedural memory—and a miscue typically results. In effect, the performer is blocking her procedural memory by deliberately trying to "practice it," instead of just "doing it" as she has already done a thousand times.

Many studies show that novice golfers perform better when they are told to focus on their mechanics. That's because they are learning something new and need their WMC to help them memorize and think about the *swing rules* to perform. Experienced golfers perform better when they perform quickly, because they have already made their swing automatic. So when they are instructed to focus on their mechanics, they perform worse than their capability—they choke.

Note the contrast: Slowing down your performance and focusing on the mechanics of a well-rehearsed skill *work against* you; slowing

down your performance in a task that requires judgment, decision, and deliberate problem-solving skills *helps* you. When we slowed down the thinking of our earlier-mentioned client (who was worried this sales meeting was the most important day of his career), it helped him, as his thinking and judgment became sounder.

Thus, choking occurs in "thinking tasks" when our concerns shrink our working memory capacity—the space that is needed for storing the relevant information we require in our pressure moments. Choking occurs in well-rehearsed tasks, such as a presentation, sports contest, or audition, when we consciously become deliberate in guiding our behavior.

To help prevent these memory systems from malfunctioning in a pressure moment, you need to learn two skills. The first is to prevent worries or concerns generated by fear and anxiety from entering your working memory.

Second, you need to learn how to prevent yourself from getting in your own way, from "mentally intruding" when your procedural memory is working—to leave it alone.

Pressure solutions help you develop both skills.

Kim and the Sharks

What memory system did Kim require to be successful on *Shark Tank?* The answer is both systems. At the beginning of her pitch to the Sharks, when Kim was delivering her well-rehearsed presentation, she did not need to think much. She had practiced this presentation so many times that the region of the brain she would draw most productively from during this part of the pitch was her automatic procedural memory. In effect, she could just get out of the way and let the words flow. And Kim nailed it. Or, at least, she delivered the presentation well enough to move successfully to the second stage of the pitch, the question-and-answer part. And that is where she needed to rely on her working memory system.

For this, Kim needed as much of her working memory capacity as possible. That means she needed to *stay focused*, not distracted by worry thoughts such as *Will I be successful? Do they like me?* These

thoughts would take up space and cause her to lose markers that she would need to answer the Sharks' questions. More storage space would help her be more effective in reading the situation, connecting to the questioner, and answering the question being asked of her. Unfortunately for many of the entrepreneurs who pitch to the Sharks, this is precisely the part of brain and memory that they risk losing when the Sharks ask questions about number of sales and growth strategy. Part of the reason for *Shark Tank*'s success is that it is so fascinating to watch entrepreneurs struggle in this incredibly pressure-filled environment.

A working memory glitch is easy to spot among the individuals in front of the Sharks. They tend to have a "deer in the headlights" look, and struggle to answer simple questions, just like an anxious student called on to recite in front of his "judging" classmates.

As working memory shrinks, "mental rigidity" sets in and the entrepreneurs become locked into a solution or behavior even if it's not working for them. This happens because the limited space on their mental scratch pad does not permit them to think of options—that space is gone. Of course, this is the exact opposite of what they need to succeed in a high-pressure moment—to think on their feet and respond skillfully to the questions that are being asked.

Kim had to respond to a series of direct questions from the Sharks. They asked about her sales, and she stumbled a bit as she explained that Daisy Cakes had just been started, but that they had sold $27,000 worth of cakes in a three-month span. The Sharks were impressed—so far so good. Then they asked her how she marketed and sold her cakes. She told them that she and her mom drove around three Southern states attending Junior League shows and selling direct to customers—and met her first major hurdle. The Sharks, understandably, could not see how she and her mom could "scale," or grow, this business. They asked if Kim could deliver five thousand cakes in a week, without killing her mother or herself in the process. Even if she and her mom worked 24/7, they would not be able to produce the amount of cakes that a scalable business would need in its current form. To the Sharks it was obvious that Kim had a regional business that might grow a certain

amount, but wasn't big enough to justify their investment. Quickly, all the Sharks except one dropped out. Kim was stunned. Her dream of success seemed to be over.

What Kim didn't know was that her answers to their questions operated on *two levels:* one had to do with the actual content of her answers (how many sales she had, what her plans were for distribution, and so on). The other level, which was less apparent to her, as it is to most people in a pressure moment, was *behavioral—how she presented herself,* which is every bit as important, if not more so, as the content of the answers.

The Behavioral Consequences of Pressure

Research shows that in venture-capital pitches, when entrepreneurs go to private equity organizations to get funded, as Kim was doing on the show, investors' decisions often turn on nonverbal factors like "how comfortable and charismatic the entrepreneur is." "The predictors of who actually gets the money are all about how you present yourself, and much less to do with the content of what you say," says Amy Cuddy of Harvard Business School, citing research by Boston College doctoral student Lakshmi Balachandra (a research fellow at Harvard Law School's Program on Negotiation).

Balachandra studied 185 venture-capital pitches and found that variables like "calmness," "passion," "eye contact," and "lack of awkwardness" were stronger predictors of success than the *actual content* of the pitch.

In high-pressure situations, pressure derails us not just by causing us to become mentally rigid, but on a behavioral level as well. When we are in a pressure moment and we are experiencing anxiety, we *behave very differently.* We are more uptight in how we show up, more defensive when tough questions are asked, less warm and a little more ill at ease, and less able to engage in humor. These subtle behavioral changes were noticeable to the Sharks who were assessing Kim and her company—but less noticeable to Kim.

For Kim to be successful, she needed to manage her working

memory so that she could think straight and not become mentally rigid, but she also had to manage her behavior so that she would be better able to connect with the Sharks.

But there was still another way that pressure could affect Kim: in her decision-making.

Decision-Making and Pressure

One of the most consistent findings in pressure research is that in all sorts of settings, pressure is a nemesis to making sound decisions.

Decisions in the Shark Tank work two ways. First, the Sharks decide whether to make an offer or not. And then, if one or more do make an offer, the entrepreneurs need to make a decision about whether or not to accept each offer. It is truly a negotiation. Assuming she received an offer, Kim would need to decide whether she could work with the person making it. After all, if she received and accepted an offer, she would have a new partner. And partners are not always easy to work with. She would need to decide whether or not she trusted the person making the offer. If they hit a rough patch down the road—which is inevitable—could she work it out with this partner? Would she trust her gut in making this decision or be swayed by the pressure of the situation?

As we saw in Chapter 1, teams facing significant performance pressure tend to default to high-status members at the expense of the most knowledgeable of the team members.

Kim was in a tricky position because the people who might make an offer to her were in a position of high status relative to her. They had the money; they were the stars who were glorified for their business success and acumen. She was a small-town entrepreneur from Spartanburg, South Carolina.

If Kim received an offer, she might defer to a Shark when she shouldn't and potentially take an offer that would not be right for her or her business. What if a Shark demanded a bigger percentage of the business than she was willing to give? Would she defer to that person?

But here Kim walked into the Shark Tank with a distinct advantage:

She had faced far tougher challenges in her life. And she truly believed in her cakes and her company. She later told us, "I have dealt with a lot of setbacks that all small businesses face, but I persisted. I have never ever given up on this. I knew in 2009 when I started doing this that it would work."

But while she believed in her product and company, only one of the Sharks agreed. The sole investor still interested in the end was Barbara Corcoran, a New York City real estate maven with one of the largest real estate companies in the country. Corcoran wasn't sure that Kim was worth the $50,000 investment that she was seeking. But Barbara noticed something on set that got her thinking. "I watched the other investors and noticed that every one of them kept eating her cake—even as they were saying they didn't want to invest. And she came on the show after lunchtime, so this told me something."

The taste of Daisy Cakes was persuasive. But Corcoran was ultimately won over by Kim's personality and the way she presented herself. "I saw a woman who really believed in what she was doing. I saw someone who had been through a lot of rough times and came out of them. She had stamina. She was going to be a fighter. The more the men, the other Sharks, asked questions, the more they degraded her to a degree about the business, the more I could see her fighting spirit. I decided to trust what I saw versus what I was hearing."

Corcoran decided to invest $50,000. Kim was ecstatic; the terms were right, and she quickly accepted the offer.

Two years later, Corcoran called her financial commitment to Kim "the best investment she has made in the *Shark Tank*." She added, "A lot of people who seem sweet really aren't so sweet, but she is. She inspires customer loyalty wherever she goes." Kim has paid off the confidence that Corcoran showed her, and is on pace to sell more than $3 million worth of cakes. And as Corcoran says: "This business is just getting started!"

In this high-pressure situation televised to the whole country, with so much on the line, Kim didn't choke, either in the initial part of her presentation where she relied on her procedural or implicit memory system, or when it was time for the questions and she had to think on

her feet. In each case she was every bit as at ease as the Sharks who were challenging her. Make no mistake, Kim wasn't perfect—but then she didn't need to be. Her best was good enough.

What was clear from Kim's experience in the Shark Tank was that she didn't have to do anything more than be herself. She just had to manage the pressure and let the rest take care of itself. The Sharks were trying to get a read on *her* as much as her business, and that is what finally won the last Shark over. As Barbara Corcoran said, "A lot of people have come on the show, and although they believe in their businesses, they don't have what it takes to convince other people to believe in them. She is a natural promoter and she can convince others to believe in her business."

Kim says, "When I look at the future of Daisy Cakes, I see no limits."

HOW PRESSURE AFFECTS OUR THINKING

The philosopher Epictetus said more than two thousand years ago, "Man is not troubled by events but rather how he interprets them." Bobby Jones, the most successful amateur golfer of all time and the designer of Augusta, the yearly home of the Masters tournament, pointed out: "Golf is played on a six-inch fairway, between your ears."

Although these oft-quoted fellows did not know each other, they both realized that *cognitive appraisal* has the power to keep us out of the rough. Psychologists today agree: It is not the event that causes our reactions but rather how we interpret the event, which makes us either confident or anxious.

Cognitive Appraisal

The mental process we engage in that helps us to define what is happening to us or around us is called *cognitive appraisal*. It is the process by which we make sense of the world around us and the situations we face. It helps us to answer such questions as: Do I have what it takes to handle the demands of the situation? Is the situation important to me? The single most important question that we face when we are under pressure is: *Do I see the situation as a crisis or a challenge?* The roots of how we appraise situations lie in the special qualities and circumstances we bring to the table that shape our personalities: family background, role models, psychological traits and health, systems of belief, fears and hopes. Self-esteem is part of the equation, as is our sense of history, pride, legacy, and entitlement, among others. These factors combine to

form the basis for the unique way we interpret our surroundings, give meaning to outside events, and appraise the situations we encounter in daily life, especially in the high-pressure moments we encounter.

Appraisal and Pressure

One of the more subtle ways pressure influences our brains and behavior is by *altering our thinking and distorting how we see events*. Many people believe that how they see events is static—that it does not change. This couldn't be further from the truth. How we appraise a situation can and often does change. And pressure is one of the most powerful influences on our appraisal.

For example, a so-so performance review at work upsets you on Monday, but by Wednesday you think it's actually pretty good. You are angry about a parking ticket in the afternoon, but the next day you realize it's no big deal. You wake up in the middle of the night in a panic about something, but by morning it doesn't feel so dire. What's changed? You still have to pay the ticket, and the performance appraisal stands. What's changed is how you are appraising the event: *This isn't fair* has become *Well, I deserved the ticket*, or *I am going to get fired* has transformed to *The review wasn't that bad; I'm just disappointed, but I can improve*. The fact that you can change your appraisals of a situation allows you to regulate the pressure you experience.

Moreover, two people can appraise the *same event differently*. You might see giving a presentation as a threat or crisis, while your teammate sees it as a challenge. Your teammate will feel less pressure. It is also true that two or more people can interpret the same event similarly. Five team members who appraise a project as threatening are sure to be in for a lot of team conflict.

Finally, an appraisal can be skewed by one's state of mind at the time. When you are angry or depressed, you will interpret a situation as more hopeless; when you are happy or enthusiastic, the same situation may be perceived with hope.

In each of these situations, the event remains the same, but your appraisals alter the feelings and actions associated with the situations. Cognitive appraisal is the "brains" of your performance thinking

component, and it is crucial to pressure management that you make it work for you rather than against you.

Cognitive Distortions

Appraisals that misrepresent the reality of a situation are known by psychologists as *cognitive distortions;* they can be likened to a computer virus in that they will cause your *thinking component* to crash and spit out errant data to your other performance components—arousal and behavior.

Cognitive distortions are so powerful they often create feelings of anxiety, helplessness, and depression or provoke needless anger directed toward those we love. People who are frequently overwhelmed by stress and anxiety are typically popular users of distorted thinking styles.

Similarly, pressure distortions are those thinking patterns that needlessly intensify the experience of pressure. Pressure distortions can surface either before a pressure moment or during a pressure moment, but in either case, their particular brand of thinking derails you. We found that there are two specific pressure distortions that are particularly harmful to our ability to perform under pressure.

Chance of a Lifetime

Consider the following statements so often made by coaches or managers or parents: *"You will never get another opportunity like this one!"* or *"This is your big chance!"* or *"Today, we make history!"*

Statements like these communicate the *singularity* of the event. We call it "chance-of-a-lifetime" thinking. And it inevitably intensifies the pressure the listener feels in the moment because it multiplies the stakes and puts self-esteem on the line. When you think along these lines, you increase the pressure from *within,* as you tell yourself *I'll never get another chance like this* or *I better not blow this.* Singularity— thinking of a pressure moment as your one shot—can exacerbate the feelings of *risk* and *loss.*

Feelings of risk and loss have powerful neurochemical effects on us

that influence our decisions and actions. Studies in behavioral science show that traders and financial advisors on Wall Street often stick to bad positions because they want to avoid a feeling of loss. Selling would confirm the reality of loss. Nobel Prize–winner Daniel Kahneman's work has shown that given a choice between risky outcomes, human beings are *twice as averse to losses* as they are attracted to comparable gains. This is one of the reasons young people over-allocate their investment portfolios toward safe fixed-income investments despite the fact that equities have been shown to be more profitable in the long run.

With athletes, loss aversion creates the behavior commonly known as "playing not to lose," instead of playing to win. How many times have we watched our team start to play conservatively when they have a lead, and appear to be a completely different team? Having worked with coaches at the Olympic and NBA level, we can tell you it drives coaches (and fans) crazy! It is one of the more difficult situations coaches face: how to change the energy and momentum of their team when they pull back and play not to lose.

For the NHL play-offs, one of the assistant coaches for the 2004 Tampa Bay Lightning came up with the phrase "Safe Is Death." The theme apparently worked. Tampa's players started extending their leads by continuing to "push the play," instead of playing cautiously and protecting the lead. They rode this strategy to victory and the Stanley Cup championship.

At work, if you find yourself procrastinating on a project or are afraid to make a mistake, it might be because you are feeling like this is your one chance and you don't want to blow it. This might have been true for prehistoric man, but your own experiences will tell you that there is almost always another chance, be it a sales call, a test, or someone new to meet (and hundreds of thousands of individuals on their second marriage will agree).

Magnification

Magnification is an extreme exaggeration of a situation. Your appraisals are making a mountain out of a molehill. At work a sales call becomes "the most important" call of your career, and the test your daughter or

son is taking is "the most important" test of your child's life. Again, for early folks, spilling a cup of water was a crisis signaling urgency to find more. Today, the urgency is to mop it up. Perceiving pressure moments as being extremely important in early times was not a pressure distortion, but today it is.

Because importance increases pressure, magnification in a pressure moment is sure to intensify thoughts of fear and anxiety, especially about failure and success. These worry cognitions become the ones *that do* stimulate real fear and anxiety and cause you to lose markers or shrink your working memory.

Magnification often comes into our thinking when we become *too attached to the outcome.* While emphasizing the importance of a test or task might increase our effort, the extra pressure we put on ourselves typically downgrades our performance.

At Stanford University, a group of students were given a test with the explanation that the results would be used by the faculty to get to know them better. An equal number of students were given the same test but with the message that the results would be important in evaluating their academic future and course planning. You may not be surprised to discover that the group that was told the test results were important to their future tested significantly *below* the other group.

The Pressure Regulator

Cognitive appraisal is one of the most effective tools we have to manage pressure because it is a *mediator* between external events and our internal brain, our bodies, and our behavior. How you appraise an event such as a pressure moment becomes a way to alter your internal brain and subsequent behavior.

This concept, that our appraisals influence our feelings and behavior, is far from new and is found in almost all branches of psychology. Decades ago, psychologist Albert Ellis introduced rational emotive behavior therapy, based on the principle that your life will be more productive if you interpret events rationally and rid yourself of cognitive "neurotic" distortions, such as "Everybody should love me," "I should never get angry."

So powerful is the concept of cognitive appraisal and its influence on feelings and behavior that researchers now investigate the process on a neuroscientific level.

A recent study at Columbia University in New York City illustrates this concept in the context of pressure. One by one, a group of undergraduate students were led into the functional magnetic resonance imaging machine (fMRI) at a lab at Columbia. This machine measures activity in the brain by detecting blood oxygenation and flow changes that typically occur during neural activity. As an area of the brain is summoned to act, it consumes oxygen to meet the demands of increased blood flow to that specific part of the brain. The fMRI charts this neural activity. The students, lying inside an fMRI machine, were informed that they would be given a few minutes to mentally prepare themselves. They were told they were to give a highly technical speech on the relationship between tariffs and free trade to a group of business leaders who had particular knowledge and expertise in business and law. The students would be graded on the content of what they said, on how they delivered it, and on the clarity of their arguments.

While they were in the fMRI machine, mentally rehearsing their speeches, the students' heart rates were monitored. They were also asked to report their anxiety level every twenty seconds. The researchers observed that the *anticipation* of giving the speech significantly increased the students' heart rates and their anxiety levels, as well as activity in the areas of the *right* prefrontal cortex related to more negative emotions such as anger, anxiety, and depression. But the interesting thing was that *it wasn't the same for everyone*. Not every student experienced the same levels of physiological change. Why would some individuals experience more activity in the right prefrontal region than others?

In the last few years, science has become more adept at charting the inner workings of the mind. We visited with some of the young new researchers who are doing cutting-edge research at the intersection point of the brain and cognition. One such person is Jeremy Jamieson at the University of Rochester in New York. Formerly, Jeremy was a postdoctoral fellow at Harvard, where he worked in the Psychophysiology Laboratory and the Laboratory for Clinical and Developmental

Research. Only thirty years old, he received his BA in Psychology from Colby College and his PhD in Social Psychology from Northeastern University.

In one study, Jeremy and his team looked at students who were preparing for the graduate record exam, or GRE, a standardized admissions test required by graduate schools to assess candidates. The students were told that they were participating in a study of how stress affects cognition. The team told half the students that recent research suggested "people who feel anxious during a test might actually do better." In other words, if the students felt anxious during the practice test, they were told, "You shouldn't feel concerned. . . . Simply remind yourself that your arousal could be helping you do well."

Simply because they read this statement before the test was administered, the students' performance improved significantly. They scored fifty points higher in the quantitative section of the practice test (out of a possible eight hundred) than the control group. A couple of months later, the students took their actual GRE test and reported back scores. Jeremy and his team were interested in seeing if the intervention had long-term staying power or whether its effects were short-lived. The group taught to see pressure and anxiety as beneficial in the lab experiment scored sixty-five points higher than the control group on the actual test. In other words, those students who were told to believe that anxiety could be helpful did markedly better.

What this study reveals is that when we feel pressure in a situation, it is not the speech or presentation or competition itself that causes increased activity in the prefrontal cortex and a faster heart rate; it is the *meaning* that we ascribe to giving the speech that dictates our response. In other words, as Epictetus said long ago, it is *how we interpret* events that causes us to respond as we do. *Changing the way pressure and anxiety are viewed* changes their negative impact on performance.

In 2010, Kathryn Minshew quit her job at the Clinton Health Access Initiative to run Pretty Young Professionals (PYP), a women's networking site she had started with three coworkers a couple of months before. She bootstrapped the company and guaranteed a small payroll with personal savings, working as an unpaid CEO and editor in chief.

Unfortunately, after an argument about how best to run the

company, the group splintered in half and the threat of a lawsuit loomed. "We split our equity on a piece of notebook paper. We didn't have lawyers; I didn't think we needed them," Minshew recalled.

You can imagine the pressure Minshew felt as her company fell apart. She had always been a star: She had excelled at school and worked at McKinsey, the prestigious consulting firm, before moving to the Clinton Health Access Initiative. She had experienced success every step of the way.

Kathryn did not recognize how pressure was distorting how she appraised the situation. As her company split in two, she had the utterly "gut-wrenching" feeling that she was blowing *her one and only chance* to be an entrepreneur. All she could think was that she was failing, *and everybody was noticing.*

The problem with singularity distortion is that it paralyzes us. After all, if this is our *one chance* to *prove ourselves,* we better *not* blow it!

Fortunately, over time, Kathryn was able to see that the breakup of her business was not the end of her career. She realized that there was nothing stopping her from starting another business. She was only in her mid-twenties when her company fell apart. In September 2011 she launched the Daily Muse (now called the Muse), and the entire staff of PYP (her original company), plus another cofounder, joined her. The Huffington Post and TechCrunch covered the launch; the site drew more visitors in its first month than PYP had at its peak. "It was painful, but being forced to start over was a unique sort of gift, because having been through a lot together, the team comes out of it with the confidence that nothing is going to stop us."

In hindsight, it is clear that the decline of Kathryn's first business was not a "chance of a lifetime," although it sure felt that way to Kathryn in that pressure moment. Her company today includes well over 2 million professionals worldwide, and Kathryn has appeared on CNN and Bloomberg, has spoken at MIT and Harvard, and was recently named to the *Forbes* 30 Under 30 in Media list and Inc.'s 15 Women to Watch in Tech.

Now Kathryn sees what this setback really was: one of *many* opportunities she has in life and a great chance to learn.

Cognitive appraisal is one the natural tools that we all have that can help us *regulate our level of pressure*, specifically by adjusting how we interpret a situation, so that our appraisals spawn productive pressure management self-statements and in the process minimize pressure distortions.

Start by increasing your awareness of the inner dialogues you have before a pressure moment so that you can begin to rid yourself of pressure distortions that derail you. Pressure distortions create distressful feelings, so use this point to your advantage. If you are feeling distress, anxiety, or fear before a pressure moment, it is a reliable sign that your thinking is being affected by pressure distortions. Fight back by "slowing down your thoughts," like our earlier-mentioned client, and then challenge the validity of what you are telling yourself. You will feel more relaxed and perform better.

Similarly, the next time you are feeling confident before a pressure moment, take a pause to reflect on your thoughts. You will see that they are positive and free of pressure distortions, a sign that cognitive appraisal is in your corner to help you do your best when it matters the most.

PRESSURE TRAPS

Can you imagine, in our current age of professional sports, the captains of two teams deciding to end a competition and accept a tie because the pressure was too intense?

In 2003, the President's Cup, a tournament where a team of golfers representing the United States competes against an international team (made up of the rest of the world's best players), ended differently from any year previous or since. With the teams tied 17–17 after four days of grueling, back-and-forth golf, a sudden-death tie-breaker pitted Tiger Woods, the top player in the world at the time, against Ernie Els, who was then rated the second best player in the world.

After three holes of the play-off failed to produce a winner, the tournament was declared a draw by team captains Jack Nicklaus and Gary Player. Amazingly, according to *Sports Illustrated* online, the "captains felt it was too much pressure for any one player" and the players apparently agreed.

What created this acute increase in pressure? After all, aren't professional golfers used to facing pressure? They are. But what they are not used to is playing on a team where there are supportive teammates cheering you on. Part of a golfer's motivation in playing the President's Cup is the prestige and camaraderie that accompanies being selected, as well as being part of a team, which is not something golfers often get a chance to experience. Els admitted that the play-off was "probably the first [time] I've ever felt my legs shaking." He explained, "You look over and see your team. You're like, 'I've got to look away. It is unbelievable pressure.'" Woods called the play-off "one of the most nerve-racking moments I've

ever had in golf." He described preparing to putt, with his red-shirted teammates in the background: "I saw all this red and I was just trying to block that out." Here were the two best golfers in the world, very experienced when it came to pressure, feeling more pressure than they *had ever felt* before simply because of the presence of their teammates.

This is a telling example of a pressure trap: Something that you think is helpful—support from a teammate—turns out to have a counterintuitive effect, *increasing* pressure and making it more difficult to perform closer to your best.

Pressure traps have three noteworthy characteristics: First, they are *omnipresent*. They can be found in our place of work, at school, on a date, or in the sports we play. Sometimes they trap us in a pressure moment; other times we are caught before we enter the pressure moment, and usually we don't even know it.

Second, like all effective traps, they are usually *well concealed*. They are often disguised as forms of motivation and support, when in fact they intensify pressure and do the opposite of what they are intended or thought to do.

Third, pressure traps are *dangerous*: Getting caught by one will likely derail us in our most important moments. They can also, if we are not careful, become more integrated into our daily routine, and they lead to pressure anxiety—perpetually feeling you have to produce and continually questioning whether you can.

While it is true that we often walk into traps of our own accord, this chapter focuses on the pressure traps we set for others—our employees, our children, and our partners. We typically do this inadvertently; nevertheless, the trap can effectively derail the people who matter most to us.

Setting Traps

In our roles as parents, managers, teachers, and administrators, we begin each day with the goal of inspiring others to perform to their best. The methods we use mirror how people tried to motivate us in the past. As a result, they are not always guided by the latest research, but we assume they are effective.

The methods we rely on—financial incentives, encouragement and support, and the spirit of competition—are often thought to be positives in terms of motivating and improving performance. But they are not always. New studies in cognitive and social psychology and behavioral economics show us that these methods are often counterproductive. In fact, they can actually *intensify* the pressure of the moment, contributing to underperformance. In effect, our efforts then make us part of the problem.

The Support Trap

Most of us grew up with the conventional wisdom that giving support and encouragement to others when they are in the spotlight helps them do their best. Yet this is not always the case. While it may seem counterintuitive, multiple studies have corroborated what Tiger Woods and Ernie Els experienced in that final showdown of the President's Cup: Support frequently *magnifies* performance pressure and often induces performers to do poorly on skill-based tasks.

Researchers Jennifer Butler and Roy Baumeister of Florida State University found, in a number of studies, that the people they tested performed less well in front of a supportive audience compared to an unsupportive audience. Why would a supportive audience cause a performer to do poorly? A proximate explanation is that supportive audiences tend to increase performers' self-consciousness, so they focus on whether they are performing correctly and what others may be thinking of them. Consequently, they move away from focusing on what they need to be doing or thinking. In other words, your ten-year-old may botch her performance because she starts to be more focused on watching herself (self-monitoring) and stops focusing on the task at hand. She is keenly aware that her parents (or, for adults, a boss in the audience at your presentation) are watching and wonders, *What are they thinking of me?* This increased self-focus disrupts the automatic execution of the skills she has practiced or rehearsed. Her procedural memory malfunctions.

But why does a supportive audience turn up the heat in the first place? Why does a supportive family intensify feelings of pressure?

Our evolutionary roots reveal the deeper answer: It has to do with our *need to be accepted,* and our primal *fear of abandonment.*

In prehistoric times, disappointing others or not doing your job led to shame, embarrassment, and even exile. Because an individual's survival was dependent on the group, exile from the group was often equivalent to a death sentence. It was a lot easier to secure food when you hunted in a group than if you did so individually. Living up to the group's expectations assured your acceptance and increased your chances of survival. Being accepted by the group gave you an evolutionary edge. Even though we no longer hunt for our food or depend on groups in the same way, we are still hardwired and inherently driven to want to be accepted by groups and others.

This is how the support trap exerts its power: On the one hand it evokes your natural feelings of abandonment anxiety, and on the other it appeals to your natural need for group acceptance. This affects us as much as the positive influence people may be trying to give us in support.

We don't worry about letting others down per se—we worry about others accepting or rejecting us. Therefore the stronger an individual's need is for acceptance and approval, the more pressure he or she is apt to experience in these situations. This effect is so powerful it can impact high-pressure performers at the most competitive levels, including, as we've seen, the top golfers in the world. Students who have a high need for parental approval also report feeling more pressure to perform academically than those who rate high on self-acceptance.

The pressure solutions we offer in Part 2 of this book will help you perform in front of a "supportive" audience by keeping your mind occupied with your task, rather than with what others think of you. This is especially important when you consider that you cannot control what others think or feel about you—influence yes, control no!

What you can control, we suggest, is your own feelings. The more you value yourself, the more confident you will become and the less pressure you will experience. This insight also has important implications for managing others and parenting: Be aware of making sure your support for others is not *contingent* on whether or not the individual achieves. When parents link their love and support to a child's

performance, the parent sets up a conditional relationship that can undermine the child's chances of becoming a confident individual.

Through therapy and coaching sessions, and pressure workshop participant conversations, we've found there is an abundance of parents who inadvertently place their kids in the support trap. Sometimes it's due to the pressure the parents feel themselves: They want their child to do well on a sports team or get into an elite school because of how it will reflect on them; they fail to see that it's *not their child's responsibility* to make them proud.

One of the ways you can minimize the pressure that performers in your life may feel is to reassure them that your support goes beyond *this one* activity or contest. It does not represent their one defining quality. Whether they win or lose, it will not affect how you see them as people; it doesn't reflect one way or the other on *who they are*.

When someone is under extreme pressure, their most basic needs tend to come to the surface—one of which is to be loved, accepted, and not abandoned. If they feel they have your full support regardless of how they do in these moments, the pressure they feel diminishes and they have a better chance of performing at their best. Perhaps more important, the pressure moment then also becomes an opportunity to build intimacy in these most treasured relationships.

Dr. Ronald Podell, a confident and successful Los Angeles psychiatrist, put it this way: "My father watched me play in a lot of golf tournaments and saw me study for a lot of tests. He always told me, 'Whether you come in first or last, you're still my horse!'" As a parent, that is the attitude you want to convey as well.

The Incentive Trap

Have you ever heard your boss say something like "Come up with something good, and you'll all get a 10 percent bonus." Or felt the lash of a negative incentive: "If you don't do well this quarter, we're not taking you to Disney World."

On the surface this seems an appropriate use of a carrot or stick approach to motivation. However, this is another example of a pressure trap that can act to decrease the other person's (or the team's)

performance. Princeton psychologist Sam Glucksberg conducted an experiment that shows how such incentives act as a trap that *increases* pressure and diminishes performance.

Glucksberg brought a group of subjects into a room in which a table was positioned against a wall. On the table was a book of matches, a box of thumbtacks, and a candle. He instructed the participants: "Your job is to attach the candle to the wall in such a way that when it's lit, the wax will not drip onto the table. I will be timing you, and I will use your results to establish averages and benchmarks."

Another group of subjects were shown an identical setup—table, matches, box of thumbtacks, and candle—and identical instructions, but with one addition: Glucksberg told them, "I will be timing you, and you will be rewarded with money based on your times. If you finish in the top 25 percent of all times, you will receive X dollars. If you have the fastest time, we will give you double that amount."

The groups who received money as a reward on average were three-and-a-half minutes *slower* than the other groups at coming up with the right answer. Why? The promise of incentives increases the pressure of the situation (there is more at stake) and causes a shift of focus from the task to the *consequences* of succeeding or failing at the task. The cognitive horsepower and focus that are needed to solve the problem are now being used to think about the possible gain or loss of the incentive. As a result, we are not giving the problem our full attention and best effort.

Another study demonstrates this, too. Published in the *Journal of Psychological Science*, the study by British researchers used functional MRI brain scans to examine people while they played a computerized game for a modest monetary reward. Nineteen subjects played the game, in which they had to catch a "high-payoff prey" or a "low-payoff prey." They performed worse when trying to catch the high-payoff prey. As in the earlier study, brain scans showed increased activity in the central mid-brain tied to motivation and reward response. The intense desire to attain the incentive causes an excessive arousal and activity in the brain that actually can interfere with decision-making, memory, and attention. These studies suggest that it's the presence of an incentive or reward that causes people to perform poorly.

Distraction and overarousal theories provide sound explanations for understanding how financial incentives downgrade performance, and their explanations help create pressure solutions. But they do not suggest why financial incentives, or other incentives, have the power to increase pressure and trap us in the first place or, more notably, why people feel pressure daily and why individuals act in ways that are undesirable.

In fact, there is considerable research that demonstrates that the desire to achieve incentives, such as a quarterly or even a weekly bonus, intensifies pressure on those seeking them, and often leads to cheating, deception, and poor employee relationships, three results that all organizations seek to avoid. Yet most organizations are set up with this kind of motivational system. Offering financial incentives is one of the bedrock tools used to drive performance in companies, and yet in financial institutions, it is often to blame for causing inside trading violations. Think of all of those bonuses and raises that are dangled like carrots before your eyes, and think about how they have caused you to feel and respond.

Why should incentives motivate us to act in ways that are often counterproductive? The answer starts with understanding that an incentive is an object or thought that has a tendency to incite or arouse one to action. Since early man's actions were directed to survival, the first incentive had to be food and water; it would be evolutionary logic to say that early man was not only motivated by the first incentive, but he had to attain it to survive, and those who consistently attained the incentive were given an evolutionary edge.

It was also true for early man that a loss of the incentive or not attaining it would threaten his survival. He needed the incentive and he couldn't afford to lose it—a feeling many have today about their incentive bonuses.

Because all early men—regardless of geographical location— needed to attain the incentive to survive and couldn't afford to lose it, it would make evolutionary sense that this mental connection between needing/losing the incentive and survival became a hardwired association that the neurosciences suggest has the capability of surfacing anytime we are aroused by an incentive, especially in a pressure moment.

Right here is the primal lure of the trap. Your inherent need for—and aversion to losing—the incentive regresses you to a primal pressure reaction, so that you actually believe and feel you *need* and must have the incentive, that without it you are doomed. The trigger that springs the trap and squeezes you is the concept of "need."

In other words, your subconscious—thoughts, associations, memories, feelings that are distant from your current awareness—is a great influence on your current emotional landscape. Primal thoughts and feelings operate in the subconscious, and no matter how distant in time they are from you today, they still play out in all parts of your life. When an executive feels and thinks that he or she needs an incentive to survive, it is not surprising that he or she will do what it takes to get it. The students who feel they need an A to survive are more apt to cheat.

We recommend you apply these points to yourself by examining how you think about the incentives you seek out and then answer this one question:

DO YOU TELL YOURSELF YOU NEED OR WANT THEM?

Multiple psychological perspectives and studies strongly suggest that those individuals who believe "I need/must have this" may achieve their incentives, but transform their world into a pressure cooker. Their belief that they need the incentive increases its importance and causes the individual to try harder and thus increases the daily feelings of pressure to attain the incentive, sometimes at any cost. Simultaneously, the individual's thoughts of not getting the incentive evoke feelings of anxiety in response to primal associations suggesting that his or her existence is threatened.

To free yourself from the incentive traps, first reflect on your *needs* and *wants*—and the difference between them. We've asked hundreds of workshop participants to perform this task, and the general finding is that individuals (as we would predict) think of needs as basics for survival. We all need food, shelter, clothes, money (or some form of social exchange currency), and love. Without attaining these basic need incentives, we would eventually not survive.

Wants can be thought of as needs *exaggerated*. As one woman put

it, "We all need clothes. That's a need. Wanting a dress with a Chanel or Gucci label, that's a want." We often think and state our *wants as needs*, resulting in the feeling of pressure intensifying. Primal associations that are stirred in our subconscious promote anxious and fearful feelings that we might lose the incentive; since we feel we "need it," we feel more pressure to attain it.

Next, short-circuit the primal association between needs and wants by recognizing that what you need is different from what you want. Then *express your wants as wants*, not as needs. "I want a nice car" is a different message to yourself than the pressure-inducing I *need* a nice car. Most people do *want* a nice car, but those who transform the want into a need will feel compelled to buy a status brand, even though they cannot afford it. When you recognize that you want a nice car but, in fact, any reliable car will do, you experience less pressure financially and in terms of being able to fulfill your needs. A Chinese proverb states: "You can tell the wealth of a man by what he can do without."

Do not miss the importance of this point when it comes to coaching and working with others: The words we use have enormous implications because of how much pressure they create within us. When JP's eldest daughter was applying to college, he learned the hard way that simple words like "need to" versus "want to" increased the pressure his daughter felt around studying and getting certain scores on her SATs and getting a good erg (stationary rowing machine) score (she is a competitive rower). Children take the literal meaning of the words we use far more than we may realize. So be careful about the language you use for yourself and with your kids or employees. Nobody wants to artificially increase the pressure others feel—especially when they already feel a lot of internally induced pressure.

The Competition Trap

It's a fact of life that we live in a competitive world. The effects of competition on performance under pressure have been studied in detail in a variety of arenas and for all sorts of tasks. Some researchers have found that competition increases student motivation and test scores and is a powerful source that challenges an organization or an individual to

adapt and get better over time. Other researchers have found that competition brings out the worst in us and is antisocial in nature, leading to cheating, poorer test scores, and distressful feelings.

Our intent is not to debate whether or not competition brings out your best or worst. It is to understand how framing competition in a certain way can act as a trap that intensifies the feelings of pressure and disrupts performance, especially as it relates to influencing others.

To start, it is important to differentiate between the two approaches or mind-sets that most people use toward competition: what we call a *ranking* mind-set and an *excellence* mind-set.

A ranking mind-set toward competition is characterized by a win-at-all-costs approach driven by insecurity and the need to prove oneself. People who are competitive in this way compete at every possible turn, even when they lack expertise. It is about proving they are "better" than another person. Even when the competition is long over, a person like this still competes and compares him- or herself to others.

When one considers the nature of early competition, it is easy to see the evolutionary utility for early man to have a ranking mind-set. Long before man hunted in groups, hunting was a solo activity. Sooner or later, the situation arose that two men would simultaneously spot and attempt to attain the same food that each needed for survival. How would it be decided who wins the prize? The men would have to compete, with the winner getting the prize—to survive and move on—and with the loser saying farewell. Early competition then was a natural pressure inducer because it set up a zero-sum situation: Somebody wins and somebody loses. This winner-take-all outcome is still prevalent hundreds of thousands of years later in competitive events.

What would be the task these two early "athletes" had to perform to settle their competition? For sure, it was not who could throw a stone farther or climb a tree faster. Much more likely, their competition was settled by physical confrontation with each other—they fought each other, often to the death—winner take all. For this reason, the competitive instinct is often called the survival instinct—your survival becomes dependent on beating your competitor. It also explains the connection between competition and aggression, as early competitive events were settled violently. Studies today tell us what nature

has evolved: Individuals with a competitive nature are also aggressive individuals. Beating his competitor gave early man the prize and, more important, the opportunity to procreate. Thus, because early competitions were winner-take-all, it was clearly an evolutionary advantage to be at the top. Your ranking decided if and when you would eat. It would also decide whom you could select as, and when you could select, a mate. Being ranked highly was clearly a goal for all.

Eons later, many individuals react to daily life challenges as competitive events in which they have to be ranked first, to *beat* their opponent so they can feel successful, while lurking in their subconscious is the primal thought that losing or coming in second would be equal to extinction.

However, as man evolved into a more social being, it became evident that it was no longer necessary to beat others to achieve success. Rather, what evolved was the requirement to cooperate with others and make a contribution to the group by doing your best. The young warrior no longer had to throw a spear farther than his teammate; he just had to do his best so that he, too, could succeed and contribute to the group, and doing so would help him advance. Today, we call this the excellence mind-set.

In contrast to a ranking mind-set, the excellence mind-set is characterized less by a focus on ranking and competition and more by a focus on developing yourself to your fullest capability. People who use this approach use the spirit of competition as an opportunity to get better—not as a way to prove they are necessarily better than someone else, but as a way of challenging themselves. They welcome, even honor, competition as a way to develop or improve their expertise and abilities.

John Child, a beach volleyball player with whom JP worked over three Olympics, is a good example of excellence versus ranking mind-set. John was internally driven to being the best player he could be; he couldn't have cared less about what other people thought of him or where he specifically ranked compared to others. This approach served him well, as he was *less* thrown off when he and his teammate Mark Heese didn't get the ranking or seed they thought they deserved going

into an important tournament. He certainly didn't lack a competitive drive—he simply had a different kind of drive. He wanted to win his matches as much as anyone, but because he was more internally driven, he was less distracted by what was happening in the stands or on the court and, as a result, was more effective in competitive, pressure-filled environments like the Olympic Games or the World Championships. In the 1996 Atlanta Olympic Games, he and Mark used their excellence mind-set to outperform their seventh seeding to win a well-deserved bronze medal.

When it comes to the traps we can set for others, how many times have we heard coaches or sales managers set up a ranking mind-set in terms of competition? The focus for the team becomes beating the competition as opposed to being their best. Managers think this technique will get a bit more zip and energy from their players or salespeople—and it might in the short term. But it is not a sustainable source of fuel. Far more powerful are the reinforcing behavior and positive performance of an excellence mind-set.

Interestingly, in organizations where ranking has been used and studied (a system that forces managers to evaluate employees on a bell curve against other employees and to let go those who fall to the bottom), it has been systematically found to be of little value, if not to actually sabotage employee effort. This system doesn't work because, like it did in early times, it sets up a zero-sum environment: "If you do well, it might result in me being fired. Better I beat you than help you." Not surprisingly, this system does not correlate well with collaboration, team cohesion, and better group results. Corporations like Microsoft, one of our clients, and many others have now gone away from this system because of its deleterious effects.

One of the consequences of habituating a ranking mind-set is that it causes greater physical arousal in our bodies because the ranking mind keeps you on edge—you always have to be ready for the "fight," always ready to beat your competitor. This high arousal state keeps us focused on winning, which in a sporting event is helpful, but when it becomes unmanageable either in the pressure moment or throughout the days, it often works against us because we become mentally rigid

and we lose our ability to generate options and consider alternatives. In the context of competition, the only thoughts we have are of beating another; we lose sight of the more worthy goal—doing our best.

Elaborating the point, relative gain is a mind-set in which we get so focused on one part of an outcome that we miss other important factors. This perspective can lead individuals to make bad decisions and commit actions that they inevitably regret. In a negotiation, you can tell the focus has moved to relative gain when things become *personal*. In a marriage, this is when relations between a couple descend into contempt or stonewalling or defensiveness. In an auction, it results in overbidding on an object just to beat your opponent, *even if bidding surpasses the object's value*. Perhaps the prime example is needless litigation that is costly and ill-advised. The individual is locked into beating his or her opponent, making it more likely that he or she will engage in behaviors that are counterproductive.

What's interesting is that a ranking mind-set and an increased focus on relative gain can lead to decisions that focus on winning even in situations where it comes *at a personal loss with no strategic upside*. In one study, the experimenter found that subjects pursue relative gain more vigorously than personal gain because they do not like receiving less than others. Gore Vidal, the American writer, is often quoted on his definition of the essence of the desire to win: "It is not enough to succeed. Others must fail."

A ranking mind-set that focuses on win-at-any-cost behavior can have another unhappy side effect: It encourages people to cut ethical corners—to cheat—in the pursuit of their goals, whether in a business deal, when taking an exam, or when playing sports with the help of performance-enhancing drugs.

There are several steps you can take that will help you keep from being victimized by competition. First, remember to frame competition as a way to become better, not as a way to prove something to someone. It is a path to excellence where all effort is worthy. Similarly, the people you coach or manage or influence do not always have to be *the* best in order to have a good outcome. There will almost always be someone who is better, richer, prettier, more handsome, smarter—these factors are things outside of your control, and focusing too intensely on them

by continually comparing and thinking you have to be better than everyone else will only breed frustration and diminished performance. Shifting your mind-set from beating others to simply doing your best will help you feel less pressure anxiety.

Second, practice relaxation. Competitive people are more easily aroused than those who are less competitive, and arousal frequently stimulates feelings of hostility toward your opponent and you are apt to do anything to win, including violating your ethics. By being more relaxed, you'll be less influenced by competitive arousal and the hazards it creates, including mental rigidity and getting caught focusing on relative gains.

Third, remember that feelings of competitiveness are hardwired in us. It is not a bad thing. In fact, when it is framed in the proper way, competition is a powerful motivational fuel that can help us and the people we are trying to influence achieve things no one might have previously thought possible, but this again is in the context of competing with yourself—to make yourself, others, or your product better and better.

If you are a parent, consider what sports psychologists at the University of Washington found out about young athletes' achievement goals and how they can change in a healthy way over the course of a season when their coaches create a mastery motivational climate (excellence mind-set) rather than an ego orientation (ranking mind-set). In other words, when parents and coaches stress teamwork and doing one's best, a child will gain the belief that he or she can accomplish more challenging goals. The opposite happens in an ego climate, typified by many professional sports coaches who create a ranking mind-set, where the focus is on winning at all cost and being better than others.

Finally, balance feelings of competition by teaming with others— even in individual sports (smart track-and-field coaches use this method). Most people in studies report strong feelings of enjoyment when they engage in collaboration and are part of a successful team; they feel less pressure because they don't feel like they have to carry the burden by themselves. The more we experience the joy of working and collaborating with others, the less our competitiveness will get the best of us.

Navigating the Traps

The best way to navigate these traps so that you do not set them for others or walk into one of your own accord is to be aware of them. Our research findings and clinical and coaching experiences point out that many managers and parents are not aware of the traps and how they sabotage their goal of making others and themselves more effective.

To avoid trapping others, remember that each trap can be managed by bringing attention to its antidote. For the support trap, be clear about what your kids—or the members of your work team—want most of all: to be accepted and not abandoned. Understanding this need can influence your communication, the support you give, and the criticism you offer. It doesn't mean you don't offer clear and strong criticism; it just means you recognize the best way to deliver the criticism and support you provide because you understand what matters most to the people you are offering it to.

If you are a parent, remember that it is *not* your child's job to *make you proud*. Don't make your support contingent on the outcome. Make sure your children know that you see them as far more than this one result or performance.

When it comes to incentives, emphasize quality of work—not the attainment of an incentive. Doing so will keep people focused on doing their best, which stimulates a mind-set of excellence, which often leads to goal attainment. When you consider that numerous studies demonstrate that the people on your team are more likely to be driven by doing meaningful work than by responding to monetary incentives, this is a transformational mind shift that is easy to implement.

As for preventing yourself from being trapped by pressure, step back and take a look at why incentives, social support, and competition can derail your performance.

To do that, recognize the common mechanism that springs these pressure traps and keeps them locked around your daily life: They all stimulate primal pressure experiences that create natural polarities; the left side being inherent aversions and the right side being inherent desires.

We are hardwired to seek "incentives" as well as hardwired to avoid

risk and loss. Perishing and abandonment are states we are hardwired
to avoid; security, acceptance, and advancement are states we're hard-
wired to seek. It's human nature to avoid threats, so we feel pressure to
make sure we don't experience the left; and because it's also human na-
ture to seek security, acceptance, and advancement, we feel pressure to
seek the right. The more we desire the right and wish to avoid the left,
the more our primal pressure thoughts and feelings come to the sur-
face and the more we have feelings of "have to" on a daily basis. These
three polarities of pressure keep us trapped and perpetuate pressure
anxiety.

Get some self-revelations about your trap reactions by asking your-
self which side drives your feelings of pressure the most:

+ Fear of not getting the reward or the need to attain the reward
+ Fear of being rejected by others or your need to be accepted by
 others
+ Not wanting to lose or having to win

Reflecting on your answers will give you some smart insights into
where the traps squeeze you the hardest and tell you which polarity
you need to move away from the most. When you're in the center,
you're feeling pressure, but it is appropriate to the context of your life
or a particular pressure moment.

Your pressure reduction "centering" lesson is the realization and
acceptance that feeling insecure or secure is not based on incentives
you attain, how many people like you, or how many times you beat the
other guy—many of you, and our clients, have been operating by these
principles for years and, even if successful, probably feel pressured to
achieve more of the same.

Instead, free yourself from pressure traps by letting your own val-
ues, interests, and goals motivate you; value yourself, and focus on
what you can control—your own efforts. Your days will be filled with
fewer pressure feelings, less pressure anxiety.

For those individuals who are unable to escape the pressure traps,
be aware that you will continue to feel the heat, even in cold weather.

THE THIRD VARIABLE

In 2011, Jordyn Wieber, at the age of sixteen, competed at the World Gymnastics Championships in Tokyo, Japan. It was her first World Championships and she felt enormous pressure. However, she did not let the pressure disrupt her performance; she won the gold medal in the women's all-around, giving her the distinction of being the world's best gymnast. Going into the Olympics in 2012 in London, Jordyn was ready. In gymnastics, the Olympics are the zenith of a career—everything leads up to that moment. Jordyn was featured, along with the rest of the US women's gymnastics team, on the cover of *Sports Illustrated*, and she had her eye set on a "fistful" of gold medals. Being the reigning world champion gave her confidence that she had what it took to take her place among the pantheon of greats in US gymnastics like Mary Lou Retton, Kerri Strug, Shawn Johnson, Nastia Liukin, and Shannon Miller, all of whom made their name at the Olympics.

Unfortunately for Jordyn, things didn't go as she'd planned. In the qualifying rounds of the women's all-around, she underperformed, stepped out of bounds in the floor routine, and placed third behind teammates Aly Raisman and Gabby Douglas. This meant that she did not move on to the finals in the all-around competition, as only two competitors from each country qualify to compete in the finals. She was *distraught*. Her coach said that he was devastated for her. "She had trained her entire life for this day." Some of the print and television media as well as other observers called it a "choke"—the "reigning world champion didn't even get out of qualifying."

But did Jordyn really "choke"? Was this simply another example of underperformance when faced with intense pressure?

Psychologist Abraham Maslow is famous for saying: "If you only have a hammer, you tend to see every problem as a nail." And when it comes to pressure and performance, we need to be careful of falling into the temptation of seeing every suboptimal performance in the same way—as a tendency to choke. This is not always the case. We need to recognize that individuals perform below their capabilities in pressure moments for a variety of reasons. Many times the causes of choking that we typically come up with are all *proximate explanations*—we use the current situational information to account for the results. But proximate explanations, especially in science, can take us off track. This is where the "third variable" comes into play.

When a psychologist conducts an experimental study, he or she is usually trying to test a cause-and-effect relationship between two variables. For instance, a researcher might want to determine if a change from a low-pressure situation to a high-pressure situation affects performance such as test scores. In order to test this theory, the researcher designs an experiment to gather data that will show whether or not increasing pressure causes a weaker performance. If the results of the study are statistically significant, it means that the results are highly unlikely to be caused by chance; instead, the researcher concludes that the weaker performance is due to a change in pressure intensity—what else could it be? Indeed, what else could it be?

Good experimental researchers know that it is always important to be aware of a potential third variable, a factor that can alter or impact the relationship between the two variables being studied. Also known as a confounding variable, it is something that the researcher might fail to control, or eliminate, which negates the validity of the experiment. In the case of understanding the relationship between pressure and performance, what other factors, or third variables, might be at work here? And how can we be aware of them?

At the 2012 Olympics, what nobody could know at the time was that Jordyn was competing with a stress fracture, a very common injury in gymnastics. A stress fracture is a tiny crack in a weight-bearing bone

that is often difficult to diagnose. Jordyn's injury not only hampered her in the competition, but it disrupted her training in the lead-up to London. After this revelation, people understood what had happened to Jordyn, given the fracture's obvious impact on her performance, but at the time of the competition many attributed her underperformance simply to choking. Her injury offers a perfect illustration of how easy it is to think someone choked under pressure when in fact there was a third variable at work. Sometimes there is more to a situation than meets the eye—the proximate explanations for behavior are inaccurate or incomplete. Just because someone underperforms doesn't necessarily mean that person choked.

It is easy to miss the third variable when we consider underperformance. Many of the studies involving psychomotor skills, such as putting in golf, or shooting baskets in basketball, or shooting a pistol in pistol shooting, are performed in an experimental laboratory or a simulator, such as a video game. This is generally not an adequate environment to test pressure. A good deal of evidence exists now to show that athletes, such as marksmen, race car drivers, and soccer players, perform very differently—not surprisingly—in game situations than in an experimental laboratory. Basketball fans might remember Allen Iverson's retort (on YouTube) to the media's criticism about his lackadaisical play in practice—"Practice! We're talking about practice. Practice! We're talking about practice! Not a game, practice!"—with the implication that he plays differently in a game. Most athletes do. Likewise, professional debaters and politicians make comments in rehearsals that they would not repeat with the camera on them.

Many game conditions that produce a third variable—such as chance events, a divot on the field, weather, personal feelings toward an opponent—are absent in an experimental laboratory. Facing the eighteenth hole at Pebble Beach is a lot different from facing a putting green in a university laboratory. This does not negate the experimental findings, but it does bring the generalization of the results into question. We need to remember that a lab is not a golf course.

There is more. Experimental laboratory studies on choking are typically defined around *a specific moment*, such as making the golf putt or shooting a basketball. Yet, in the real world, the corresponding tasks

play out differently. There is no major golf tournament that is just a putting contest, or NBA game where players restrict themselves to foul shooting. Golfers make poor shots all the time, and each one is not attributable to distractions and/or other factors that cause choking. A bad golf shot could be the result of poor club selection rather than the mechanics of the golfer's swing. A missed putt could be caused by a wrong grip or taking a caddy's poor advice, rather than thinking too much and choking.

A female student who chokes on a math test is not necessarily responding to the belief that if she performs poorly, she is proof that "girls aren't good in math," as former Harvard president Larry Summers implied in his speech at a 2005 economic conference to explain why women were not prevalent in top science positions. Perhaps the morning of her exam, she overheard her parents talking about divorce, and that's the thought that interferes with her doing well on the exam, not her concern about some silly stereotype that she knows doesn't apply to her.

The Problem with the Label

A sad consequence in missing the third variable is our tendency to mislabel people as chokers when it is unwarranted, and this label can have a serious long-term effect on them. Take Donnie Moore. He was a pitcher in 1986 who gave up a home run to Dave Henderson, blowing the save in Game 5 of the American League championship series, costing his California Angels the championship against the Boston Red Sox. Unfortunately, Moore couldn't handle being labeled a choker, and on July 20, 1989, he took his life. "I think insanity set in. He could not live with himself after Henderson hit the home run. He kept blaming himself," Moore's agent, Mike Pinter, said.

What people didn't know about Donnie Moore was that he had a bone spur near his spinal cord, and he pitched the whole 1986 season in significant pain. It was a heroic effort. He had tried to use nerve-blocking agents, cortisone, and other medications to deal with the pain, all to no avail. There is a code in major-league sports, however, that you never blame a performance on an injury, so nobody ever knew about Donnie Moore's third variable until it was too late.

Frequently in organizations, someone gets a reputation because of a single, significant underperformance under pressure. Sadly, few people wait to see if there is a pattern or not before they affix the label to someone. This negative moniker can have many significant effects on a promising employee: It can become a stigmatizing reputation; the employee may fail to get challenging jobs or to get promoted, and this starts to affect how engaged he or she is in the job or how much discretionary effort—extra effort—the employee chooses to give. It can feel hopeless even to try.

This is one of the reasons why it is so important for managers or leaders to be effective under pressure themselves: It allows them to see beyond the proximate explanations for the behavior of their direct reports. They are more aware that a third variable may be at work in their directs' actions. Maybe they are underperforming because there is a "chemistry" problem on the team—people aren't getting along—or because they are having an issue at home that is causing them distress, something that has nothing directly to do with getting tasks done at work. When a manager or leader can manage his or her own emotions intelligently, it gives that leader the ability to tune in, have more empathy, and see more clearly what is going on for his or her people, and not reactively judge them for underperforming.

The second problem with missing the third variable and mislabeling someone as unable to manage pressure effectively is that it promotes the use of the wrong solution to the problem. Because most of the research into choking uses proximate explanations, current situational information, to account for the results, and most people observing pressure situations do the same, the result is that experts tend to offer proximate interventions that may not be effective at all.

This is like the fifth grader who has a cold, probably caught from a classmate. That is a proximate explanation—it attributes the cause to what we know currently about the child's life. Given his symptoms, he will probably be given some cold medicine to treat them. However, a child who *consistently* gets a cold, on a regular basis, is a different issue, and it raises the question of *why* this keeps happening. For appropriate treatment, the physician needs to determine the *root cause*. The physician's investigation may lead to discovering a deficiency in the child's

immune system that started when he was two and went undetected until now. The cause is different, and so is the treatment. Sticking to a proximate explanation when more information is needed could be hazardous to the child.

The twenty-two pressure solutions we provide in Part 2 are proximate solutions. They treat the symptoms of choking—but not the cause. There is great value in that, as there is in taking cold medicine to stop a runny nose. If you have a sinus infection, however, it won't be effectively treated unless you are also prescribed antibiotics.

For most of us, treating the symptoms of choking is sufficient; it helps us get through high-pressure moments. For example: It helps the financial advisor when she presents to her clients; it helps the lawyer when he makes his closing deliberation; it helps the student on test day; it helps the downhill racer in her Olympic trial; it helps the real estate agent when he's showing a house; it helps military and law officers do their job. For most individuals, pressure management is simply about performing to their capability. Every once in a while, they will drop the ball. We all do that, just like every once in a while a top quarterback throws an interception or a professional golfer misses a three-foot putt. We all blow an opportunity now and then. But with enough practice and some anti-distraction and anti-worry strategies, we have a better chance of performing closer to our best. For many individuals, pressure solutions are the perfect prescription. Yet our work as psychologists, coaches, and consultants to elite athletes and executives reveals another group of individuals—much larger than you would suspect—that *face a significant and ongoing uphill battle.* These individuals are well prepared and well rehearsed, and have extensive expertise, yet they are up against what feels like an insurmountable obstacle.

When It's More Serious

A patient of Dr. Weisinger: "I am good at what I do, but ever since my second year of law school, every time I have to stand up in front of others and speak, I start to perspire. I find it embarrassing," says Sarah, a thirty-one-year-old attorney, who graduated from a top ten law school. She is an example of someone with a more serious problem. "What is

worse is that when I meet with a new client or explain a position to my boss, I get really anxious—not thirty minutes prior to the meeting but the day before. I don't get distracted or lose my focus. . . . I am always complimented for my work, so I should feel confident. My first appearance in front of a judge, it was a *nightmare*. The judge was pleasant and it was just a hearing—no trial, no jury. Yet my heart was racing. I wasn't concerned with the outcome—I wasn't even thinking about it. I just felt really uncomfortable, like something terrible was going to happen. I wanted to run out of the courtroom. When asked to state some facts, I had them right in front of me—I just couldn't communicate them the way I had rehearsed, even when looking at my notes. I spoke quickly and probably sounded a little incoherent—the judge asked me to speak slower. I wanted to—but I couldn't. I just wanted to get out. A few weeks later, we had a firm party—a couple of hundred people. For some reason, I didn't want to go. Just the thought of going was making me perspire."

There are countless people like Sarah. Their fear of facing pressure situations can prevent them from advancing, because they avoid being in the spotlight—for fear of choking. Characteristically, these individuals say before a pressure moment, "I hope I don't screw it up," or "I hope I can get through this."

Early humans were hunter-gatherers. An ongoing problem for them was that much of what they ate was dangerous to catch. They had to survive in a harsh environment in which what they hunted also wanted to hunt them. There are various ways in which man and other animals evolved to adapt to this challenge. Some creatures evolved defenses, such as claws, razor-sharp teeth, or sword-like beaks. Human beings did something different. We became social beings. We hunted in packs and evolved ever more complex forms of communication and tools that enabled us as a group to defeat our prey. Our social skills and bigger brains allowed us to dominate the planet over time. We were able to successfully avoid being the hunted.

We humans had a natural emotional signal that told us we were vulnerable—anxiety and fear. Anxiety cautioned us to be careful and to watch the environment closely for threats. Inevitably, early man

would come face-to-face with a predator—say, a saber-toothed tiger. Threat then became *concrete danger*.

Anxiety is heightened by uncertainty. Experiencing uncertainty in a life-or-death situation, Navy SEALs and Marines will tell you, can be costly: "He who hesitates in the face of his enemy is dead" is how General George Patton put it to his troops. For early man to survive such an encounter, he would have needed a *fast reaction to a perceived threat* that enabled him to remove himself from danger before being attacked. In other words, a *panic response* or, as Walter Cannon, a professor and chairman of the Department of Physiology at Harvard, called it in his book *The Wisdom of the Body*, published in 1932, a *flight-fight response*.

The reaction originates in the amygdala and causes a neural response in the hypothalamus. The initial reaction is followed by activation of the pituitary gland and secretion of the hormone ACTH. Almost simultaneously, the adrenal gland is activated and releases the neurotransmitter epinephrine. The release of chemical messengers results in the production of cortisol, a hormone that increases blood sugar and blood pressure and suppresses the immune system.

Some humans are born with a stronger fight-or-flight response than others. And tens of thousands of years ago a stronger fight-or-flight response was an advantage. Those of our ancestors who couldn't panic fast enough had a lower chance of passing on their genes to their offspring. That helps to explain *why* exaggerated anxiety and panic (disorders) can run in families. Indeed, anyone who seeks treatment for anxiety or depression will be asked about the prevalence of the condition in his or her family.

At the *immediate onset of a perceived danger*, our bodies launch into a panic response by shooting up our heart rate so that we can take immediate, high-energy action, and by focusing our minds in such a way that we are fully alert to the danger and can take decisive action, while at the same time shutting down all nonurgent bodily functions, such as processing food, so that our bodies can be fully devoted to the task of avoiding the danger.

In Ridley Scott's Academy Award–winning movie *Alien*, there's

a scene in which one of the female crew members comes face-to-face with the alien. Despite another crew member yelling at her to move, she can't. She is frozen, overwhelmed by her terror. This happens in the real world, too. A popular Navy SEAL expression is "movement is life"—it is their reminder not to freeze when they are attacked. An athlete who panics performs poorly; the same is true for a student who panics at the thought of taking a test.

In our ancestors, such a highly developed panic mechanism would have been an advantage that natural selection favored because the threat was *real*. Today, however, overresponding with *excessive anxiety* in a situation—whether you are giving a presentation, playing basketball, or doing math—can be detrimental if not disastrous.

A Biological Predisposition for Intensity

The National Institute of Mental Health reports that 18 percent of the population eighteen and older, more than 40 million individuals, have anxiety and panic disorders. In other words, there are a lot of people who, because of their natural makeup, experience a greater amount of fear and anxiety than others in a pressure moment. While we all share common responses to pressure, these individuals experience specific responses much more intensely and thus are more at risk to do poorly in a pressure moment. For instance:

Distorted Threat Perceptions. Feeling *threatened* in the *absence* of genuine threat is a common occurrence to those individuals who experience anxiety and panic disorders. Individuals diagnosed with these disorders, for example, interpret the famous Rorschach inkblots as more threatening and hostile than those without such a diagnosis. They tend to perceive the world as a more hostile and threatening environment.

Spiked Arousal. The physiological responses of anxiety and panic—increase in heart rate, respiration rate, and muscle contraction—are present even when there is no immediate threat. Many people sweat and have a racing heart before a presentation or interview, for example. Anxiety, panic, and choking seem to be different shades of responding to a threatening situation. They are different in intensity

but are part of the same family. People who fear pressure moments experience these responses sometimes days before a potentially high-pressure event.

Avoidance Behavior. Highly anxious individuals rarely look forward to a presentation and may seek to avoid one. Socially anxious individuals report that they stay home more than those who are low on the same measure. Socially anxious college students are less involved in student activities than those who aren't. Anxiety creates uncertainty, so they hang out in a "safe college dorm room."

Insecure Subjective Experience. Individuals with anxiety and panic disorders have an *external locus of control*—they believe their behavior is driven or influenced by external factors. They also tend to have feelings of insecurity—perfectly natural if you perceive your environment as hostile and threatening. Individuals who do not suffer from these disorders more often have an *internal locus of control*—they believe they are in charge of their lives. As a result they find it easier to manage their emotions.

The bottom line is that there are a significant number of individuals who are, by the luck of the draw, behind the eight ball when they encounter a pressure moment. Their inherent *biological disposition* to perceive a situation with an exaggerated perception of threat triggers a degree of panic that becomes a third variable unseen to most observers. They experience a sudden sensation of fear that is so strong it dominates logical thinking, replacing it with overwhelming feelings of anxiety and fear, reminiscent of the primal but realistic panic present-day attorney Sarah's ancestors experienced in their face-to-face encounters with predators. This biological disposition makes pressure moments for Sarah and others like her even more intense.

If you experience this range of reaction to pressure situations, you might need more personalized help than what this book offers. You may want to consider what Sarah and others like her have explored: a pharmacological and/or talk therapy approach to pressure. Do not feel embarrassed if this is your experience. We have witnessed firsthand the benefit of these more significant interventions and have seen how they can change an individual's life. Once Sarah had her anxiety and panic under control, she found that she benefited enormously from the

solutions found in this book. While the short-term pressure solutions in Part 2 proved helpful to her, she found she was even better served by the longer-term solutions found in the third section of this book: the COTE of Armor strategies that helped shield her from the exaggerated anxiety and fear she and many others face. This, along with help from her psychopharmacologist and therapist, was her "smarter" approach to being able to handle pressure. She now can be in an anxiety-inducing situation of pressure more easily, stay in the moment, and perform closer to her best.

PART 2

REGULATING, REDIRECTING, AND RELEASING THE FLOW OF PRESSURE

After successfully landing a damaged Airbus on the Hudson River and saving the lives of hundreds of passengers, United Airlines pilot Captain Chesley Sullenberger, cited for his poise and calm demeanor during the crisis, told investigators, "I immediately took over flying from my co-pilot and made a series of command decisions. I knew that for 42 years, I'd been making small, regular deposits in this bank of experience: education and training. And on January 15 the balance was sufficient so I knew I could make a very large withdrawal."

After a year in which his team failed to deliver on an already low-ered business plan, Jim Breach, VP for customer development at Unile-ver, realized he was "doing things just to save my job": "Under extreme pressure, I was making decisions just to please my boss. Finally, I took a step back and looked at the broader picture and realized that there were only three people—myself, my wife, and God—that I needed to care about being judged by, and I decided to go down swinging. I took the pressure as a challenge as opposed to a threat, and it made all of the difference." The result? Still lots of anxiety but also more courage in approaching as opposed to avoiding the big issues.

When ESPN New York talk show host Michael Kay asked two-time Super Bowl champion quarterback Eli Manning, "Is handling pressure in your genes?," the quarterback answered, "No, it's because I practiced the plays thousands of times in all different scenarios. . . . In pressure situations, I never think of failing; I think of all the past times I have succeeded."

Inadvertently or not, each of the individuals quoted above is using

a *pressure solution*—a strategy, technique, or method that allows you to regulate, redirect, or release the pressure of the moment so you can perform to your potential. Pressure solutions immunize you to the pressure of the moment because, in one way or another, they:

+ Reduce feelings of anxiety, stress, fear, embarrassment
+ Avoid distraction
+ Regulate your arousal
+ Guide your behavior
+ Help you focus on what helps you

All of the twenty-two pressure solutions we present in the pages that follow are self-contained strategies that are powerful in their own right. But they are more powerful when combined with others. Each pressure solution has been derived from research and years of clinical expertise in corporate, educational, and health care settings, with the military, and with elite athletes, developing the most effective methods to modify and apply the solution.

Based on the privileged front row seat we have had to the numerous pressure moments our clients have faced, we will point out when a specific pressure solution will be especially helpful. But each pressure solution can be used in all sorts of high-pressure situations. Some of the pressure solutions come into play *before* the pressure event; others can be utilized *during* a presentation or a high-pressure game or an interview. Experiment with them to see which are most effective for you.

Some of the pressure solutions influence how you *think* about pressure moments; others immunize you by directing your focus to *specific mental imagery*; and others serve to depressurize you by managing your *physiology*.

We hope you will find each of the pressure solutions to be *concise* and *easy* to use. Most important, they do not require that you "rise to the occasion," only that you use your natural tools—thinking, arousal, senses, voice, and body movements—to perform to your capability, which more often than not is good enough to be successful.

You'll likely find that the more selective you are—using the right

strategy or strategies for the right situation—the more effective you will be. Test which strategies work best for you. Everyone is different— just because your teammate or workmate uses one strategy for a specific situation does not mean that it will necessarily be the right one for you.

The biggest obstacle that individuals face in using pressure solutions is their inability to free themselves from *past responses*. When these ineffective past pressure responses become *habitual*, they resurface without the individual's awareness in a high-pressure situation.

To prevent being held hostage by your past responses under pressure, use any feelings of pressure that you experience as a cue that it is time to employ one or more of the twenty-two pressure solutions.

Pressure Solution 1
BEFRIEND THE MOMENT

Carroll Ann Scott, president of the Arizona Rodeo Club, sums up her sport this way: "You walk in the arena, you get on that horse, and you get on that bull, whatever you're doing, that's pressure. And that's intensity. Our events don't take longer than ten seconds most of the time, and so you have ten seconds to give it all you got." But the pressure doesn't buck rodeo world champion Justin McDaniel. "I like pressure; it makes it fun and exciting, so I lay it on the line every time."

Basketball star LeBron James was asked on ESPN *Sports Center* how he would handle the pressure of the deciding game against the tough Indiana Pacers, who had just won Game 6 to force a Game 7 in the 2013 NBA playoffs. His response: "There's no pressure. It is going to be fun, a great game, and I look forward to meeting the *challenge*." He played sensationally and the Heat won.

LeBron's answer and Justin McDaniel's attitude are ingrained in this pressure solution:

THINK OF PRESSURE MOMENTS AS A CHALLENGE OR OPPORTUNITY/FUN

Do you see high-pressure situations as threatening or as challenging? Do you embrace such moments, or do you dread them? Threat

perceptions are the root cause for choking. This pressure solution is your pressure insurance against a primal pressure reaction, but you must use it *frequently* before your pressure moments.

Our data indicates that an overwhelming majority of individuals in the working world see pressure situations as threatening—as do-or-die. Seeing pressure as a threat undermines your self-confidence; elicits fear of failure; impairs your short-term memory, attention, and judgment; and spurs impulsive behavior. It also saps your energy. Our blood vessels are lined with smooth muscle; when we see a pressure situation as a threat, our body releases noradrenaline, which acts to vasoconstrict these muscles. The lungs become constricted by noradrenaline as well, so there is less oxygen exchange. The end result is that you tire far more easily as you get less oxygenated blood to the tissues that need it. All of these results handicap your performance at the very moment you need to be most effective.

On the other side of the coin, individuals who perceive a task or situation not as a threat but instead as a challenge, an opportunity, or fun are far more likely to perform up to the level of their ability, increasing their chances for success.

Feeling challenged is an *inherent* performance steroid—your body releases more adrenaline than noradrenaline, which means the smooth muscle in your blood vessels dilate, as do your your lungs, and now you have more oxygenated blood going to the tissues that need it. Your body has more energy and your brain can think more clearly.

When you see the pressure situation as a challenge, you are stimulated to give the attention and energy needed to make your best effort. One group of eighth-grade math students were given the assignment "Challenge yourself to see if you can do these problems," while another group of eighth graders were given the same problems with the comment "Here is your homework assignment for tomorrow." The group for whom the situation was framed as a *challenge* attempted more problems and scored a better percentage correctly.

When we perceive a pressure moment as fun, the arousal we experience is enjoyable and exciting rather than uncomfortable and unsettling. Positive arousal translates into enthusiasm, a powerful emotion in overcoming anxiety and fear. Think of the high-pressure situations

you've been in, and the times you've performed well. You were probably enjoying the moment despite the pressure, just like Justin McDaniel and LeBron James.

The student who volunteers to tackle a difficult problem in front of the class, the manager who takes on the impossible job to turn around a department, the fireman who leads the way into a burning building, and the basketball player who asks a teammate for the ball to take the last shot are all examples of individuals who view the task as a challenge or opportunity to test themselves and show off their stuff. Their attitude makes them the go-to person. *They are not thriving on the pressure as often thought; they are thriving on the challenge.*

Those who execute this pressure solution tend to use statements like "I want to see how good I can be." Miami Heat basketball players expressed this attitude before they repeated as world champions by winning the 2013 championship game. What they said was, "Now we will see if we are as good as last year and where we need to get better."

A creative director in a global advertising firm describes her use of this pressure solution this way: "My parents always told me an exam was an opportunity to test myself, to show my stuff or to have fun when I tried out for a team. I have the same attitude when I pitch a client. I see it as an opportunity to show off my creativity. The pitch is fun for me, not pressure-packed like it is for so many of my associates."

Before you go into a high-pressure situation, convince yourself it is a *challenge* or an *opportunity*. Such a positive mind-set will help your performance. To build "challenge thinking," try the following exercise: Think of your tasks and responsibilities as *daily challenges* to strut your stuff. If you are a project manager, tell your team, "I challenge you to make this your best work ever." A sales manager might tell his sales force, "Here's the challenge—let's see if we are up to it." Or "Hey, it's great that we get opportunities like this to show how good we are!"

Focus on the fun aspects of your life. Celebrate the positive aspects of your work, the part that you find enjoyable. Remember these thoughts the next time you feel under pressure, with too much to do.

A final point: It is important to bring positive thinking to the task

at hand, as well. Remember to do this, and draw on pressure solution #8, as well—"Use Your Positive GPS System."

Pressure Solution 2
MULTIPLE OPPORTUNITIES

In prehistoric times, a hunter who saw a herd of antelope knew that if he missed with his first arrow, there would be plenty of other opportunities to bring down his prey. There was no need to rush; sooner or later he would succeed. The same attitude can make us successful today. NFL quarterbacks report that they feel less pressure to win a game in the first half of the season than in the second half, because in the first half they have many opportunities to prove themselves. These examples illustrate an important point about how we experience pressure: When you know that you have more than one chance to get it right, you feel under less pressure. This pressure solution suggests you convince yourself before any high-pressure moment:

THIS IS ONE OF MANY OPPORTUNITIES

In one study, a group of auto mechanics were told they had one chance to demonstrate their ability to assemble an engine that they had been practicing on for the previous two weeks. To increase the pressure on them, they were told that if they assembled it correctly within the time allotted, they would be in line for a supervisory position they all desired. A second group was given the same task and the same promise of promotion. But they were also told that if they made mistakes, they would be given additional opportunities to show their competence. The group with only one chance felt more pressure, made more mistakes, and took longer to assemble the engine.

The fact is, it is realistic to think that additional opportunities will come your way. Think back to your academic career in high school and college. Remember how many tests you had? How many times you got an opportunity to show how well prepared you were the next week? Consider the number of people who needed multiple opportunities to

succeed: Oprah Winfrey was fired from her first job as a news anchor in Baltimore. Steven Spielberg was turned down by the University of Southern California School of Cinematic Arts several times. J. K. Rowling was turned down by thirty publishers who told her that her book about a young wizard was unsaleable. Each of these individuals probably felt like Oprah did at the time: that she "blew her one and only chance." Think about how many of us get divorced and then marry a second time. *The fact is we each get multiple chances over and over again in life.* Keep this in mind, and you will find your life less pressured.

Before an interview, presentation, or sales call, depressurize the moment by telling yourself: "I will have other interviews [or presentations or sales calls]." When your kids audition for a school play, help them to reduce the pressure they are apt to feel by telling them, "Do your best. And if you don't get it, you will get other opportunities."

In another seminar, a young financial advisor quipped, "How could I use this to make the first call to a girl I like? I feel a lot of pressure when I make that call." Another participant, a few years older, boomed out: "Just tell yourself there are plenty of other girls waiting to be called!" The class broke out into laughter, but it was true.

Pressure Solution 3
DOWNSIZE THE IMPORTANCE

Of the individuals listed below, who do you think is under the *least* pressure?

+ A golfer leading by a stroke going into the final round of the US Open
+ A cardiac surgeon prepping for a quadruple bypass
+ A baker beginning to roll the dough for his best friend's birthday cake

Most of us would probably say the baker. But in fact the answer depends on which of the individuals above practices the following pressure solution:

SHRINK THE IMPORTANCE OF THE PRESSURE MOMENT

A golfer who appraises the final round as "just another round" and a surgeon who perceives her task as "*only* a quadruple" are on their way to doing their best, while a baker who appraises his task as "This is the most meaningful cake I've ever made" might bake one that does not rise to the occasion.

This pressure solution is spurred by the well-documented fact that the *more important* we appraise an event to be, the *more pressure* we feel—that is the nature of pressure. Pressure distorts our perceptions, often to an irrational take on the moment, and this *distorted thinking* downgrades our cognitive success tools, such as judgment and decision-making, and motivates impulsive behavior. Super distortions get you back to primal pressure. Sales reps make more errors when they are instructed to believe that a presentation is very important, compared to those who are told to speak about their product as though they are "shooting the breeze," and track sprinters have more false starts when told their time is important and will be recorded as opposed to being discarded and used for training purposes. Your friends who tell you before your interview, "Don't make a big deal of it," are giving you good advice.

It may feel awkward, but you can depressurize the moment by minimizing its significance. A day before the Super Bowl, "I treat it like any other game" is how Baltimore Ravens' Joe Falco put it before his championship performance.

Tell and teach your kids that their grades aren't the most important thing in life, and they will feel less pressure at school, enjoy learning, and be less likely to cheat. Even when a potential account is on the line, we'd recommend telling your team to "treat it like our other projects," not "This is the most important project we have ever had," a pep talk that will lead to conflict and stifle creativity.

One popular and effective use of this pressure solution is when performing with an audience—presentations to your senior staff, an audition, a PhD oral exam, being observed by supervisors. Social psychology studies clearly indicate that the individual experiences more pressure as the status and size of the audience increase. Thinking, *This*

is really an important and knowledgeable group will most likely make you nervous, and not as articulate as you hoped to be. You will probably be more effective if you approach the presentation with thoughts about the audience that *diminish* their status—we'll leave the specifics to your imagination. Also, depressurize the moment by periodically focusing on a few individuals; you'll be less susceptible to the "big audience effect."

We've heard many people push back with "It's unrealistic to tell yourself that something isn't really important when you know it really is."

Our response is that overexaggerating is equally unrealistic, and because of the nature of pressure, you are apt to overexaggerate the importance of a pressure moment to the point of hurting your performance, whether it is your performance on an exam or on a golf course. Furthermore, overexaggerating is apt to stimulate primal pressure and push you toward choking and panic.

To counter and prevent primal pressure thinking, you need to *under*exaggerate or generate thoughts that minimize the significance of the pressure moment. These minimization thoughts will help you counter the pressure distortion magnification and thus help you regain a more realistic perspective of the pressure moment. For most, the battle between exaggerated importance and *shrinking to fit* is continual and one that minimization must win if they are to develop nerves of steel.

A powerful antidote is to be *mindful* of what is most important in your life. Making a list will help you. Right before a pressure moment, reflect on your "most important" list—it will help you keep your current moment in proper pressure perspective.

Of course we recognize that the pressure moment is defined as important; but it is also important not to exaggerate its significance.

Pressure Solution 4
FOCUS ON THE MISSION

There is probably no easier pressure solution to use before and during a pressure moment than this:

FOCUS ON YOUR MISSION

This solution suggests that you stay clear on what you are trying to accomplish—your mission. It could be to shoot a clean round of golf (regardless of score), have a strong interview (independent of how other interviewees do), or just be an excellent employee. Increasing your awareness of your mission before and during a high-pressure moment helps to depressurize the situation quickly.

First, it prevents distracting thoughts generated by self-consciousness or external distractions. Such thoughts can derail your efforts.

Second, focusing on the mission keeps you on track because it cues you to do the things you need to do to achieve the performance you are looking for. To write an excellent paper, focusing on the mission will cue you to do your research.

In an extended high-pressure scenario, such as writing a research proposal or working on a long-term project, reiterating the mission helps you and your team stay the course.

Remember, focusing on your mission is different from focusing on the outcome. Focusing on the outcome steers your thinking into whether or not you will suffer negative consequences if you do not succeed; worrying over failure can distract and derail you.

In contrast, focusing on your mission creates a mind-set that helps you recognize the best way to accomplish your mission is to simply do your best on each task. In this way, you stay anchored in the moment.

Pressure Solution 5
ANTICIPATE, ANTICIPATE, ANTICIPATE

Have you ever played the "what if" pressure game? It's educational and you can play it anywhere, alone or with others. Kids like it; there are no pieces to lose, and best of all, the game conditions you to use this pressure solution before any high-pressure event:

EXPECT THE UNEXPECTED

The rules are simple. Select an upcoming high-pressure situation. Let's say it's *giving an important presentation*. Now ask yourself a bunch of *what-if questions—what if something bad or unexpected happens?* Here are some examples: What if your PowerPoint slides malfunction when you're presenting to your senior management? What if you are told a minute before you start, "You can only have five minutes instead of the expected twenty to make your case"? (That's happened to both of us.) For more fun, make your questions a bit more surprising: What if you are in the middle of a presentation and someone has a heart attack? (This has happened to JP.)

Anyone can use this technique. If you're a mountain climber, ask yourself, what if the weather charts are drastically wrong, or your guide breaks a leg? If you're a race car driver, ask yourself, what if on the final lap your car starts to malfunction at 180 mph? Or at school, let's say your son or daughter is expecting an essay test. Ask them, what if the teacher throws a curve with a multiple-choice test format?

The reason this is a good game to play is because most of us respond to unexpected events in high-pressure situations with a sudden spike in arousal that disturbs our thoughts and actions and throws us off course, sometimes to the point where we can't recover. "He lost his composure" is the way sports analysts describe a golfer who can't recover from a terrible fluke shot.

The operative concept in this pressure solution is to *anticipate the unexpected*. It can protect you from a pressure surge by allowing you to *prepare* for and thus be less startled by the unexpected. Instead of your heart rate zooming and your actions becoming impulsive, you are able to maintain your composure and continue your task to the best of your capability.

Over the last one hundred years, one sports team has had the best winning percentage of any team in any sport in the world. It is not the New York Yankees or Manchester United or the New England Patriots or the Montreal Canadiens. It is the New Zealand All Blacks rugby team. They have been consistently the most successful (and most

feared) team over the past century. There is only one problem: With the exception of the first Rugby World Cup (RWC), which they won, at every other RWC, the All Blacks have gone in as favorites and succumbed to pressure and inexplicably lost.

In 2011, they again entered the RWC, held in New Zealand, as the prohibitive favorites. This time they brought a different approach to the competition. Their new team motto was "Expect the Unexpected." They went in with the expectation that especially when the pressure to win increased something would happen that they hadn't planned for. And it did.

The All Blacks lost not only their starting fly half (similar to the quarterback position in football), Dan Carter, considered the best in the world, but their second and third string as well. They had to call a fourth stringer, Stephen Donald, to come play in the final. He received the phone call from the coach while whitebait fishing on one of New Zealand's beautiful rivers. This was the "Unexpected."

But the All Blacks were ready for it, psychologically. They were determined not to let the injuries to their stars affect their play. The result? In the pressure-filled championship game against France, fourth stringer Donald stepped up to kick the winning three points that brought them the 2011 world championship, 8–7.

Anticipating glitches like this enables you to work out responses in advance and build your confidence by practicing or mentally rehearsing them. It also teaches you to be adaptive and flexible in any high-pressure moment. Knowing that you can adapt to changing circumstances provides you with a sense of *control*, no matter what happens.

Our prehistoric ancestors who anticipated the glitch that they might encounter on a hunt gave themselves an edge—they wouldn't be caught off guard if a predator appeared, or if bad weather struck. Anticipating and rehearsing a response eliminates panic.

In a video-simulated driving test, student drivers who were told what obstacles would come their way—cars darting in and out, pedestrians running across the street, quick traffic light changes—reported "feeling less pressure" than those performing the same test but without being told what situations to anticipate. Furthermore, the results

generalized to real-world driving situations, in which student drivers who were told in advance that they would encounter heavy traffic reported their driving experience to be less pressured compared to those not warned, and also were rated better drivers by their driving instructors, who were kept in the dark about the warning.

Try playing the "what if" game with your staff. Ask them to list their upcoming high-pressure moments, and then give them what-if questions. Play the game with your kids. Even better, teach them to play it by themselves. Like most games, the more you play, the better you get. Those who train astronauts, NFL quarterbacks, and Israeli pilots play it all the time.

You don't have to be a movie buff to appreciate the quote that endorses this pressure solution: "Chance favors the prepared mind."

Pressure Solution 6
RECOGNIZE THAT YOU ARE WORTHY

Do you recall a pressure moment in which you didn't do as well as you hoped? That was you in the past. Today is a new opportunity to show what you can do.

Whether you are thinking about an interview, a presentation, a sales call, a test, a tournament, an audition, or a first date, here is something you can do to depressurize yourself so that you perform to your best:

AFFIRM YOUR SELF-WORTH

Acknowledging the experience, skills, and other positive qualities you possess is an effective way to buffer yourself from the pressure you face.

Underlying this pressure solution are a group of studies, perhaps best exemplified by a study published in the journal *Psychological Science*. In the experiment, subjects had to perform a difficult task that

required self-control. Before the task, half the subjects were given an exercise that affirmed their self-worth. While the subjects performed the task, the researchers studied their brain activity, with particular focus on a neurological signal called ERN (error related negativity), a neural alarm signal that is triggered when we make a mistake.

Those who affirmed their self-worth ahead of time made fewer errors performing the task than those who did not. Even better, their brains seemed to learn more easily from the errors they had made—self-affirmation seems to make us more receptive to correcting our mistakes.

Clinical psychologists would add that validating your self-worth is an important tool for bolstering your ego "strength." Ego strength helps to prevent you from being overwhelmed by "threats," so you can handle yourself more adeptly in situations that are stressful, anxiety-arousing, and pressure-packed. Stronger ego strength also contributes to your cognitive resiliency—your ability to bounce back from failure. Here are some proven suggestions that will help you affirm your self-worth before your next high-pressure moment—and, equally important, after a high-pressure moment has derailed you.

1. List your values and their importance to you, so you realize that your identity is not tied solely to the work at hand.

2. List your positive attributes; in fact, take a minute or two every day to appreciate them.

Practicing these activities helps to make this pressure solution automatic, so pressure situations become less threatening. You become more relaxed and better able to perform to your ability.

Help your staff depressurize before a presentation by pointing out that you are proud to work with great people. Before your daughter's piano recital, remind her that she is a great kid, and that you love her. Be specific.

We're sure that your family and friends think that you are a worthy person. But remember, when the heat is on, it's important that you believe it, too.

Pressure Solution 7
RECALL YOU AT YOUR BEST

In winning the 2010 National Indoor Archery Championship at Louisville, Kentucky, Bridger Deaton learned a powerful pressure solution that he uses frequently: "[Competing in the championship] was the most pressure I ever felt, and after winning, I knew I could make the shots when it counted. It was a confidence booster. I think about it before every shot I make." You can increase your chances of winning if you use this pressure solution before and during high-pressure moments:

FLASH BACK TO YOUR PREVIOUS SUCCESSES

A lack of confidence in high-pressure situations is common to many of us, so this pressure solution is sure to come in handy. The basic idea is that by visualizing your past successes in similar situations, you stimulate the same type of responses that helped you before. Pressure moments are filled with uncertainty—you are uncertain that you will deliver the goods. Remembering your past successes *ignites confidence*—you did it before and you can do it again. As your confidence increases, uncertainty (anxiety) and pressure are diminished, freeing you to approach the task with your best effort. Nervousness becomes transformed into positive enthusiasm that is directed to the task, rather than anxious thinking that is distracting. "I've done it before. I can do it again" is the mantra of this pressure solution.

Research shows that the thoughts and behavior associated with our past experiences are imprinted in our brain; the more frequently these experiences are thought of, the more firmly implanted they become, and the more likely they are to resurface in a current experience. On the other hand, someone who frequently recalls the anxiety of a pressure moment is more likely to repeat that sense of anxiety.

In the same way, an athlete who keeps his or her *muscle memory* alive by thinking about past actions that were successful has a better chance to repeat those same actions in the next performance. In

an interview with *Basketball Digest,* two-time NBA MVP Steve Nash states, "Before I shoot a foul shot, I think of the thousands I've made, and do it the same way." The more you use this pressure solution, the more automatic it becomes, and the more confident you will feel.

Flashing back to your previous successes is also helpful to you in pressure situations that call for a strong performance over a sustained period of time, like supervising a months-long project at work. For these pressure scenarios, take a page from someone who successfully climbed Mount Everest: "One of my most useful strategies to keep me positive, confident that I'd make the summit, was to think of past climbs, or even earlier moments in the current climb. These images helped me a lot. I'd get a surge of energy when I needed it, and it made going through the tough time easier."

Here's an exercise to help you perfect this pressure solution:

1. Make a list of the times you were successful (when you were at your best) in pressure moments.

2. Sitting in a comfortable chair, regulate your breathing to a comfortable level.

3. Relive these successful pressure moments, focusing on all the right things you did in each situation. Take your time: The point is to use all your senses—sounds, sights, smells—to relive the experience.

4. Conclude each scene by saying, "I did it."

5. Repeat the process until you find yourself momentarily flashing back to your successes in your pressure moments.

The night before a big exam, remind your son of how well he's done on previous tests. One way to depressurize your staff and build their confidence for an ongoing project is by prepping your interactions with them.

If you have an interview or presentation coming up, or if you find yourself writing under deadline pressure, remembering a past success will remind you, *I've done it before.* Recalling that, you will probably do it again.

Pressure Solution 8
USE YOUR POSITIVE GPS SYSTEM

"We went on a lot of missions but we never worried about coming back. We always assumed we would be successful. A lot of it was our training, but *we were pretty positive people,* too. We never got rattled when the action started."

Now eighty-eight years old and living in Santa Monica, California, World War II fighter pilot Lieutenant Marvin Tanner's words reflect the perfect recipe for this pressure solution:

BE POSITIVE BEFORE AND DURING HIGH-PRESSURE MOMENTS

Each of us has an inherent internal GPS that is programmed to give us a positive attitude. When you have a positive attitude, you are more apt to attend to the necessary task with confidence and the knowledge that you can succeed.

In prehistoric times, those of our ancestors with a *positive attitude* had an evolutionary advantage; the attitude motivated them to approach their tasks with a minimum of fear and anxiety, two factors that lead to poor performance under pressure. Because positive individuals were more successful, and better able to pass on their genes through the process of natural selection, positive thinking became a natural attribute in our species, to help us succeed.

However, for many of us, life circumstances and a pattern of ineffective responses have instilled a tendency to think negatively. People who do so are at a disadvantage in high-pressure moments; pressure short-circuits their positive thinking system by adding anxiety and fear of failure, which distracts them and takes them off course.

This pressure solution helps you depressurize the moment by rebooting your inherent tendency for positive thinking.

Belief in a successful outcome can prevent you from *worry* that can drain and distract your working memory. Anxiety and fear are stripped from the equation, allowing you to act with confidence.

You can incorporate this pressure solution into a high-pressure situation with little effort.

+ Positive images can foster your tendency to think positively. As a Mount Everest climber reported, "Every day during my training, I started out by imagining myself at the summit. I pictured all the details of my surroundings and saw myself dancing around like Rocky. That image energized my training and, *during* the actual climb, motivated me to succeed."

+ *Assume* a positive outcome. Lieutenant Tanner would tell himself and his men, "*when* we get back," as opposed to "if we get back." The day before a critical client meeting, a manager might say to his or her staff: "when we get the client," or "after the client says yes," as opposed to "if we get the client," which creates anxiety and pressure. When success is assumed, you and your staff can focus on the details for success.

+ Use a variety of *encouraging* and *confidence-building* statements, such as "I am going to be great," "I'm going to be successful." Make a list of such statements. Keep them visible or available for those moments when you encounter a high-pressure situation.

If you have a high-pressure event coming up, and you feel ill prepared, or haven't had the time to ready yourself, *act as if you are positive*. Studies show that individuals' feelings and moods respond to their actions. Acting depressed leads people to feel depressed; acting euphoric creates feelings that match. That is why a marine drill sergeant orders nervous "newbies" to "stand up straight," so that they will feel confident, like the Marines they are training to be.

Pressure Solution 9
HERE AND NOW

When psychologist Fritz Perls introduced Gestalt therapy to the world by establishing the Gestalt Institute in New York in 1952, he probably

wasn't aware that he was also introducing what would become one of the great clichés in terms of pressure: "Stay in the moment."

Gestalt therapy focuses on what is *happening now*—what is being done, thought, and felt at the present moment—rather than on what was, might be, could be, or should have been. To do this, we need to let go of the past and ignore the future, or we will be unable to focus on how we are responding now. The Gestalt therapist's goal is to keep the patient in the here and now or, as thousands of athletes and coaches instruct us, to help the patient "stay in the moment."

Unfortunately, most individuals, athletes included, have trouble following this advice if it doesn't instruct them *how* to stay in the moment. So Perls taught his clients how to do it, and his method is the impetus for this pressure solution:

TUNE INTO YOUR SENSES

When Dr. Perls observed his clients drifting into the past, or focusing on the future, he would return them to the present by instructing them to *experience their senses*. "What does your breathing feel like?" he might ask. "What do you see right now? What sounds are you hearing?" These are the kinds of questions Dr. Perls used to anchor his patient in the *here and now*.

These same questions can help you *depressurize* a high-pressure situation. The pressure you experience is intensified by thoughts of future consequences, fear of repeating past mistakes, or simply letting your mind wander. Careless errors can occur and well-coordinated skills become disjointed. Performance slips.

Whether you are experiencing pressure from an unrealistic deadline or from performing a task under intense scrutiny, your chance of doing your best is improved when you focus on the here and now. In one study, Air Force pilots were given a repetitive task to perform that lasted thirty minutes. Those who were told every five minutes, "Pay attention," performed faster and with fewer errors than those left to their own devices. A teacher who tells a student, "Pay attention," is attempting to keep the student's focus on understanding the problem,

the here and now. (The instruction is less effective when said with anger—or emotion of any kind.)

To get yourself in the habit of tuning into your senses, practice the following exercise a few minutes a day. Your goal is to *increase the frequency with which you turn to your senses* to keep you in the moment, whether you are speaking to your staff or listening to your son or daughter.

1. Pay attention to your breathing. Is it fast, slow, comfortable? Keep focusing on it until you regulate it to a comfortable level.

2. What do you see? Where are your eyes focused? Scan the room.

3. What are you hearing? Close your eyes and verbally describe the sounds you hear, including your own internal noisy chatter.

4. For a few seconds several times a day, ask yourself the above questions, especially when you are in a pressure situation.

The next time you feel jittery before you are about to tee off with a client or a friend, or if you find your mind wandering when you are being told important information, or you have to get behind the wheel of a car in bad weather, tune into your senses so you can stay in the moment and do your best.

Pressure Solution 10
BE A CONTROL FREAK

For many of us—athletes and regular employees as well—a pressure moment can undermine our performance because we focus on factors we can't control. When you focus on "uncontrollables," you intensify the pressure; it boosts your anxiety to the point of disturbing your physiology, creating distracting thoughts that undermine your confidence. If you want a shot at being your best when it matters most, apply this pressure solution before and during a high-pressure situation:

FOCUS ON WHAT YOU CAN CONTROL

Baseball pitcher Greg Maddux was never considered a high-potential prospect when he came up through high school; he received no scholarship offers to play in college. He was only six feet tall and didn't have a ninety-mile-an-hour fastball or other great "stuff" like many pitching prospects. What he did have, however, was an intense focus on the things that mattered most to performing under pressure.

Maddux was asked after a game one day to assess his performance. His assessment surprised people: He didn't talk about whether he got the win, how the other team hit him, or even the number of runs they scored. Instead, Maddux's answer was: "73 out of 78." Reporters and teammates didn't understand. What Maddux meant was that in his simple assessment, seventy-three out of the seventy-eight balls he pitched left his fingers in the desired way, which was a good day in his estimation. Everything that happened to the ball *after* it left his fingers was beyond his control and irrelevant to him. This mental discipline of focusing on only what he could control served him well: He won the Cy Young Award a record four times in a row.

To execute this pressure solution effectively, you have to be able to know (a) what you can control, (b) what you cannot control, and (c) *when* your focus shifts to things you can't control, so you can snap it back. Practice the following procedure to bring a focused mind-set to bear during high-pressure moments:

- Sitting in a comfortable chair, practice this three-minute procedure once a day for the next two weeks.

- Identify an upcoming high-pressure scenario, or one that you frequently encounter.

- List the factors involved that you cannot control.

- List the factors involved that you *can* control.

- Visualize the high-pressure moment; think about the things you can control, and imagine those going well.

- Now think about the things you can't control. Visualize your performance going astray.

- Bring your mind back into focus on what you can control, and visualize yourself getting back on track.

Tune in to the obvious: your responses to the things you can control—your thoughts, physical arousal, and actions. These are the factors that determine how you perform.

A few minutes before your interview, focus your mind. Do not think about how many other candidates applied for the position, or whether or not the interviewer will like your attire, or whether he or she has a bias against your accent, skin color, the college you received your degree from, etc. Do not let yourself think about whether a decision will be made immediately or not, or whether it might rain this afternoon.

Instead of worrying about what other candidates might say in an interview, focus your energy on learning about the company and rehearsing what you want to say about what you can contribute to it. Those are things that are within your control.

Consistently using this pressure solution will force you to focus on how you can manage your responses and behavior to leverage more effectively the factors you can influence in a high-pressure situation. It will give you grace under pressure. And if you perform with grace under pressure, while you might not get into the Hall of Fame, you will easily throw more strikes than balls.

Pressure Solution 11
CARRY A PRESSURE-TUNE

The Iowa State Ultimate Frisbee team had played in several national tournaments. Yet it consistently underperformed in high-pressure situations. In important games, especially in the later stages of the game, the offense struggled to execute the fundamentals: making smart decisions, completing simple throws, catching the disc.

The team's lackluster performance was not due to a lack of physical skills; rather, the team underperformed because of pressure. Under pressure, a player's focus tends to narrow and turn inward, leading to missed cues, muscle inefficiency, and poor timing. Internal focus causes athletes to overanalyze their mechanics when performing well-practiced skills, such as throwing and catching. Muscle inefficiency

leads to fatigue, causing poor concentration and decision-making. When their timing falters, players are either too late or too early with their passes, leading to turnovers. With team expectations rising every year, the Iowa Frisbee club desperately needed help.

A collection of studies offered the team a pressure solution, one that is especially effective when you need to perform a well-practiced behavior or task:

LISTEN TO OR SING A FAVORITE SONG

In several studies, researchers induced pressure on athletes performing a variety of tasks, such as foul shooting, bowling, and marksmanship. Those athletes who used headphones before and during their athletic event to listen to a song they liked performed better. Furthermore, those instructed to focus on the song's lyrics performed the best of all and closest to their proven capability. There is a reason that track stars, skaters, swimmers, and skiers listen to music on their smartphones or iPods before their events.

What makes this pressure solution so effective is that it reduces the culprit behind choking—increased anxiety. Increased anxiety causes us to worry about our performance; listening to music distracts us from the anxiety.

Listening to music seems to distract us just enough to get the job done. In interviews, players reported that when they listened to music, they focused less on mechanical details such as how to make a shot (they were less self-conscious) and were able to block out the distraction of the audience, making it easier to focus on making the shot. Those who listened to music experienced fewer worry thoughts and kept their physiological arousal at manageable levels.

Executing this pressure solution is easy. Pick out a song or two that you like that will distract you from the task at hand. The goal is to put yourself in the zone. Listen to your music choice right up to the moment of your interview, presentation, or sales call. You'll reduce your anxiety and start confidently on track. Obviously this doesn't work in every situation. If your son can't listen to music in class, have him mentally "play" the song in his head. What if you are suddenly called

before your boss for an explanation of your department's performance? Hum or mentally "play" a tune you like in your head as you walk down the hall.

Caution: Remember that when you are trying to learn a *new* task, music can interfere with your concentration and ability to learn. It's hard to do math homework, or master a new company procedure, when your mind is distracted by the music you are playing.

But in pressure situations, the sound of music, contrary to conventional wisdom, is often better than the sound of silence.

Pressure Solution 12
USE AN "ANCHOR"

Think of a high-pressure situation you've experienced recently. Next, visualize the task you had to perform. If it was a sales call, visualize yourself interacting with your client, speaking about your products; think about how and where you are sitting, and other details that give you a complete picture of the scene. Now come up with *one word or image* to broadly describe the best way to perform what you do. That's the essence of this pressure solution:

USE A HOLISTIC WORD/IMAGE "CUE" TO GUIDE PERFORMANCE

One reason many of us do poorly in pressure moments is that we tend to overthink what we are doing. This self-consciousness distracts us from the task at hand, and our performance suffers. A baseball player who swings a bat, or a football player who throws a pass, in a jerky movement is usually overly self-conscious about how he is performing. The same is true if you are giving a presentation or are in the midst of a sales call and your thoughts turn to how you are doing. Suddenly you're off course and out of rhythm.

In Daniel Gucciardi and James Dimmock's 2008 study, which took place at the University of Queensland and was published in the journal *Psychology of Sport and Exercise*, experienced golfers (handicaps ranging from zero to twelve) played under three different conditions. In the

first instance, they were told to fixate on specific components of their swing, such as the motion of their hips or keeping wrists straight. In the second instance, the golfers were asked to focus on irrelevant words such as "white" or "blue." In the third, the golfers were instructed to focus on general aspects of their intended movement in the form of what psychologists refer to as "holistic cue words." With athletes, we call each of these an "*anchor*." For example, instead of concentrating on their stance or wrist movement, the golfers thought of an adjective that was descriptive of their best strokes, such as "smooth" or "balanced." To add to the pressure all the golfers were under, the researchers offered a cash reward to the victors.

The results? The first two groups performed worse under pressure, while the experienced golfers who used a holistic cue word were unaffected.

How a person learns a task affects how a person performs the task in a high-pressure moment. We often learn a task through explicit instruction or education—a strict sequence of steps necessary to performing a skill. In other cases, an athlete, for example, is given a metaphorical or analogical image that describes how to perform the task. It appears that those who have been taught to use such an image to focus on or anchor their thoughts before or during a high-pressure moment stand a better chance of depressurizing the moment and performing at their best.

At the University of Hong Kong, psychologist Wing Kai Lam had inexperienced female volunteers chosen to shoot basketballs. The task was to be learned and performed under pressure. Those taught by explicit instruction were given eight steps, including specific details about posture, wrist motion, and follow-through. Those taught by analogy were told, "Shoot as if you are trying to put a cookie into a cookie jar on a high shelf." Each group had two days of practice. On the day of the test, players had to shoot in front of an expert who evaluated their skills, monitoring their performance with a video camera and scoreboard. The women were offered money for good scores, and money was taken away from them for bad scores. The results showed that both groups learned how to shoot equally well, but when pressure was added, those who had learned through explicit instruction did worse

than those who were taught by analogy. The latter group performed as well as they had in practice. They also exhibited less cognitive anxiety than those who'd been taught explicitly.

Studies like these show the effects of an anchor or holistic cue word and metaphorical images. Using an anchor does not require a lot of effort or attention. In other words, performers may still succumb to pressure and lose focus, but they do so without having to think about the specifics. Focusing on a word, a very short descriptive phrase, or a metaphorical image can be a clever distraction from thinking too much, as well as a stimulator to the actions you need to perform at your best.

Before your next sales call, audition, negotiation, presentation, exam, or golf outing, focus on telling yourself the holistic cue word or metaphorical image that you've established. Tell your kids and those under you at work to do the same.

Pressure Solution 13
PRESSURE YOURSELF

He's called Ax. He is one of the leaders of an elite special ops force that is in a league of its own. Working in Afghanistan and without wearing a bomb-proof suit like the one in *The Hurt Locker*, his job is to lead troops through "hell on earth"—minefields hidden with hundreds of antipersonnel devices. It's his responsibility to decide when it's safe for the troops to proceed. One wrong step could end his life. His Green Beret trainer, Chris Corbin, says of Ax, who is an elite special ops dog, "Pressure doesn't bother him. He feels invincible. He wasn't trained to fail."

How Ax was trained to withstand pressure is the focus of this pressure solution:

PRACTICE EXPERIENCING PRESSURE

Ax went through rigorous training in which he was constantly exposed to pressure and stress. He was pushed, shoved, and blocked as

he tried to reach his "prize." He was bombarded with the noise of exploding bombs and had to squeeze his body through narrow obstacles, work in the dark, and perform other training exercises that mimicked what occurs under battle. The goal: for Ax to become *familiar with feeling pressure* so that he could learn to ignore it and do his job, no matter how stressful it got.

Feeling pressure is uncomfortable for most people. Pressure moments are loaded with stress and anxiety and distressful feelings. We naturally avoid distress, so we try to avoid pressure moments.

The logic of this pressure solution is the opposite. Since high-pressure situations are inevitable, you might as well get used to the feelings of pressure, so that you are able to perform at a high level in spite of pressure. In psychological terms, the goal of this solution is to desensitize yourself to the discomfort of pressure, so that it has little effect on you. To do so, you need to train yourself like Ax; you need to practice under pressure.

This was precisely the goal of professional concert pianist Bernard Gabriel when he started the group Society of Timid Souls to help performers counter stage fright. Performers like Flora Cantwell.

Ms. Cantwell came to Gabriel's Manhattan apartment to engage in an unusual approach to learning to perform under pressure. While Ms. Cantwell set up her instrument, the others in the room appeared normal, quiet, and respectful. But when she launched into an étude, "pandemonium broke loose: [other musicians like] Miss Simeon blew the Bronx cheer, Mr. Carr whirled a watchman's rattle, Miss Cohen sang, Mr. Hokins slammed the door. She plowed ahead with Mr. Gabriel banging the keyboard of the piano not in use, shouting, 'You're playing abominably, don't stop!' She didn't. She concluded and remarked that she could play in a boiler factory after that."

Through this ordeal of practicing under pressure and distraction, musicians like Flora Cantwell get an opportunity to find within themselves the inner grit that they need to perform on stage in front of audiences in the hundreds. Gabriel's methods proved so popular that pretty soon his apartment was bursting at the seams, filled by many kinds of performers, from musicians to Broadway actors.

The goal is to put yourself through the same conditions—or

worse—that you'll face when you have to perform for real. While you can't completely replicate the stress and pressure of real-world situations in a practice setting, training under pressure conditions can improve your ability to perform closer to your capability in high-pressure moments.

Before Roger Reid arrived to coach Southern Utah University's basketball team in 2007, the team ranked 217th in free throw percentage. When Coach Reid took over, he integrated pressure into practice by randomly stopping and bringing his players to the free throw line to make a shot that would decide whether the player could take a breather or would have to sprint around the court. It worked. By 2009, the team was ranked number one in free throw percentage.

When your son is preparing for a test, help him depressurize the test moment by suggesting he take practice exams under the same or shorter time limit he'll have on test day and without the use of study aids. If possible, tell him to practice in the same room in which he'll be taking the actual test, using the same type of paper.

If you're preparing for a presentation, challenge yourself to make your points coherently in a shorter-than-expected time frame. Add more pressure to your practice by handicapping yourself—no notes and a blaring television. If it's a psychomotor task you need to perform, play your practice like Phil Mickelson—one hundred three-foot putts in a row before he can call it quits.

A manager told us that his daughter complained that he was putting too much SAT pressure on her. He told her, "Sweetheart, I'm helping you. This is baby pressure compared to what you get in the real world so you better get used to it."

Pressure Solution 14
WHEN YOU'RE IN A SQUEEZE: SQUEEZE

In a workshop for Concordia University MBA students entitled "Pressure and the Job Interview," a job seeker volunteered her plight: "I've had a few interviews. Each time, I am well prepared. I think about what I want to communicate and how I will express it. Then, when I am in the

interview, I fall apart. It never comes out the way I want. I always feel the pressure. What can I do? Why does this happen?"

"Look at a happy picture on your iPhone," one student recommended. Another offered, "Just stay focused on the points you want to make." There were a good many other suggestions. But nobody recommended using this pressure solution:

SQUEEZE A BALL

If you're a student, this scenario is familiar. You find yourself in a pressure moment—often a competitive one—well rehearsed and motivated to perform. Yet, instead of delivering a stellar performance, you unravel, like a golfer losing a big lead; the debater fails to make his scripted points. Here's the explanation that was given to the student as to why she chokes during her interviews:

When we learn and practice a new skill, we rely on the left frontal lobe of the brain. As we practice the skill and it becomes more *automatic*, the skill and associated behaviors pass over to the right hemisphere of the brain, where performance is automatically and unself-consciously controlled. In other words, it's not just your rehearsed responses that pass over; it is also your voice tone, mannerisms, speech, body posture—all of which become part of your performance.

In a competitive moment—an interview, an audition—anxiety is triggered by a desire to do well, coupled with a heightened fear of failure. Together, these emotions boost activity in the language areas of the left hemisphere of the brain. This activity manifests itself with increased self-focused attention and a conscious reflection on "how I am doing." When you are learning and developing a new skill, such reflection is helpful. But once you have mastered the skill and have to execute it in a high-pressure situation, such reflection is to your detriment.

Choking occurs when a well-rehearsed skill fails; because the person brings self-conscious thinking—"how am I doing?"—to the critical moment he or she has to perform. This self-conscious thinking disrupts the person's response. A skill that would normally be performed effortlessly misfires because the self-focused left-hemisphere processes interfere with the right side of the brain.

Surprisingly, even a mindless exercise like squeezing a ball with your left hand will give you a better chance to do your best. Juergen Beckmann, PhD, chairman of Sport Psychology at the Technical University in Munich, found that athletes were less likely to choke when they squeezed a ball or clenched their left hand before competition, to activate key parts of the brain.

In studies conducted with experienced badminton players, judo experts, and soccer players, the athletes' skills were tested during practice and then in a pressure competition before a large crowd or video camera. The results showed that right-handed athletes who squeezed a ball in their *left* hand before competing were less likely to choke than right-handed players who squeezed a ball in their right hand.

The explanation for the results is that closing the left hand over a soft ball primed the right hemisphere of the brain, the part associated with fluent, automatic, and largely unconscious neural pathways controlling the skill. Activating the right hemisphere like that also tends to suppress the left hemisphere, and therefore tone down our thoughts about success and failure.

The next time you have a job interview, before you go in, clench your left fist, or get yourself one of those fuzzy little balls and squeeze it.

The same advice is useful for a surgeon who is about to operate, a machinist before he uses a dangerous tool, or a golfer before she putts.

Pressure Solution 15
WRITE PRESSURE OFF!

+ A student worries about her upcoming SATs.
+ A lawyer is anxious about a closing argument.
+ An engineer is apprehensive about being observed by his supervisors the next day.

Those individuals may be on their way to a subpar performance. Whatever the task, worrying about doing poorly can sabotage your performance and prevent you from doing your best. But by using this pressure

solution the night before or a few hours in advance, you can improve your odds:

WRITE OUT YOUR CONCERNS ABOUT THE HIGH-PRESSURE SITUATION YOU ARE FACING

Worrying about what can go wrong diminishes processing power in our brains, known as working memory capacity, or WMC. WMC is housed in the prefrontal cortex; it allows you to keep in mind the information that is critical to the task you are performing. When we are concerned or worried about something, our working memory capacity is overtaxed. Students taking their SATs need all of their working memory capacity to do calculations, as does the manager or lawyer who needs to remember key facts to make his or her case. In short, concerns generated by pressure are a detriment to your best performance.

A wide body of research shows that writing about a traumatic or emotional experience over a few weeks is an effective technique for decreasing worry in clinically depressed invididuals. Psychologist Sian Beilock has found that writing out your concerns can help you avoid choking and permit you to do your best.

College students were asked to take two math tests. On the first test, students were instructed to do their best. Before taking the second test, the researchers increased the pressure put on the students via a combination of financial incentives, social evaluation, and peer pressure. Students were told that they could earn money by performing well on the test, and that their performance would also decide whether other students would get money.

Half of the students were the control group and were told to sit quietly for ten minutes. The other half were given ten minutes to write down their thoughts and feelings about each upcoming test. The results showed that the control group choked under pressure (they experienced a 12 percent drop in accuracy between the two tests). That did not happen with the group told to write down their thoughts ahead of time.

Similar results were found in a classroom study. Ninth grade students had their test anxiety (the degree to which they became anxious

in a test situation) measured six weeks before they took their first high-school-career final exam. On test day, students were given instructions either to write down their thoughts and feelings about the forthcoming exam or to think about subjects that would not be on the test.

The results: For students who didn't write out their thoughts and feelings, there was a high correlation between test anxiety and performance—the more anxious the student, the worse the performance. In contrast, those students who wrote about their test thoughts and feelings showed no relationship between test anxiety and performance. In fact, the highly anxious students did as well as the less anxious students. The bottom line is that students who wrote down their thoughts and feelings achieved a final grade average of B+, compared to the control group, who achieved a final average of B−.

Writing out your specific concerns before a high-pressure situation helps you to minimize distractive thinking, which eats up your working memory capacity. Expressing your concerns in writing increases your insight into the sources of the pressure. These insights allow you to reexamine and reappraise the situation in a way that decreases your tendency to worry when you need your "A" game.

If you see your daughter feeling the heat over an upcoming test, encourage her to write down her thoughts and feelings about the test. The same is true for an anxious coworker the day before his presentation, or a friend before an upcoming interview or sales call.

Invest in an old-fashioned pad and spend a few minutes writing down your feelings about upcoming pressure moments. The short time investment can give you strong performance returns.

Pressure Solution 16

PUT AWAY SELF-CONSCIOUSNESS

If you have a video camera or a smartphone (and who doesn't these days), you can use it to improve your ability to perform in a pressure situation. Michigan State researchers, led by Dr. Sian Beilock, designed a study that shows that while explicit monitoring (making subjects

self-conscious) of a task can be a cause for choking in a task that has been highly practiced, it can also be a boon for tasks that are new to an individual.

Fifty-four novice student golfers were put into three groups, and all were trained to a high level of skill on a putting task. The golfers were trained under different circumstances. The first group practiced under normal conditions. The second group practiced putting while simultaneously engaging in a secondary task—listening to words presented on a tape recorder and repeating a target word every time they heard it. The third group practiced under a condition that *increased their self-consciousness*—they putted in front of a video camera and were told to pay close attention to their performance because it would be reviewed by golf pros.

When practice was completed, all three groups were given a low- and a high-pressure test. In the low-pressure test, the golfers performed a sequence of putts in a distracting environment. In the high-pressure test, the golfers were told prior to putting that they had to improve their performance to receive monetary awards for themselves, and that a partner was depending on them.

The results showed that all the groups putted equally well on the low-pressure test. But in the high-pressure test, the single-task group and the distraction group performed significantly worse under pressure, whereas the self-conscious group actually improved. Apparently, increasing your level of self-consciousness while you practice a *new skill* helps in the learning process and immunizes you against the intrusion of self-conscious thoughts when it is time to perform.

If you can't practice in front of others, take advantage of the fact that videotaping yourself, while it initially heightens your tendency to be self-conscious, over time *decreases* your self-consciousness as you become desensitized to being videotaped or watched. Practice your presentation in front of a video camera. When it comes time to present, you will be less affected by the fact that others are observing you. Without these interfering thoughts, you can simply focus on your presentation. Airline pilots whose simulated landings were observed by senior pilots made fewer procedural errors in their landing tests than

those whose simulations were not monitored but who were then observed by instructors in their performance assessment. A sales trainer who videotapes those he or she is training will both increase their technical expertise and, equally important, minimize their tendency to become overly self-conscious when pitching their product.

Don't lose sight of the point that videotaping yourself performing a skill that *you already do well* can be helpful, as well. A lawyer giving a closing argument to a jury may feel the pressure to perform and begin to think too much about what she is doing—and then stutter or lose her train of thought. If she practices and videotapes her closing argument several times, chances are she will develop her confidence to the the point of having no need to observe herself when performing in court.

Get your daughter to give you a preview of her music recital in your living room; you will be desensitizing her to the pressure she will face in a filled auditorium.

What should you do if you are called to give a presentation on the fly in front of management, or are asked to pinch-hit for a coworker on a sales call? Make a trip to the bathroom and practice for two minutes in front of the mirror. You'll see your self-consciousness diminish and even disappear.

Pressure Solution 17
MEDITATE

Have you ever tried meditation? You might consider using this pressure solution before your next high-pressure moment:

PRACTICE MEDITATION

How does meditation help you to depressurize? That's a fair question.

In any high-pressure moment, it is imperative that you are able to regulate your thoughts, emotions, and behaviors. The more effective

you are in regulating this trio, the more adept you become in minimizing the adverse effects of pressure.

A study conducted at the University of Oregon used magnetic resonance imaging to scan students' brains while they rested. Students were then randomly assigned to participate either in an integrative mind-body training (IBMT) meditation program or in a relaxation program. The meditation procedure stressed a state of "restful alertness"—a high degree of awareness of your body and mind so unwanted thoughts are less likely to hijack your attention and distract you. The training sessions were divided into thirty-minute sections over a one-month period for a total of eleven hours. Upon completion of the program, students were again subjected to an MRI.

The researchers found that the meditation training altered for the better the white matter that connects the anterior cingulate cortex (ACC) to other structures in the brain. In other words, after meditation training, your ACC is able to regulate your thoughts, behaviors, and emotions more effectively and thus help you respond more effectively in pressure moments.

There are a lot of meditation practices to choose from. But the study suggests that whatever meditation procedure you choose, it should include three components: relaxation, mental imagery, and mindfulness training. The group that participated in just relaxation for the same amount of time did not show the same results; it is the combined components that help your brain depressurize. Practice your meditation method for thirty minutes a day over the next month—more if you are enjoying it.

Olympic bronze medalist in volleyball Mark Heese, with whom JP worked at three Olympic Games, would be considered a conscientious user of this solution. Mark would mindfully meditate every morning during training and on days in which he had a competition, as a way to be more present, nonreactive, and alert.

The fact is, even if your brain doesn't change, the skills you are practicing—*relaxation, mental imagery,* and *mindfulness*—are all tools that will help you to depressurize. Need more encouragement? NBA Hall of Fame coach Phil Jackson will tell you it helped him win eleven

NBA Championships, to say nothing of being able to manage some of
the biggest stars in the game.

Pressure Solution 18
BE OBSESSIVE AND COMPULSIVE

A VP advertising executive tells us: "Ten minutes before I pitch a client,
I go in my office, close the door, pull the shade down, and boom!—I do
a few minutes of the Ali Shuffle—I bob and weave, throw a few jabs like
I'm making my points, and when I feel I float like a butterfly and sting
like a bee, I'm ready for that client. I tell myself, I'm ready!"

This executive is using a pressure solution that is utilized by just
about every athlete, actor, surgeon, musician, and other professional
who has to perform under pressure *and* perform at his or her best:

CREATE AND PRACTICE A PRE-ROUTINE

As the term suggests, this pressure solution involves the creation
and practice of something that you consistently do before you compete
or present or perform. Two-time NBA Most Valuable Player Steve
Nash, for example, *always* bounces the ball twice and bends his knees
before he shoots a free throw. Watch a golf tournament and you'll see
every player go through a pre-shot routine.

When you engage in a pre-routine, a few things occur that help
you to depressurize. First, the pre-routine prevents you from being
distracted, whether by worrying about the competition or thinking
about your last failure. Second, by helping you avoid distraction, a pre-
routine keeps you focused on the relevant information and behavior
that you need to integrate into your performance, whether it is sales
data or a smooth golf swing. Most important, because the pre-routine
is a routine, it tells your body to take over and helps get you in the
"zone," ready to perform. Studies demonstrate that individuals engag-
ing in a pre-routine are less affected by pressure.

An effective pre-routine consists of a series consisting of mental ac-
tivities, imagery, relaxation, positive self-talk, and finally, some arousal

or activation. You need to integrate and apply these skills in a well-established pattern that helps you *feel* comfortable. Approach each performance the same way and you will become somewhat immune to the pressures of a big moment.

Be careful not to confuse a routine with a ritual. A routine is a mindful way to get you into ideal psychological and physiological position to deliver your best effort on that day. A ritual is a mindless activity that is repeated to bring you luck. If your routine ever becomes an empty ritual, develop a new routine. These guidelines will help you develop an effective pre-performance mental routine:

- The routine should be relatively short (three to five minutes).
- It should be done immediately prior to the high-pressure situation.
- It should include a mental component—reviewing your key points, analyzing your club selection, contemplating how you will approach each math problem, using your list of things that really matter to you, etc.
- The routine should include a physical component as well—consciously breathing deeply, stretching, striking a power pose, wiggling your toes as a means of acknowledging that you are in control.
- Part of the routine should deal with kinesthetic imagery—visualize yourself performing at your best.
- Upon completion, say a mantra or use an anchor word or phrase that signals that you're ready for showtime.

The VP we met above told us that he doesn't always get the client, but "I don't choke."

Pressure Solution 19
SPEED KILLS

When we are in a high-pressure situation, we typically speed up our thinking, causing us to jump to erroneous conclusions, fail to consider

relevant data or alternative viewpoints, and respond without readiness. In effect, a speedy response often kills our chance for success. Studies show that when dealing with tasks that require *working memory*, you will get smarter results if you practice this pressure solution:

SLOW DOWN YOUR RESPONSE

Doing so helps ensure that your working memory isn't overly taxed by stress and worry, factors that typically downgrade your comprehension, judgment, and decision-making and thus lead to ineffective responses that are often disastrous.

In the 1980s, psychologist Micki Chi investigated what caused individuals to succeed or fail at difficult problem-solving in high-pressure situations. She gave a set of basic physics problems to a group of Physics professors, Physics PhD students, and undergrad students. The undergrad students had completed only one semester of Physics.

As expected, the professors and the PhD students performed better than the undergrads. The surprising finding was that the professors and the PhD students *took longer to get started solving the problem than the undergrads did.*

Before putting pencil to paper, the profs and the PhDs paused, presumably to think about the problem and the underlying principles. Once they had a grasp of the problem, they were able to solve the problem quickly and correctly.

The undergrad students, on the other hand, jumped right into the problem without mulling it over. This caused them to get distracted and stressed over irrelevant details, which were often the direct cause of their incorrect answers; their working memory became taxed.

Develop "slowdowns," responses that give yourself more time, be it a minute or day, so that your cognitive operations have the best chance to succeed. If you're taking an important exam, instead of frantically rushing into solving the problem or writing the essay, slow yourself down. Give yourself two minutes to think it over and make an outline.

If a travel agent presses you to lock up your vacation with a deposit, tell the agent, "I want to sleep on it."

If a client says he or she needs something "right away," slow yourself

down. Tell the client, "It's top priority," without committing to a fast schedule. If you're faced with an unforeseen problem at work, slow yourself down by taking a five-minute walk to think in a less pressured way. When a big decision needs to be made around priorities at work, ask yourself if it absolutely has to be made at that moment. Many times it does not, yet we act as if it does. Heather Tulk, a senior vice president at Bell, says she learned an important lesson when she was coming up through the ranks: *Not everything is urgent.* In high-pressure meetings, when you are in the middle of a big decision, it can feel like the decision needs to be made now. Sometimes it does. But many times it does not. We know that pressure can distort our thinking, and make us believe a matter is more urgent than it is. In these cases, you may want to invoke the "twenty-four-hour rule": Choose to not make a decision in that moment and, instead, come back to it the next day, after everyone has had a chance to think it over and see it in a new light.

When you slow down your response in working memory pressure moments, you reduce your arousal, which in turn allows you to think more flexibly, creatively, and attentively, all forces that help overcome pressure. Slowing down your response in a high-pressure moment gets you smarter results.

Pressure Solution 20
BREATHE NATURALLY

In a pressure situation, when you're on edge, with senses heightened and adrenaline pumping, it is likely your natural breathing pattern will become shortened and labored. This is a sign that you are close to losing your composure, that you are no longer in control of the outcome. Before panic sets in, use this pressure solution:

REGULATE YOUR BREATHING

Losing composure is a common scenario in sports. A golfer with a lead makes a terrible shot, loses his composure the next time he gets

the ball—and does it again. It also happens when the presenter is asked a difficult question, or the college graduate is thrown a curve by the interviewer.

Being able to depressurize is dependent on your ability to *regain your feelings of control* so that you can reduce your anxiety and overcome the sense that the situation is slipping away. At the same time, you want to put yourself back in control and restore your sense of confidence. The fastest, easiest, and most accessible way for you to do this is to bring your physical arousal under control via your breathing.

Body functions, such as heart rate, body temperature, breathing, blinking, and digestion, are controlled by the autonomic nervous system, or ANS. You are unaware of the workings of the ANS because it functions in an involuntary, reflexive manner. However, one of the responses you *do* have control over is your breathing. The strategy here is to use your natural act of breathing as a bridge back from mindless panic to an optimal condition to perform.

Anxiety speeds up your breathing, forcing you to breathe high up in your chest. By consciously slowing your breathing down and making sure you breathe from your diaphragm, you will be able to quickly calm yourself down.

The strategy, conceived by Lieutenant Colonel Dave Grossman, is taught to soldiers and police officers to quickly calm themselves down and stay focused in high-pressure situations like firefights. Practice the following procedure two minutes a night for a week:

+ Inhale through your nose, deeply, expanding your stomach for a count of four—one, two, three, four.
+ Hold that breath in for a count of four.
+ Slowly exhale through your mouth, completely, contracting your stomach for a count of four.
+ Hold the empty breath for a count of four.

The next time you feel your anxiety rising, or you experience pressure, in the midst of an action, regulate your breathing and calm yourself down.

Pressure Solution 21
YOUR FIRST ADVANTAGE

The only requirement for using this pressure solution is that you be in a situation in which you are able *to choose* when you want to perform— first, second, third, or last. It could be in a staff meeting with your boss who says, "I want to hear from all of you." It might be a potential client who says to you and your competitors, "You all have two minutes to pitch your idea." Or an audition where the performers are given a choice in terms of who reads first.

If you follow conventional wisdom, you might sit back and see how others do, to get a feel for the situation. This is a good strategy if you want to increase the pressure you feel. But you are likely to perform below your capability. If you want to depressurize the moment, then:

> GO FIRST

Studies of World Cup soccer and the National Hockey League show that when shoot-outs determine the winner, the team (or player) that goes first has a strong statistical advantage. Follow-up interview data with the athletes confirms that those who perform first feel less pressure than those who perform second.

The "first advantage" is seen in many other competitive situations as well. In one study, researchers investigated how individuals' performances of a cognitive task in a high-pressure competition were affected by their peers' performances. Data from the National Spelling Bee showed that when the immediate predecessor was correct, a speller had a much greater probability of making a mistake than if the predecessor was incorrect.

What causes the first advantage? Consider a best-of-ten foul-shooting contest with your kids. If you go first and make the shot, your son *has to make* his shot just to tie. If you miss your first shot, your son still *has to make* his shot to go ahead—he is thinking, *I've got to make this.* The conditions of going second intensify pressure.

When you go first, *you do not have distracting thoughts* caused by the performance of those who went before you. Your working memory can fully focus on the task at hand, whether spelling a word correctly or making a judgment/decision.

Competition is also lowered because going first frees you from comparing yourself to others; instead you can focus on doing your best, rather than *trying to beat* someone else. The latter often causes you to change your performance for the worse.

These two first advantage factors make it easier for you to be positive and approach the task with enthusiasm, enhancing your chances to do your best.

Besides helping you depressurize the moment, there is another advantage to going first, one that can give you an edge in a competitive situation: You put more pressure on those who go after you.

Note: This strategy applies only to performing familiar tasks. For novel tasks, it is often better to go second, if observing the task *helps you learn how to perform it*. In that circumstance, watching the first competitor perform might reduce your anxiety and enhance your confidence.

Pressure Solution 22
SHARING PRESSURE

Recall how you felt after you disclosed to someone else the feelings of pressure you were experiencing about an upcoming event. In line with our coaching experiences and what we've learned from evolutionary and social psychologists, we're guessing you probably felt relieved or, as we say, depressurized. That's because you executed this pressure solution:

> COMMUNICATE YOUR FEELINGS OF BEING UNDER PRESSURE

Studies show the act of *sharing distressful feelings* reduces anxiety and stress. Sharing your feelings also allows you to examine them, challenge their reality, and view a pressure situation in a realistic manner.

Often, others will provide you with helpful suggestions and strategies that put things in perspective.

Next time you're feeling the heat of an upcoming presentation, deadline, or important client meeting, share your feelings with a friend, colleague, or peer, or with your client or boss.

In a team meeting when it's obvious everyone is under pressure, raise the issue with the group. Talk about it. We think you'll find that the entire team will be relieved when it's out in the open and people realize, *It's not just me.*

This is what Dave Bialis did when he faced one of the most intense pressure-filled situations of his career. Bialis is senior vice president and general manager at Cox Communications. He realized he had to let seven hundred people go from a call center unit. While Dave and his senior team understood the need for Cox Communications to take this action, given the competitive environment the company faced, it didn't make Dave's job any easier. One of the decisions he made early on was to share the news with his senior team, as well as how he felt about the change. The effect was to galvanize them around Dave. On the day he had to convey the news to the seven hundred who were going to be let go, he didn't use the usual corporate scripting that most organizations have their lawyers draw up. Instead, he chose to speak from the heart about how he felt. He described how sad he felt about the situation, and how he recognized how this would impact everyone in the room. It helped that Cox provided generous severance and opportunities to relocate employees to other parts of the organization. But the way Dave handled this difficult situation went a long way to helping him and others deal with the pressure more effectively. If you are collaborating with someone else, and starting to feel pressure from a deadline, sharing your feelings will make it easier to effectively confront the task. And you'll realize it's not all on your shoulders.

Next time your daughter has an important test coming up, have a "pressure conversation" to get her to share her feelings.

There are plenty of studies to suggest that the *act* of verbally expressing your feelings, whether in a journal, to a tape recorder, or in an empty room, helps to diminish feelings of anxiety, stress, and pressure.

There is no shame in feeling pressure, but if you don't share your feelings, there is a good chance pressure will shame *you*.

Keep in mind that all twenty-two of our pressure solutions are short-term strategies. They are "proximate" solutions; they help you in the moment when it comes to handling pressure anxiety. Those who want longer-term solutions, however, will need to build a COTE of Armor.

PART 3

On October 18, 1924, Grantland Rice penned for the *New York Herald Tribune* the most famous passage in the history of sports journalism:

> *Outlined against a blue, gray October sky the Four Horsemen rode again. In dramatic lore they are known as famine, pestilence, destruction and death. These are only aliases. Their real names are: Stuhldreher, Miller, Crowley and Layden. They formed the crest of the South Bend cyclone before which another fighting Army team was swept over the precipice at the Polo Grounds this afternoon as 55,000 spectators peered down upon the bewildering panorama spread out upon the green plain below.*

Judging by the fact that Notre Dame went on to beat Stanford in the 1925 Rose Bowl, to win the national championship with a perfect 10–0 record, and that none of the most fabled quartet in football history stood taller than six feet or weighed more than 162 pounds, Mr. Rice would not have been inaccurate to have scribed, "In success lore they are known as Confidence, Optimism, Tenacity, and Enthusiasm."

If you were to ask, "What are the personality attributes of the most accomplished individuals, those who enjoy the greatest mental and physical health, are engaged in positive relationships, and experience the most joy in life?" What are the attributes of individuals who can play their best under pressure? The answer is the aforementioned characteristics. All of the Four Horsemen were elected to the National Football Hall of Fame, and went on to distinguished coaching careers

and later success in business and law. We believe the attributes they are known for are part of the DNA of success. They help you do your best in pressure situations.

The Old Testament tells it differently; but in the annals of sports lore and "success lore," the Four Horsemen will always represent Confidence, Optimism, Tenacity, and Enthusiasm.

In this section of *Performing Under Pressure*, we provide you with a COTE of Armor manual: guidelines, procedures, techniques, and practices for developing and strengthening your natural pressure management tools. For we all have natural tools we were born with to help us counteract pressure. Of course, there is a caveat, and it is a large one: You must sharpen these tools if you want to obtain results. We will provide you with the information, step-by-step strategies, powerful examples, colorful illustrations. And we will endeavor to make them easy to use. But it is *your responsibility* to develop and regiment them into your life.

Our Methodology for Building a COTE of Armor

Our blueprint or "building plans" come from several sources.

First, we draw from research studies and academic journals from the fields of evolutionary, social, cognitive, positive, and sports psychology; neuroscience; organizational behavior; and economics. All provide a theoretical framework and empirical data that corroborate the positive relationship between COTE and managing pressure. A second source of information is our clinical, consulting, and coaching experience. And a third source is the research we've collected from individuals via online surveys, as well as our ongoing study of twelve thousand people from around the world. They have helped us to develop proven strategies for implementing our advice.

Most of us learn best by doing. The individuals who are most successful in building their COTE of Armor are those who fully engage in the activities we discuss, just as those who are most successful in weight reduction and exercise programs are those who follow the diets and do the exercises. You must experience the attributes of confidence, optimism, tenacity, and enthusiasm firsthand if you are to strengthen

the natural pressure management tools within yourself. You will find that the activities suggested here are often connected to one another; activities that will help you develop your self-confidence are reinforced and made more effective by activities that develop optimism, tenacity, or enthusiasm, and vice versa.

Learning new skills, of course, takes time. You have to practice these activities over and over for them to be effective.

You will need some time to process the information we are presenting, in order to integrate what you are learning into your thinking. Give yourself a few minutes a week to think about the attributes we will discuss and explore. Don't skip through the activities, or do them haphazardly, or you will not get the results you want.

Bottom line, the more you do the activities we discuss, and the more support you have to incorporate these attributes into your behavior and life, the more likely it is that you will develop the natural protection against high-pressure situations that these attributes confer.

The attributes behind our COTE of Armor originally evolved to help our ancestors overcome the pressure to survive in prehistoric times. They equipped them with the characteristics to be successful in the face of the high-pressure situations—the life-and-death situations—they encountered.

Take the act of hunting, literally an early *do-or-die* pressure moment. Young hunters who threw "incompletes" over and over were doomed to feel ineffective and helpless—either they starved to death or they found a different vocation that earned them a share of the food. Those who either by chance or skill hit their target experienced success, and thus their self-confidence was born—they started to *believe* they could throw their spear accurately when their prey suddenly appeared.

Confident self-talk would tell this bunch they could accomplish this goal, and this *appraisal* allowed them to be courageous and put fear aside so they could embrace hunting. Since early hunters often came up empty-handed, they would have bad days at work, but sooner or later, some would be successful, leading them to think that in similar *future* situations, they would also sooner or later be successful—they became *realistically optimistic*, and this prevented them from being pulled down by distressful feelings. Needing strength and determination to improve hunting skills and knowing that success was only a matter of time kept them *tenacious* to provide the mental toughness needed to stay committed to their goal, even when frustrated, so that they could turn setbacks into comebacks and achievements. When they did this, they experienced *enthusiasm*, which energized them with

positive feelings that made them even more confident and optimistic, as well as helped them infect those around them with confidence and optimism, too.

In evolutionary terms, these attributes became *psychological success adaptations*—response patterns that help individuals thrive. Through the process of natural selection, they become hardwired into our brains. Throughout history, those individuals with the most confidence, optimism, tenacity, and enthusiasm tended to be those who survived, had children, and passed on their genes. These attributes are part of our human heritage. And by strengthening and developing them, we can better handle the pressure moments we face today.

These attributes have been hardwired into us as an "open system"—in other words, they are dynamic and susceptible to growth. *Not all* attributes/traits that humans possess can be developed, but the fact that these attributes *can* be makes an important evolutionary point: *They continue* to give you an edge. Those who choose to regularly strengthen them navigate their lives more effectively. No matter the pressure situation we face, whether at work or at home, confidence, optimism, tenacity, and enthusiasm protect us from pressure's injurious effects. They free us to do our best, whether it is the first day of work, the middle of a project you are managing, or a sales presentation.

Nonetheless, the COTE of Armor we describe in the chapters ahead will not materialize out of thin air. To create it, you need to start with the core attribute: confidence.

As Simon Tedeschi walks out onto the stage of Melbourne's darkened Hamer Hall, all he can see amid rows of empty seats are three shadowy figures hunched over a makeshift desk. The judges sit in silence, notebooks in front of them, as Simon makes his way to the piano. Excitement and fear course through him. To get his blood pumping, he starts throwing his arms out, shadowboxing his way across the stage.

His fear is as much about himself as it is about this moment. This performance can make or break his career. He has spent endless hours—in fact most of his life—practicing, honing his skills, preparing for this. And *this is it*. As he sits down, he realizes he has to put it all on the line, playing as close to the edge as possible. With a deep breath he begins playing.

The occasion is the early round of the ABC Young Performers Competition, an international piano competition. For all practical purposes, Simon Tedeschi has spent the last fourteen years preparing for this moment. For ten years he studied piano in Australia with Neta Maughan, as well as with Noretta Conci in London, and with Peter Serkin in Boston. Over the next few minutes, he will play literally thousands of notes at breakneck speed, and with an artistry aimed to rival the greatest musicians in history, in order to best the other pianists in the competition.

When we think of performance under pressure, we typically think first of professional athletes, because of our culture's obsession with sports. But the life of a young classical musician like Simon Tedeschi might be a better example of pressure, just based on the numbers. The

sobering reality is that only a few competitors will ever establish careers in music. In a given year, very few, often none, will become household names. Their careers are every bit as precarious, competitive, and cutthroat as those of elite athletes. Gaining acceptance into a top conservatory such as Juilliard is fiercely competitive, and only the first step in a pressure-filled path that only *might* lead to a professional music career. Even if one succeeds at school, there's no automatic portal to a profession in music. In the US alone, some eight thousand pianists graduate from professional schools with piano performance degrees each year (and many thousand more come from China and the Pacific Rim), with almost no jobs available to them in their field. Their only hope to gain attention is to win a significant piano competition.

These competitions, therefore, are crucial gateways to landing professional representation and building a reputation. And even then, winning is no guarantee. In this environment there isn't a "three strikes and you're out" attitude when you play for a panel of judges. Instead it's one mistake and your career's over. One mistake. One wrong note.

For Simon to succeed in this high-wire life of intense pressure, his piano training, like that of his competitors, must be boiled down to a very limited number of musical works. Many musicians from the nation's best music conservatories graduate with the ability to perform only a handful of musical works at an elite level—a few knuckle-busting sonatas and a flashy concerto—just enough for one recital or competition. The pressure to *not* make a mistake is so intense that most pianists rehearse only a few pieces, which ironically limits their repertoire rather than expands it.

Simon was inspired to start playing at a very young age, by an unlikely source. "I heard a fellow student in first grade bashing away quite incoherently at the piano and I was completely stunned by the power and the breadth of the instrument. The young boy actually had cerebral palsy and was playing piano as part of his physical therapy program." At just nine years of age, Simon performed a Mozart piano concerto in the Sydney Opera House, and by 1998 he had entered the ABC Young Performers Competition.

So did Simon falter under all the pressure?

In fact, Simon Tedeschi beat the odds—he won the ABC Young

Performers Award. It cemented his career and allowed him to get a manager and professional engagements.

Simon went on to be named the Symphony Australia Young Performer of the Year and was the recipient of a $10,000 Queen's Trust Overseas Study Award. His career trajectory continued in other competitions, and he won various awards and scholarships, including the Open Age Concerto Series and the top prize in the keyboard section of the Royal Overseas League Music Competition in London in 2002. He is now often described by critics and musical peers as one of the finest artists in the world. But it hasn't been easy. Simon described to us his experience of pressure when it is time to perform.

> As an "elite" musician, I suffer from pre-performance anxiety like any other sportsperson or indeed any person where their occupation carries with it a certain degree of risk. Like most musicians, I feel an elevated heart rate and, sometimes, clammy palms just before walking on stage. When you're consistently performing at such a high level under extraordinary pressure in an industry with too few jobs for too many contenders, it can be overwhelming.

Not everyone manages with these pressures. Stage fright and the continued pressure of performing cut short the careers of some of the twentieth century's most esteemed musicians. Pianists Vladimir Horowitz and Glenn Gould curtailed their careers from the weight of anxiety; cellist Pablo Casals endured shortness of breath, a racing heart, and shakiness, even as he played into his nineties. Historically, performers have carried around flasks of Scotch, which they sipped from before walking on stage. Other musicians have relied on Valium and similar sedatives. Today, many performers tackle pressure with a newer chemical, a family of prescription drugs known as beta-blockers.

As far back as 1987, this new drug of choice was making itself known in the concert world. A survey in 1987 by the International Conference of Symphony Orchestra Musicians (which represents the fifty-one largest orchestras in the US) revealed that 27 percent of their membership used beta-blockers to reduce their nervousness. Known as the "musician's underground drug," these drugs are intended to treat

irregular heart rhythms, high blood pressure, chest pain, and related tremors. Beta-blockers act to mute the effects of epinephrine, one of the hormones released by the body that mediate its response to pressure. We surveyed a group of accomplished musicians in New York City in 2014 about the use of beta-blockers and were astounded to hear that "any claim you make about the abundance of beta-blockers is probably *understated*."

In January 2013, Simon Tedeschi confessed to using beta-blockers to improve his performance. "I've been living a lie." His disclosure was heard around the world. Beta-blockers, which had once remained an industry secret, had gone public. As Blair Tindall, a professional oboist and author of the book *Mozart in the Jungle*, says, "the little secret in the classical music world is that the drugs have become nearly ubiquitous."

"The pressure was just overwhelming," Tedeschi told us. "I couldn't stand it anymore. The jittery hands, the racing mind, the fear of messing up." He said that he had taken beta-blockers for the last decade. In an open letter to the concert piano world, Tedeschi came clean and described how hiding his use of the drug affected him:

> From Sydney Opera House to Campsie RSL, my performing career has been an exercise in subterfuge. . . . My recordings, noted for their slow tempi, should have had another name on the liner notes. Its scientific name is Metoprolol, but it is most commonly known by its generic name: beta blockers.

Simon and his fellow musicians (and their steroid-using peers in athletics) know how to perform—they were practically born training to perform. But in high-pressure situations, they experience the physical and psychological manifestations of pressure we all experience at times. The feeling can be overwhelming. What these elite performers are searching for is anything that can help them manage pressure more effectively. What they want is an *antidote* to the pervasive, universal, negative effects of pressure. Most of us can't pop a beta-blocker when we face a pressure situation. But we can develop an attribute that will inoculate us against pressure, acting just like an antidote to its sabotaging effects. This magic "pill" is *confidence*.

The Nature of Confidence

Confidence impacts virtually every aspect of our lives. Few executives and managers will back a project that is being pitched by a nervous, fumbling employee. Countless studies show that self-confident people are more attractive and sought out than those who aren't. Self-confident people inspire confidence in others, and gaining the confidence of others is often a key to success in our careers.

Your behavior, body language, how you speak, and what you say all reflect your level of self-confidence. The confidence some people feel is so tangible that we almost feel we can touch it. How do you rate yourself in terms of confidence?

+ Do you assert your beliefs even if you know others are sure to disagree?
+ Is it easy for you to admit your mistakes?
+ Do you take risks to get ahead or make things better?

Confidence is often defined as the degree to which you believe you can influence a specific outcome, but for most of us it is a *sureness of feeling* that we can master the *task at hand*. It's rooted in a belief in our ability, the belief that *we can do it*. In the psychological literature, confidence is often understood as *self-efficacy*, a term first introduced by Stanford University social-cognitive psychologist Albert Bandura. Self-efficacy refers to feeling confident in your ability to affect a situation; to perform a specific task and reach your goal. Your daughter might be confident that she will do well on a math test, but her confidence may plummet when she is doing the gymnastics module in physical education class in front of her peers. Similarly, you might be a very self-confident individual in a sales situation but would feel totally overwhelmed if you had to return a professional tennis serve or sit in the cockpit of a 747 (whereas professional tennis players and pilots have *high self-confidence* in those situations, even if they lack confidence in many other areas of their lives). None of us feel confident in situations in which we have no experience or training. But we want to feel confident in the areas where we know we are expected to excel.

There is a big difference between *thinking* you can do something and feeling a sense of conviction that you can do it. Sometimes you can fool others into believing you are feeling self-confident, when inside you know your feelings are telling you otherwise.

As your self-confidence (sureness) increases, your anxiety is reduced, making it more likely that you will be able to perform closer to your best in a high-pressure situation. People who are self-confident rarely panic in a pressure moment. And individuals who *do* panic tend to measure low on confidence.

Our goal in this chapter is to help you *feel* confident. Feeling confident is what allows an employee to give feedback to his or her manager or a shy person to approach a stranger at a party. It is what allows us to better manage high-pressure situations. First, a few facts.

Our level of self-confidence can change over time. We all know people who lacked self-confidence in high school and now are brimming with it. Others, for one reason or another, may lose their sense of confidence in themselves—perhaps they have been in a job that has not sufficiently challenged them or been in a relationship that has eaten away at their confidence.

Our self-confidence is malleable. It can be strengthened or weakened by events, or by our performance. For example, you may feel your self-confidence eroding as the result of a bad sales year, a poor presentation, or bad luck. Mike Vanderjagt, the most accurate field goal kicker in NFL history, encountered such a moment during the 2006 NFL playoffs. With eighteen seconds left in the game, the Indianapolis Colts field goal kicker stepped onto the field to nail a routine (for him) forty-six-yard field goal that would tie the Steelers and send the game into overtime. But Vanderjagt missed, and the Colts lost the game and the chance to go to the Super Bowl. The miss eroded his confidence to the point that he was soon out of the league. "I lost my confidence," he admitted. Confidence can also be elevated by a single incident: a home run, a perfect score on a spelling test, making a date with the person you have a crush on, closing a big deal. Such experiences help you believe you can do what you set out to do.

Self-confidence should not be confused with self-esteem. As early as the 1970s, the idea that the general feeling that we have about ourselves—

self-*esteem*—affects success became a revolutionary new approach to helping children and adults realize their potential. After all, who could argue with the logic of it? If you feel good about yourself, you perform better. But as it turned out, the research into self-esteem did not live up to its initial promise.

According to Roy Baumeister, a professor at Florida State University and one of the most highly acclaimed psychologists in the world, a new read of the literature finds that self-esteem does not have the magic powers many ascribed to it. In schoolchildren, self-esteem does *not* help children do better in high-pressure situations, such as testing or producing better grades. College students who had mediocre grades who got regular self-esteem strokes from their professors ended up *doing worse* on final exams than students who were told to apply themselves more and try harder. The same applies for adults at work.

What our level of self-esteem *does* change is our perception of our performance. Individuals who feel better about themselves rate their own performance better—they see themselves as smarter and more attractive than their peers. But neither objective tests nor impartial evaluators can detect any difference in the quality of work.

While psychologists, educators, and parents have touted the importance of self-esteem in producing well-adjusted children and students who can do better under pressure, there is ample evidence that the *direction seems to be wrong*: Feeling good about ourselves comes *after* we succeed, not before. It is the *result* of our success, not the cause of it. Research studies suggest that kids with high self-esteem do indeed have slightly better grades. But that's because getting good grades *leads* to higher self-esteem, rather than the other way around.

Similar confusion exists in companies and other organizations around the issue of job satisfaction. For many years, organizations have organized their company's performance management systems around the idea that an increase in job satisfaction leads to an increase in productivity. It stands to reason: If you do all of the things that make people feel more satisfied at work, they will perform at a higher level. Unfortunately, it turns out not to be true. Employees are not productive *because they are satisfied;* they are satisfied *because they are*

productive. High satisfaction is the *result* of high performance, not the cause of it.

So as a parent or manager, be clear about what you are attempting to build: Praising your kids or employees to make them feel better about themselves whether they deserve it or not is not the path to helping them perform better. The "everyone gets a medal" mentality has been officially discredited. Your children and employees will perform better under pressure if you help them build the self-confidence that comes from doing or achieving, not from your attempts to make them feel better about themselves by persuasion. This is why your goal should shift to putting them into situations where they are challenged. This will build the confidence that will help them when they need it most.

How Confidence Helps Us

Confidence as an Antidote

When we are confident, it acts as an *antidote* to the negative effects of pressure that can result in doubt, distorted thinking, and physiological overarousal or -stimulation. Feeling confident doesn't mean you don't experience doubt. In fact, every single elite athlete and Olympic or NBA coach and manager and leader we have worked with or studied has experienced doubt. As two-time gold medal–winning hockey player Sidney Crosby said: "Show me an athlete who does not have doubts and I will show you an athlete who is *not telling the truth.*"

Over a thirty-year period, research consistently found that people with a great deal of confidence see high-pressure situations—when they are tested—as challenges to be overcome, as opposed to crises to be confronted. In so doing, they find themselves *immunized* to a great degree against the deleterious effects of pressure and are better able to perform at a high level even when the pressure is intense.

Individuals with a higher degree of confidence work harder, persist longer, are more optimistic and enthusiastic, show more grit and determination, and choose more difficult and higher goals than those

with less confidence. Ideally, our schools should build confidence in our students at every stage of their academic careers. And indeed, by the time students reach college, their level of confidence is *more strongly related to their achievement than to any other measure.*

When students or employees or athletes feel the physical manifestations of pressure, confidence acts to fortify them, because deep down they know that *they can do it.* When they feel the effects of pressure—increased anxiety and self-doubt—they know they do not need to give in to it. Because they know they can do it, they simply recognize the signs of pressure as an early warning system that it is *time to perform.* Knowing that they can handle the moment increases their sense of control. And when any of us feel more in control, we are psychologically stronger, feel more centered, and are less afraid to approach as opposed to avoid pressure-filled situations.

As Elie Wiesel, Holocaust survivor and Nobel Laureate, said: "First we must understand that there can be no life without risk— and when our center is strong, everything else is secondary, even the risks."

Confidence in Action

On the morning of January 4, 1988, a fire erupted at the Cargill fertilizer storage facility in Maysville, Kentucky. Just as the story was being broadcast on CNN, Jim Prokopanko, a mid-level manager at the facility, received a call from Cargill's CEO. "Are you aware of the fire?" Jim was witnessing the first images of it on his television screen. His manager was away on vacation. Cargill's CEO told Jim, "I need you to go down to Kentucky. I need you to take care of the people and the reputation of the company."

And in an instant Jim found himself responsible for the twenty-five hundred residents who were being evacuated from the area, and for the reputation of Cargill, an American multinational corporation founded in 1865 and based in Minneapolis, one of the largest privately held corporations in the world.

Jim felt a moment of panic. He knew the chemicals in the storage facility could include ammonium nitrate, which if ignited could

explode. The facility at times held four hundred tons or more of am-
monium nitrate, among other chemicals, but he wasn't sure if there was
any on the site now.

"You ask yourself, what to do? There was so much unknown, so
much uncertainty. I had no experience with this. I wasn't aware of what
was in the inventory at that time. . . . What are the health risks if it is
ammonium nitrate and it blows?"

He told us he couldn't help but think, "My career *is over*. Right off
the bat, there is an embarrassment factor. It is on CNN! It couldn't
have been worse. This could harm the community, the people, and
the company. Your mind is spinning. When it hits you out of the blue
like this, there is this sense of being overwhelmed, of being out of con-
trol. . . . I didn't feel like I could finish a single thought. . . . I was start-
ing to panic. I knew I needed to slow things down."

Although Jim was filled with doubts, he was also confident in his
abilities. "While I could feel things spinning out of control, I also knew,
deep down, that if I slowed things down, if I got a group of trusted ad-
visors together, we could take care of this situation."

This is where confidence plays such a big part. Jim felt anxious, his
thinking was distorted ("my career is over"), and his body was physi-
cally reacting to the adrenaline and the pressure. But at the same time,
he also knew that he could handle this. And that surety acted as a
brake to the doubt and the physical manifestations of the pressure he
was under, helping to diminish his anxiety.

Jim's first thoughts about the accident were prescient: "I expected
the first info I was going to hear from CNN or other sources was prob-
ably going to be wrong." And it was.

He realized that if he was going to be effective in this situation
he needed to first manage himself. "I couldn't worry about the small
things. I had to take care of the 'elephants,'" the big things. And he re-
membered what Cargill's CEO had told him—"take care of the people
and the reputation of the company." Those were the elephants.

Next he got a group of trusted advisors together and walked
through a calibrated response. "We assessed the situation and did
it as logically as we could. I got a team that included people who
were very good at what they did—medical personnel, fire experts,

financial people, insurance adjusters—and we worked very closely together. I became so much smarter in that moment of bringing these people together.

"I realized it is not the event that causes pressure—you cause it in yourself. It is your physical and mental reaction to the situation. So you need to trust in your ability. You are rarely blamed for the event—but you will be remembered by your response. I had to take myself out of the equation, think less about how this would affect me personally and focus on the key issues. If you think about yourself, you feel more pressure and your performance goes down. I realized that if I was going to get our team to work together I needed to be candid and open. If I made a mistake, I had to admit it and move on. I had to not pretend I knew more than I did. The key was to put our team in a good place to make good decisions, and that started with me."

And with that in mind, Jim and his team successfully handled the situation. They went out of their way to take responsibility for the fire and take care of the people whose lives had been disrupted. They made good if imperfect decisions under pressure. By all accounts—the community's, the media's, and their company's—they succeeded.

Months later, after things were sorted out, Cargill, in a review of their operations, decided there was too much risk in the storage business, especially in strong chemicals like ammonium nitrate, and decided to sell the business.

But the experience served Jim well in facing challenges later in his career. He has gone on to become CEO of Mosaic, a public company that is the world's leading producer of concentrated phosphate and potash crop nutrients.

Jim continues to use the experience of the Kentucky fire in his job today. As CEO, he faces many pressures in the job—delivering on yearly goals, implementing change, expanding into new markets, giving his team feedback. It was his experience with Cargill that gave him the confidence that he could handle whatever comes at him. It also is one of the events that has distinguished him in the eyes of others as a leader. Through this experience, he built a reputation as someone who can be trusted to lead under pressure.

Building Confidence

An individual's level of confidence does not magically develop on its own. It takes effort, a thoughtful approach, and execution.

To start, you need to:

1. Assess your current level of confidence

2. Engage your brain using the latest findings in neuroscience

3. Develop confidence habits

Getting Started: Know Your Starting Point

Being overconfident or needlessly underconfident can make it difficult to develop self-confidence and perform at your best. Both can be overcome by developing your ability to *accurately assess yourself.* An accurate self-assessment tells you where you stand now. With this information, you can develop a plan to strengthen your sense of confidence. You will also have a baseline from which to measure your improvement. Knowing that you are improving acts as a positive feedback loop to increase your self-confidence and reduce anxiety in pressure situations. But conducting an accurate appraisal is not as easy as you might think.

Each of us falls prey to overconfidence at times. When we are overconfident, our judgments about our skills are greater than our skills warrant. Most people, for example, consider themselves better-than-average drivers. Yet by definition we can't all be better than average. Nobel Prize–winning economist Daniel Kahneman has spent years of research showing that we all have "cognitive biases" that throw off our assessments of ourselves; we tend to remember our successes and forget our failures, overestimate our knowledge and ability, and so on.

According to research by Kahneman and others:

+ Ninety-five percent of professors report that they are above-average teachers.

⁺ Executives were asked questions about their own industries and
 then asked how confident they were of the answers. People in
 advertising gave the answer that they felt was 90 percent correct.
 In fact they got *60 percent wrong*. People in the computer industry
 thought they were 95 percent right. In fact they got *80 percent
 wrong*. This overconfidence, by the way, is a gender-linked trait.
 For example, men drown twice as often as women because they
 erroneously think they can swim across the lake. They can't.

When you are deluded by an overconfidence bias, often perceived as
arrogance, it is much harder to see yourself objectively. Most home sell-
ers, for example, overestimate the market value of their house. Banks
know that, so they seek assessments by an independent appraiser who
can be objective. An objective appraisal minimizes the chances the
bank will make a risky investment in granting a mortgage to the buyer.

An overconfidence bias can also get in the way of our ability to
learn. One of the biggest problems with overconfidence takes place
when someone tells us something that we don't want to hear: We im-
mediately dismiss what they are saying and miss the opportunity to
learn from the information or feedback. Jamie Rooney, president of the
NFL Houston Texans, and somebody JP has worked with, says that
"growing from feedback and getting better each day matters far more
than looking good." According to Jamie, being overconfident in the
NFL interferes with the players', coaches', and leaders' ability to learn
and meet their organizational goals: "At the Texans, we have what we
call our 'three imperatives': winning championships and creating mem-
orable experiences and doing great things for the community. It is a
long journey and we simply cannot deliver on these imperatives if we
fail to learn because we think we know everything."

*Under*confidence can be every bit as damaging as overconfidence.
If we are needlessly underconfident, we get inundated with worry and
lose valuable working memory. We can't think straight, recall critical
information under pressure, or perform at our best. We also *avoid*
pressure situations.

A basketball player avoids a shot because she is not confident she
can make it; a student stops giving it his all during a test because he is

not confident in his math ability, whether justified or not. For people with low self-confidence, merely contemplating an anxiety-provoking pressure situation can cause them to "awfulize" about all that could go wrong and make the situation more pressured than it needs to be. This, in turn, makes it even tougher to approach the situation. When they shy away from the pressure situation they *know* they have avoided, they experience a spiral of internal recriminations that can lead to guilt and regret and even self-loathing and shame, all of which diminish their confidence even further.

Accurately assessing yourself begins by acknowledging that self-assessments are purely subjective. Numerous studies show that our subjective appraisals are filled with self-deception. So it does not make sense to use them as the sole source for your evaluation. We have found two key strategies to help you accurately self-assess your confidence: using the *perceptions of others* and using a *benchmark*.

Using the Perceptions of Others

You can counteract your cognitive biases and inherent subjectivity by using the perceptions of others in your self-assessments. Businesses have boards of directors to provide, among other things, an unbiased point of view to the president or CEO. This can be extremely valuable in the decision-making and planning process for a business. It is no different for individuals. Getting an unbiased point of view about your strengths or decision-making can be invaluable. Unfortunately, very few people reach out proactively to others for feedback. One of the ways you can do this that is very powerful is by creating your own *board of directors*.

For the past ten years, JP has been part of a small group of individuals who meet every two months to act as one another's personal board of directors. Over the course of the evening, each person in the group gets an opportunity to hear each of the others' perceptions on how effectively that person is handling particular situations. Hearing one another's thoughts helps them all see situations more clearly and reminds them that they are not alone in the challenges they face. It also challenges assumptions they are making, or gives them feedback on how to improve themselves. It provides a more realistic viewpoint of

their abilities, as well as a plan to improve. Group members find their confidence levels increase following these meetings, and this results in a greater likelihood of taking action and, for our purpose, helps them handle pressure more effectively.

Start a board of directors among a group of peers. Whom you select for your team is up to you. But make sure they are available to you, and that you feel comfortable in discussing various issues in your personal and professional life with them. The goal is to have people you can reach out to about any aspect of your life in which you need support or guidance. However, if it feels like too much of a challenge to organize a group like this, there are other ways you can use others to help you build confidence.

Another strategy for using the perceptions of others is role-playing a pressure task. For instance, a participant in one of our executive education classes at Wharton believed that her interview skills were top-notch, but she had not been successful in landing a corporate position. When she role-played in front of the other executives (and used a video camera), the reason for her lack of executive job offers quickly became apparent to her. She didn't interview well. This realization was surprisingly positive. By role-playing she gained insight about how she was performing and was able to make meaningful improvements. She learned that she frequently interrupted the interviewer, made poor eye contact, and communicated in vague terms. With this information, she was able to work on those things, which helped her perform better.

Parents can use role-playing to help their children perform better when they are facing a pressure situation like a college interview or giving a class presentation. Videotaping can be a powerful tool for giving them a real-time critique that aids self-assessment, and besides, the videotaping will reduce the self-consciousness they might feel in their upcoming interview.

Use a Benchmark

If your daughter is preparing for SATs, taking practice exams will tell your child how she is doing, and how much and where she needs to improve. The same is true for a sales rep who needs to improve his closing

rate. Gaining clarity about how his closing rate compares to a benchmark can help him focus on improving the area that needs the most attention in order to meet his sales quota. Gaining such information does more than help people accurately assess their performance—it gives them a baseline to measure their improvement and thus allows them to observe that improvement. *Knowing* they are improving propels them to self-confidence territory.

Another way to use benchmarks to help individuals in organizations understand how they perform in high-pressure situations is through use of our "360" assessment tool evaluating how they manage pressure. (See Appendix B.) This tool, which more than 120,000 people have participated in as either a target (the person being assessed) or a rater (the person doing the assessing), allows people to get feedback from those they work with, such as direct reports, managers, peers, and key clients, and also from people like family and friends. Each person provides anonymous feedback. At first glance this can feel intimidating to the person being assessed, but when it is done well, managers and employees gain valuable information that not only helps them more accurately assess their performance, but gives them a baseline to measure their later improvement. Again, seeing their improvement gives them more self-confidence.

In a broader perspective, the subject's response to an accurate assessment suggests an important empirical finding about self-confident individuals that may seem to be a contradiction: They have a level of humility that allows them to look closely at themselves in order to learn and improve. In fact, research points out that confident people *extract three to five times* more information from the same opportunity to learn as the average person. In this way, they end up with a more *realistic viewpoint*—best defined as meaning that they see things as they really are. Their thinking is void of exaggerated distortions of failure that create self-blame and plague those who do poorly in pressure moments. They do not exaggerate the significance of their success, so they are not prone to arrogance and overconfidence. Nor are they unjustifiably underconfident, causing them to avoid pressure situations. By accurately perceiving their skills and talents relative to the skills and talents of others, they keep their sense of themselves in perspective and

thus reduce needless pressure. Their everyday realistic appraisals continually help them stay attuned to who they are, how they are doing, and what they need to do to move forward, not just to prepare for a pressure moment.

A second path to building confidence is by applying some of the exciting advances in neuroscience to your approach.

Get Your Brain Involved

In sports, leadership, and neurological science a pattern has emerged linking effective leadership and performance under pressure with a particular neurochemistry. For example, we know that leaders who perform closer to their best in high-pressure situations have higher levels of testosterone and lower levels of cortisol.

Testosterone has gotten a bad rap among the general population as being linked to physical aggression and even violence. The story is far more nuanced. Testosterone has a number of powerful effects on the brain and body, all critical to helping us perform under pressure: It makes us *feel more confident* and increases our level of motivation and willingness to engage in risk-taking behavior. This helps us beyond the typical physical pursuits that most associate with testosterone. Research has found that testosterone crucially helps us take risks that are *normally constrained by fear*. It does this by acting on the amygdala (the emotional part of our brain that codes for fear), tamping down the fear response and helping us access our cognitive resources to think more clearly. It removes the emotional wariness we have toward uncertainty and helps us perform more cognitively as opposed to more emotionally.

To perform under pressure in any domain, there is a need to enter into fear-based situations *in spite* of what we feel physically, and to take action. Testosterone predicts which chess player will play better under pressure as well as the performance of elite surgeons, because, in each case, these performers need to be able to take the necessary risks to be effective even when they feel a level of fear. The research points out that testosterone does not lead to taking "stupid risks." Rather testosterone keeps emotions from interfering with our cognitive processing, allowing us to think and behave more, *not less*, rationally.

At the same time, individuals who perform better under pressure also have low cortisol, which means they are less anxious when it comes to managing pressure. They are able to stay the course even when things aren't going smoothly, and they are more able to be nondefensive when they get feedback. In effect, higher testosterone and lower cortisol allow them to be the "calm person in the boat."

The brain of each of us is constantly fluctuating in its neurochemical levels, and these hormones affect our levels of confidence and the type of behavior we choose to engage in, especially when it comes to pressure situations. What most people miss is that they have a choice in their neurochemistry—they do not need to leave it to chance. There are a number of small things you can do prior to entering a high-pressure moment that will increase testosterone and decrease cortisol. In this section we will identity three ways you can get your brain involved to do this: through your posture and by using a split between the other two ways—visualization and focusing on micro-success as ways to use what psychologists call the "winner effect" to your advantage.

Posture and the Brain

Amy Cuddy grew up in a small rural town in Pennsylvania. She studied for her undergraduate degree at the University of Colorado at Boulder. In her sophomore year, however, she was in a serious car accident and suffered a significant head injury. She was told that she would never fully recover her previous cognitive ability and would have trouble finishing her undergraduate degree. Her IQ fell thirty points. Her diagnosis was devastating, both for Amy and for her family.

Fortunately, Amy was also very hardworking and resourceful. Over time she found a way to relearn what she had lost, and although it was extremely challenging, she was able to complete her degree, four years later, and go on to study for her PhD at Princeton.

As she advanced in her studies, Amy experienced what many people feel as they grow their careers: that she was out of place, that she was an imposter. She felt she didn't deserve the success she was enjoying. She lacked self-confidence. And of course these doubts were exacerbated by her brain injury. Had she really regained all of the

mental abilities she had lost? Several times along the way she considered quitting.

One such time she went to her advisor at Princeton, Susan Fiske, to let her know that she would not be continuing in her program and was going to quit her pursuit of a PhD. Susan, one of the top researchers in her field and a strong advocate for women in science, refused to accept Amy's resignation. Instead, Susan insisted that Amy "fake it until she made it."

An interesting thing happened when Amy adopted this strategy. In faking it, Amy stumbled upon an insight into how the brain works that has become one of the most powerful findings in social psychology and brain science today. In effect she found that *tiny tweaks in how we behave can lead to massive changes in our brains.*

Amy found that our posture has a huge impact on our neurochemistry. For years we have known that our nonverbal communication makes a big difference in how we are perceived by others. Amy's work found that our nonverbal communication—in particular our posture—makes a difference *internally* to us and to our brain chemistry.

When we engage in what she terms a "high-power pose" where our bodies are more *open and expansive*—arms open as opposed to closed across our chest, standing straight with shoulders back as opposed to hunched with shoulders folded forward, occupying more space versus less—our brain and body respond by increasing testosterone and decreasing cortisol. Testosterone levels go up by 20 to 25 percent, and cortisol goes down by 20 to 25 percent.

In one study Amy taught high- and low-power poses to two groups of subjects prior to engaging in simple risk-taking activity that involved gambling for a few dollars. She had subjects take a saliva test before and after the test to measure testosterone and cortisol levels. One group adopted high-power poses for one minute, while the other assumed low-power poses for a minute. Then they filled out questionaires measuring power and risk tolerance, before proceeding to the gambling test.

Amy found that those who had engaged in high-power poses had a massive increase in their testosterone levels and a massive decrease in their cortisol levels. She found that 80 to 90 percent of the

high-power-pose subjects took more risks and used more approach be-
haviors than the low-power posers did, who took a risk only 50 percent
of the time. The results have been replicated in subsequent studies. The
effect is found equally in women and men.

In another study, Amy and her colleagues had experimenters tell
subjects to wait while they went to an adjacent room. Before leaving,
they gave each subject either an iPhone, an iPad, or an iMac to use
while they all waited. As part of the protocol to the study, the experi-
menters never returned. What Amy and her colleagues were curious
about was how long it took each subject to interrupt the experimenter
who had left them, based on the size of screen they were using while
they waited.

They found that those who were using the larger screen of the
iMac, and thus were sitting more expansively, came almost immedi-
ately to interrupt the experimenter in the adjoining room, wondering
what was taking so long. The subjects who used the smaller iPad took
much longer to find out what was keeping the experimenter. And the
subjects using the iPhone, who were more closed in their posture as
they hunched over the smaller screen, did not come out to interrupt
the experimenter at all. In fact, the scientists conducting the experi-
ment had to institute what is known as a "floor effect" and stop the ex-
periment, because it was taking so long for these lower-power-posture
subjects to interrupt them.

In effect, the smaller screen promoted a low-power condition. It
affected the subjects' brain chemistry and levels of confidence to such
an extent that it caused them to *avoid interrupting the experimenters.*
Small tweak, big change.

These neurochemical changes don't just affect us in small tasks,
however; they are important, too, when we are in high-pressure situa-
tions like a job interview or a public presentation.

Amy Cuddy and her colleagues at Harvard Business School con-
ducted another study that replicated the pressure that comes with a
job interview.

Interestingly, the subjects who performed high-power poses scored
significantly higher according to independent evaluators on a number of
different criteria for effectiveness, but they did not come across to the

evaluators as *smarter*. The difference was in their levels of *confidence and presence*. A short two-minute power-pose intervention made all the difference. It is something each of us can do to help improve our performance in a high-pressure situation. An example of someone who was able to use power posing to perform under pressure is slam poet Ian French.

In the 1980s slam poetry emerged as a new kind of performance art, a competition in which poets read or recite original work to an audience. It can sometimes take the form of a rap, as some poets will use different cadences and rhythms in their recitation. Members of the audience are chosen by the organizing committee or host to act as judges for the event. After each poet performs, the judges award a score for that poem, typically ranging between zero and ten. In slam poetry, Ian French told us in our 2014 interview, "the points are not the point, the poetry is the point." There are no costumes, props, musical instruments, or covers (using other people's material). Time starts as soon as the poet engages the audience.

Picture a hundred people or so squeezed into a crowded bar. Each poet gets up, recites his or her poem, and is then judged on the quality of the content and the presentation and how it moves the crowd. It is the epitome of a high-pressure situation.

Ian French, a filmmaker, musician, and father, came to slam poetry late in life. While most slam poets start to slam in their twenties, Ian began when he was forty-five. He was always the "old guy" at these events.

The winner of the 2013 Buffalo International Slam, Ian has performed at various festivals, including the prestigious Word on the Street and Words Aloud festivals. His poems channel "the wisdom of spirit, the rage of the wounded and the yearning that resides in every human heart." He says, "Every poem I write is a 'shout-out' to the sacredness of our days, a three-chord party jam, and a tribute to the triumph of love over fear."

We worked with Ian in preparation for the national poetry slam championships, where he would perform over three nights in a packed auditorium to more than one thousand people. The winners of each round would go on to the next evening of competition. The overall winner would go to Paris for the World Championships. We taught

Ian to do power poses while doing a form of mental rehearsal where he pictured himself *being at his best*. He would do a ninety-second intervention fifteen to twenty minutes prior to going on.

The goal was to put his body in a posture or pose that made him feel strong and powerful and open and expansive. For Ian that pose was arms up and out, hands open to the sky, head slightly raised, legs comfortably apart, eyes closed. After taking a few breaths to center his body, he would see himself at some past competition where *he was at his best*, where he felt strong and powerful, connected to the audience, and at the top of his game. He would stand there open and expansive, seeing himself having a huge impact on the audience, really moving them. He would visualize what he saw, felt, heard, smelled, and thought as he was at his best. He would tune into how energized and excited he felt and how calm and decisive he acted.

"Before I started doing this different type of preparation," Ian says, "I would often find myself, prior to getting up on stage, feeling the pressure affecting my body and my thoughts. I would feel agitated and be thinking about the worst-case scenario. I would focus on potential problems or how I might offend people with my remarks. Or how they might not get it. Slam poetry is a different form of art. It can seem weird to people. Especially for people who come to watch from my church who are pretty straitlaced or who come from my business." (Ian is a very successful entrepreneur, having started Northern Lights Direct, a leading maker of television commercials that use direct response technology, with offices in Chicago and Toronto.)

"This approach helps me turn anxiety into empowerment. I picture myself being successful at past events and it reminds me that I have done this before. *I can do this again.* I realize I don't need to be panic stricken by the show. . . . After ninety seconds or so, I feel more confident and I am ready to go."

In essence, Ian is flooding his brain (and his body) with chemicals; as Cuddy's research at Harvard found, he is increasing his level of testosterone and decreasing his level of cortisol. He is tamping down the fear response in his amygdala in order to put himself in the best position possible to take the risk necessary to manage pressure and deliver his best performance. Ian used this preparation, as documented in the

award-winning documentary by Kim Saltarski, *IF: The Poet*, to win the national championship by 0.3 of a point, the smallest difference in the history of the competition. He is now off to Paris for the world championship. Again, small tweak, big difference.

Using Visualization to Turn On Your Brain

Self-confident individuals frequently visualize positive images of themselves; they tend to "see" themselves as successful in a wide variety of activities. This is, in effect, what Ian was doing: a form of mental rehearsal or visualization that included power poses. Athletes, clinical and medical practitioners, salespeople, astronauts, students, and entrepreneurs have all used visualization to prepare for a specific task, whether kicking a field goal or handling an emergency situation. There are countless explanations as to why visualization and mental imagery enhance performance. One is that they allow the individual to create a mental model of perfect performance that shows what ideal execution looks like. The individual can then use this *covert model* to guide performance. Another is that visualization reduces performance anxiety, allowing the individual to successfully deal with unexpected or troublesome situations.

Maybe the most important explanation comes from some new research in neuroscience that found that when humans mentally rehearse a physical action they execute the same neural operations that are used during the actual performance. In other words, the *same neural pathways* are recruited and the same neurochemicals are secreted when we visualize doing something as when we engage in the actual activity. In one fascinating study, two groups worked with a finger muscle exercise for one month. One group actually did the finger strengthening exercises while the other group merely visualized doing the same exercise. At the end of the study, the group who had actually engaged in the exercise increased muscle function by 30 percent while the other group, who had only visualized doing the activity, increased their muscle strength by 22 percent. What this study points to is a way to access a phenomenon called the *winner effect* without stepping onto the field or into the meeting room.

The Winner Effect

Studies have shown that when we experience a victory or what we *perceive* to be a victory, no matter how small or how "virtual" (as in visualization), the probability that we will win our next contest goes up significantly.

When animals or humans win or perceive that they have won a competition of any sort, they experience an increase in testosterone. Again, testosterone helps us under pressure as it increases our motivation and our tolerance for risk-taking behavior—all critical to making us *feel more confident*. And that feeling of confidence contributes to our ability to win the next match or fight or competition. This phenomenon was first identified in animals.

In one study, researchers had two mice fight. One mouse was drugged so that he was a less aggressive opponent. Not surprisingly, the drug-free mouse won. Then the researchers had the winning mouse fight another mouse that was its equal in physical size. And the probability that the same mouse would win again increased. Even when they put the winning mouse up against a bigger, more aggressive mouse, the probability of the first mouse winning rose significantly. This winning effect has been found in several species—including humans.

A study by John Coates and his colleague Lionel Page used a very similar protocol to test professional tennis players. Drawing on a database of 623,000 professional tennis matches, the researchers identified matches where the opponents were very close in ATP rankings—only one seed apart at the time of the match. They next identified a subset of matches that went to a tie break in the first set. In other words, the players had been evenly matched over the course of the year, based on the ranking criteria, and they were playing evenly in the match itself, based on the tie break at the end of the first set. Focusing only on these matches out of this very large database, the researchers found that players who won the first-set tie-breaker had a much greater *probability of winning the match*. The player who won the first set and had an increase in testosterone went on to win the match 60 *percent of the time*.

Testosterone has another important effect: It increases levels of

dopamine, the feel-good chemical in the brain that mediates the reward network. Pay raises, compliments, sex, experiencing any kind of success—all result in increased levels of dopamine in the brain.

But it is our perception of success that has the biggest hit on this part of our brain. When dopamine levels are high, they engage our frontal cortex, where are our "executive function" exists. The frontal cortex is where our most important cognitive processes take place, including problem solving, planning, task flexibility, and working memory. Working memory is where we hold chunks of information that allow us to think on our feet and be flexible in solving a problem in the moment. When dopamine increases, we increase the number of chunks of information we can hold (up to five or six chunks). We are able to see more options in front of us and think more quickly and decisively in a pressure situation. Each time we experience a win, our brains are flooded with dopamine, allowing us to think and react more quickly.

The Neuroplasticity of Winning

The winner effect also has a longer-term impact on the brain, due to a phenomenon called *neuroplasticity*. Neuroplasticity is the process by which the brain rearranges itself based on what it experiences. The brain, we've discovered, has the capacity to rewire itself, to create new neural patterns. A central part of this change occurs in the communication between nerve cells, where an increase or decrease in the number of receptor cells in the brain occurs in response to brain activity generated by new and repeated experiences.

New research has conclusively shown that our brains change well beyond early childhood and puberty. One of the most powerful times that the brain is molded, according to cognitive neuroscientist Ian Robertson, an international expert on neuropsychology, is when we win.

In a series of studies he conducted, he found that winning not only increases testosterone and dopamine levels in the brain in the short term, but over the long term it *increases the number of receptors* for testosterone in the brain. These extra "receiving stations" for testosterone

mean that when you are in future tennis matches, for example, you can use the testosterone that is present in your brain more effectively and experience more of testosterone's effects. All of this becomes a "virtuous cycle," enhancing the winner effect. This, in part, is why the mice and the tennis players went on to win subsequent competitions.

The important takeaway is to know that you don't have to wait until you win something to access the winner effect: You can do it in any moment by engaging and getting proficient at mental rehearsal or visualization.

Try using visualization as a tool to improve your performance in a specific task. You can do what poet Ian French did and engage in a power pose while you visualize yourself *being at your best*. You can also do a powerful procedure we call "split visualization":

1. Stand in a comfortable position, legs body-width apart. Put your body in an *open* and *expansive* stance or posture. You can do this by putting your arms up and out as if you have just won a sporting contest or a victory of some sort. Chin up. Find a position that makes you feel strong and powerful. If you do not feel like using the power pose, you can also sit in a comfortable chair.

2. Relax yourself by breathing deeply (eventually you will be able to practice this exercise on the move).

3. Visualize a high-pressure moment. Detail is essential—color, sound, location—the kinds of details a top film director would look for.

4. Visualize yourself performing to your capability. See yourself "on your game"—connecting, sharp, anticipating what you need to do and executing it. All is going well.

5. Interrupt your successful image with a negative one. See yourself losing control, crumbling in front of others. Think about how your body feels. Imagine your anxiety and fear. See yourself fumbling the ball, the crowd dismayed at your failure.

6. Just when all is lost, visualize yourself making a spectacular recovery, regaining your composure. Take control, and finish with a bang.

Hear the applause, imagine the smiles of the crowd, imagine what that *feels* like.

The more visual and auditory detail you include, the better. You might find that the exercise takes a long time at first. But eventually, you'll be able to do it in only a minute or two.

Split visualization like this gives you practice in overcoming your concerns about the issues and problems you may have to confront. Confident individuals think about the negatives in order to *problem solve*. With athletes, we call it a refocus plan. They mentally rehearse solutions to their concerns. As a result, their worries diminish or disappear, and their confidence increases. Split visualization helps to do this by *limiting our time spent on the negatives*, while giving us ways to overcome them. You can also choose to do what Ian did at the slam poetry competition and visualize a time when you were *at your best*—going back in time and seeing yourself in an actual pressure situation where you delivered successfully. Again, bring as much color as you can into your mind. Really see yourself succeeding and tune into all of your senses: how you feel, what you see, hear, smell, and think.

Beyond changing your posture and using visualization, the final way to get your brain involved and increase testosterone and decrease cortisol is by using micro-successes.

Create Micro-Successes

Most people view success in the context of big events—a job promotion, winning a key account, acing a midterm or final, putting out a fire in Maysville, Kentucky. Sure, achieving these sorts of milestones or wins certainly helps our future performance. But we now know that even small victories, or *micro-successes*—a productive conversation with your boss, or a positive phone call with a client, a compliment from a colleague or friend—can have the same impact. They stimulate the winner effect, causing the release of testosterone and dopamine, which in turn build confidence. And because micro-successes happen in our lives far more frequently than the big victories, they may be even more

important. Acknowledge these micro-successes. Celebrate them. They will start to create positive feelings within you to fuel self-confidence.

Micro-successes begin with goal setting. For example, instead of saying you are going to lose thirty pounds, decide to lose just five pounds over, say, the next month. Set a goal to have a healthy snack at your desk every day or to walk five minutes a day. Or if you are thinking of changing careers, make your first goal to interview one person who is currently in that profession. By achieving these small goals you can use the winner effect to gain momentum on achieving bigger goals. Essentially you feel more confident.

Micro-successes are not, however, limited to goal setting. We achieve smaller victories every day, which we tend to overlook. A small victory can involve making some progress, however small, on a large project you are working on. A short, productive conversation with your boss or a positive phone call with a client would count, as would receiving a compliment from your partner or a friend. Tuning into these moments of success will start creating positive feelings within you. Micro-successes can also be *created* by redefining success in terms of how you perform, rather than the outcome you achieve. A great interview or a presentation *is* the success—not getting the job does not negate your successful performance. According to Teresa Amabile at Harvard Business School, these micro-successes or small wins matter far more than people think. In the same study in which Teresa found that pressure leads to less creativity rather than more, she analyzed more than twelve thousand diary entries of primarily white-collar knowledge workers (15 percent were blue collar) to try to establish the most important driver of an employee's emotions, perceptions, and motivation at work. She found somewhat surprisingly that it was *not* recognition, incentives, or interpersonal support that mattered most. It was seemingly minor steps forward, or "small wins." Simply *making progress had the most prominent positive effect on employees' emotions, perceptions, and motivation.* As Professor Amabile said: "Some of the progress that people made seemed almost trivial to us on the outside, really incremental, even mundane, but it ended up having a big impact on pride, confidence, emotions, and intrinsic motivation."

Professor Amabile went on: "These small wins matter more because they are *so much more likely* to occur compared to the big breakthroughs in the world. If we only waited for the big wins, we would be waiting a long time. And we would probably quit long before we saw anything tangible come to fruition. What you need instead of big wins is simply the forward momentum that small wins bring."

Comedian Jerry Seinfeld lives by this process. Each January, on a prominent wall in his apartment he pins up a calendar that has the entire year on one page. On days when he writes new material, no matter how little, he will draw a big red "X" over that day. Over time a chain develops of crossed-off days. His goal is *not* to write brilliant comedy; his goal is to *not break the chain*. He says, "Just keep at it and the chain will grow longer every day. You'll like seeing that chain, especially when you get a few weeks under your belt. Your only job next is to not break the chain."

This is the idea behind micro-successes. We need to mark the small wins, no matter how insignificant they might seem. For a team doing technical work in pharmaceutical trials, a small win can be sitting down at the end of the week to discuss the smaller and perhaps less significant progress members are making toward the bigger goal of bringing useful new drugs to the market. For a client services team, it can mean getting through the week without any major hiccups. For a human resources team, it can mean getting a couple of key managers on board for a training initiative. These micro-successes are at the heart of building confidence. According to Amabile, "The more frequently people experience that sense of progress, the more likely they are to be creatively productive in the long run. Whether they are trying to solve a major scientific mystery or simply produce a high-quality product or service, everyday progress—even a small win—can make all the difference in how they feel and perform."

If you are a manager, a parent, a spouse, or a friend, using micro-successes and small wins is a very effective way to build confidence in others. When you encourage and point out micro-successes, no matter how small, you improve others' performance and motivation, build confidence, and increase the likelihood of their achieving more success.

Celebrating such micro-successes is even more important for parents eager to help their children. In today's fast-paced world, we sometimes risk overlooking our children's smaller wins.

Whether you praise a child for a true win or you mark a micro-success he or she has achieved, you leverage the *winner effect* and change your child's neurochemistry .

The final way to instill yourself with confidence is to habituate confidence habits.

Engage in Confidence Habits

There are a number of proven smaller strategies you can use. High performers use these strategies as habits—engaging in them every day as a way to be more in control and feel a little more confident.

Be at Your Physical Best

Silverback gorillas spend hours polishing their coats to luster. They are attuned to the fact that the better their coat looks, the more they attract others. This seems to make them feel more confident, at least according to naturalist Dian Fossey, who observed many of them over the decades. "You could tell the confident ones," Fossey said. "They move freely, keep their heads up and seem to stand taller than the others. Their coats are the shiniest and they project pride."

Looking your physical best is a way of taking action and makes you feel better about yourself. Countless clothing retailers, hairdressers, cosmetologists, and psychologists will vouch that their clients feel better about themselves when they like how they look.

Take Responsibility for Your Actions

Positive psychology pioneers Martin Seligman and C. R. Snyder have spent much of their careers demonstrating that when you believe you are responsible for your actions, you can influence, change, and *improve* your behavior, and become more self-confident.

Those who do not take responsibility for their actions put themselves at a disadvantage. They blind themselves to their own role in shaping the behaviors they are perpetuating.

If you decided you were responsible for your happiness, your financial security, your safety, and your physical health, what would be different? What benefits do you get by not taking responsibility for these things? We tend to feel better about ourselves in areas where we have more control. A student who blames her test grade on the teacher's "unfair grading" or a lecture she missed isn't acknowledging her lack of preparation. On the other hand, the student who sees the connection between her preparation and her test score has the ability to improve.

The most successful athletes are those who, after a disappointing game or a team slump, look to their *own behavior* for the solution. When the New York Knicks were in the midst of a losing streak and were subjected to harsh criticism, star Carmelo Anthony stepped forward in MSG's postgame interview show to take the heat: "We know that the problem is the way we are playing. We, I, have to play better if we are going to win. Nobody's making us play bad, we're doing it ourselves. Poor passing, not getting second shots, not enough rebounds, it's all us and if we are going to win, we need to play better starting now. There's nothing else to say. It's on our shoulders; but that's what we want."

Find Unorthodox Ways to Practice

Here is how a spelling bee champion describes how he prepared for spelling tournaments:

> I was eight when I had my first spelling success. I came in third place at my school spelling bee. I had beaten almost all of the big kids. I missed I-R-R-A-D-I-A-T-E, but I went home and made a decision. I wanted to win. As a sixth grader, I placed 9th at the state bee, coming in ahead of more than 200 other kids only to lose on A-V-U-N-C-U-L-A-R. That's when the practicing really began. I mean hard-core. The word lists in the booklet published by Scripps each year were not enough. My mother was my coach, and as a school teacher, she knew how to help me learn the words. She began

collecting the word lists from previous years, and buying dictionar-
ies of odd words. We'd practice all waking hours. I'd be in the bath-
tub and my mother would be in the hall asking me words. We'd go
to the market and up and down the aisles she's quizzing me. We'd
go to the beach and jumping waves, I'd be spelling. We had boxes
and boxes of notecards and posted them all over the house. We
studied in the car in the morning on the way to school and in the
car on the way home from school. My friends cheerfully showed up
to make flashcards, look up obscure meanings to see if they could
stump me. Before dinner, during dinner and after dinner spelling
words were a constant. Before bed too, and in the morning my
alarm clock was: "How do you spell . . ." No matter where we went,
no matter what the hour, we were practicing. It paid off when I won
the Alaska State Spelling Bee as a seventh grader with I-N-F-R-A-
N-G-I-B-L-E, which means incapable of being broken.

Our point is not that this person won—he lost in his next contest. Rather, it is the unorthodox preparation he went through—spelling everywhere, every day, a sharp contrast to those who prepare by studying in their room or library for a set number of hours a day. In effect, this person was developing what psychologists call his *fluid intelligence*—the ability to solve new problems independent of the knowledge or experience we have. It is the ability to reason quickly to solve unexpected problems. Self-confident individuals tend to rate high on fluid intelligence. And because they believe in accountability, they spend a lot of time practicing the tasks they have to perform. They may mentally rehearse their presentation while waiting in line for a movie, or when they're cooking dinner. Show us a kid who can play his violin unashamedly on a crowded subway and we will show you a musician who will perform closer to his best in his audition.

Seek Criticism

Mel, a freelance writer, told us, "I spend a lot of time on my work so when I finally turn something in, I am in a state of high anxiety until I hear from my editor. Her feedback will decide how I spend the next few

months of my life, even if I don't agree with it. If the criticism is really bad, the project can even be canceled. Then what would I do? It's not easy to sell something. The process is nerve-wracking to me. Minutes before I hear her reaction, I'm drenched, incredibly nervous. And I get defensive as soon as she opens her mouth."

The ability to accept criticism is crucial to building confidence. Why? Criticism provides you with information that can help you improve in your next effort. Confident individuals tend to respond to criticism productively.

Why do so many of us respond defensively to criticism? For most of us, criticism gets exaggerated in our own minds, causing us to think, *I'm terrible, I'm in trouble, my career is over, they don't like me.* These exaggerated statements promote defensive behavior. And they are typical of the way couples who visit the Love Lab, which we introduced in Chapter 1, process each other's criticism—negatively.

A better way to think of criticism is as it was originally conceived by Aristotle: an evaluation whose intent is to improve. Using this mind frame will better enable you to accept and benefit from the feedback of others. It will lead you to a more accurate assessment of yourself, and provide steps for improvement.

It's not easy to adapt this view of criticism. Most of us have been responding defensively to criticism for years. It is even trickier when you add the fact that most people give criticism ineptly. To start, take a few minutes to repeat the mantra "Criticism is information that can help me grow."

Practice accepting criticism by proactively reaching out to others and asking them to tell you how you can perform better or more effectively (not what you are doing wrong). This will help you get used to hearing comments in a useful manner.

Challenge the Accuracy of Your Thoughts

While we suggest that you accept criticism from others in a way that can help you get better, we want you to be wary of your internal critic. Most people with low self-esteem and lack of self-confidence (and those who experience clinical depression) use language loaded with

self-blame. They tend to exaggerate their flaws and voice a great deal of self-doubt. Those with positive self-esteem compliment themselves appropriately, have more realistic expectations, and accurately appraise their capabilities.

Think about how you speak to yourself. Are your thoughts helpful or debilitating? Here is a simple, empirically grounded method cognitive therapists use to help their patients develop the habit of asking the question "Are my thoughts helping me or hurting me?"

1. Spend a few minutes a day paying attention to your internal dialogue. Note how you speak to yourself: Are you supportive or critical, realistic or exaggerated in your perception? Do you talk to yourself in a helpful or hurtful manner?

2. Ask yourself: "Are my thoughts helping me or hurting me?" Doing so will help you identify and discard sabotaging thoughts.

3. Use distressful feelings as a cue. If you discover that you are condemning yourself, tell yourself, "STOP!" and speak to yourself in a helpful manner. On an index card write down some generic statements that will be helpful to you in difficult times. Keep it nearby, on your desk or night table.

Putting It All Together

Over the years, we have worked with many elite performers—Navy SEALs, Olympic and professional athletes, entertainers, and successful executives—all bursting with self-confidence. We've asked these individuals how they maintain their sense of self-confidence in the face of setbacks. One secret we discovered: They are all methodical in their preparation. Here, for example, is how they would prepare for a presentation before an audience:

1. *Practice the basics.* Run through your presentation again and again. Make sure you know it cold, so you can perform it on autopilot; that way you can turn some of your focus to reading the room instead of having to think about every word you are saying.

Next, think about likely questions or interruptions, and rehearse your responses. Then think of additional questions or interruptions, and how you would handle them.

2. *Rework the basics.* Your initial presentation will result in a sequence or series of steps: To really know your stuff, change the order. Start with step 5 and work backward. Skip a couple of steps.

Rehearsing the material in a different order helps to reinforce your knowledge of the material. It also prepares you for those inevitable moments when the client says, "That sounds good so far . . . but what I really want to know is this." When that happens you won't need to say, "We'll get to that later," and frustrate your client. You'll be fully prepared to get to it now.

3. *Practice pressure solution #5, "Anticipate, Anticipate, Anticipate."* Once your presentation is in good shape, prepare for things that could cause you to choke. What if your software locks up? What if your client is delayed and you get only ten minutes to present instead of thirty? Decide in advance how to shorten your presentation so you still hit key points. What will you do if you get questions you aren't able to answer? Think of outlandish scenarios, and decide how you'll handle them.

Do this while engaging in a power pose—open and expansive—as a way to get your brain involved. You can apply this approach to almost any situation, from business to career to personal: giving an employee evaluation, pitching investors, handling a confrontation, winning over a potential client, playing a sport, dating.

When musician Simon Tedeschi walks onto a stage around the world or Jim Prokopanko faces a situation like the fire in the fertilizer plant in Kentucky, they are looking for something to help them handle the acute pressure they face when it is time to perform. Like a beta-blocker, confidence acts as a neurochemical antidote that allows them—allows each of us—to move forward even when we are feeling the physical and psychological manifestations of pressure. It is a feeling, a knowing, that we can do what we need to do to take the necessary risks to be successful. When we are clear about where we stand (accurate self-assessment), when we take charge of our neurochemistry

by using power poses or visualization or micro-successes, and when we practice the habits of confidence, we put ourselves in the best position possible to think, act, and perform closer to our best.

We will still feel pressure—and the doubt and anxiety that accompany it—but confidence acts as an antidote to immunize us against its sabotaging effects, and we have a better chance to effectively perform. It is not surprising that confident individuals are also found to be optimistic, the next fabric to weave into your COTE of Armor.

If you ask pessimists what they have to look forward to as they get older, they will likely not respond with a comment that will bring a smile to your face. Their answer, spoken with earnestness, will likely be the three constants of the human condition: disease, old age, and death. With this in mind, it is not surprising that so many pessimists have the attitude professionally and personally of "What's the point of trying?"

Elie Mechnikov recognized the three "evils" of disease, old age, and death, too, but through a very different lens. Born in the village of Ivanovka near Ukraine, he was the youngest son of Ilya and Emilia Mechnikov. His father was a guard officer and his maternal grandfather, Lev Nevakhovick, was the first Russo-Jewish writer and founder of the Haskala movement in Russia. His parents were devoted to each other and are said to have provided a warm home. Family dinners were the norm and the house was often visited by friends.

Elie spent much of his youth playing in the woods, intrigued by the wonders of his surroundings. He developed a penchant for examining the bark of trees.

His brother Lev became a prominent geographer and sociologist, and doubtless influenced Elie's passion for natural history. When Charles Darwin's *The Origin of Species* was published in 1859, Elie fervidly undertook testing and teaching its principles.

A good student, he was told by his mother that he was free to make his way in the world by using his brains and following his interests. He did both. He attended Kharkiv University, where he studied natural sciences, completing his four-year degree in two years. Upon his

graduation, he studied marine fauna on the small North Sea island of Helgoland in Germany, and then at the University of Giessen, the University of Göttingen, and the Munich Academy. In 1867 he returned to Russia as a docent at the newly established Imperial Novorossiya University (now Odessa I. I. Mechnikov National University, named for him), eventually taking the appointment of titular professor of Zoology and Comparative Anatomy.

Mechnikov agreed with pessimists that the three constants of disease, old age, and death hang darkly over our heads, but it did not occur to him to passively await the inevitable. Instead, he thought about how to defeat these evils.

He proposed the establishment of a new scientific discipline called *gerontology* and suggested that science should be encouraged and helped in every possible way in its task of removing the diseases and habits that prevent human life from running its normal course. In his classic text, appropriately titled *Prolongation of Life: Optimistic Studies*, he proclaimed himself an *optimist* and found in biological science a hope toward which to work, to possibly achieve that goal. In 1908, for his efforts, Elie Mechnikov was awarded the Nobel Prize.

We won't leap ahead to the conclusion "Be an optimist and you will win a Nobel Prize." But we do claim that having an *optimistic thinking style* makes it *easier* to win one. It's easy to see why optimism is part of our natural COTE of Armor.

"Optimism" is a word that is both overused and misunderstood in popular culture. People talk about optimism and pessimism as if they were characteristics that quickly can be put on or shed, like a winter sweater. "I'm just an eternal optimist," people say, when they are trying to put a positive spin on something, or "I'm not optimistic that it will work," meaning that their relationship to a future event is pessimistic. While these statements simplify the concept, the truth is that you'd be wise to develop your optimism.

The Optimist Advantage

Bill and Melinda Gates, speaking to the 2014 graduating class at Stanford, made it very clear that it was optimism, above all else, that

propelled them forward. "There are many remarkable things going on here at this campus," Bill said. "But if Melinda and I had to put into one word what we love most about Stanford, it's optimism." They went on to describe how optimism was behind the important work of their foundation and the new graduates' chance for success: "Even in the most dire situations where our foundation works, optimism can fuel innovation and lead to new tools to eliminate suffering." The Gates' observation of what it takes to build a great company like Microsoft or their foundation or a successful life fits with what fifty years of rigorous research has found: Optimism helps you advance your life. Better physical and mental health; a better marriage; better high school, college, and graduate school grades; and greater resiliency sum up some of the benefits of being an optimist.

The same is true for work, especially under pressure. Our research at the Institute for Health and Human Potential found that those individuals who were in the top 10 percent—the high-performing twelve hundred out of a sample twelve thousand people in high-pressure environments we have studied over the past ten years—scored higher on our scale for optimism in our multi-rater assessment (meaning their manager and seven to fifteen other people assessed them). They were more *positive about the future* and were able to *handle setbacks more effectively* than the rest of the sample of twelve thousand people we studied. Here is what raters said about some of the individuals in the top 10 percent:

> *Westley always believes it will work out. We have been part of a team for over ten years and he has this incredible ability to let go of a setback, even difficult ones—it's as if it never happened—and just go forward. He just works and works until he does succeed. He is incredible. I find being around him helps me let go and join him in pressing forward.*

> *Brigitte, though you would never know it by how quiet and unassuming she is, has this incredible power. We had this very difficult client project we were working on. We were late and not going to make a couple of key timelines but she just willed it to happen—expected it would work out—and it did. She outworked everyone.*

Similarly, Duke economists Manju Puri and David Robinson consistently found that optimists earn greater pay and work harder and longer than pessimists. It makes sense: Optimists are more deeply engaged in their work because they have positive expectations about the future, and they work hard to make that success happen.

The optimism advantage extends to high-pressure situations outside of work as well. Optimistic children perform better in school and engage in more social activities and team sports than their pessimistic cohorts. Optimistic swimmers bounce back quicker from losing efforts than pessimistic swimmers, and optimistic pitchers and hitters do better in pressure moments than pessimistic players who frequently choke. And you can be sure that Las Vegas bookies know that optimistic NBA teams are more likely to cover the "point spread" than pessimistic NBA teams.

Interestingly, there is one profession where optimism *does not* predict overall performance under pressure: the practice and study of law. Pessimistic law students, on average, fare *better* than their optimistic peers. They outperform more optimistic students on the traditional measures of achievement, such as grade point average and law journal success. There is a reason: Pessimism is seen as desirable in law. The capacity to look for and pick up on the potential range of complications and problems that most people do not see is a highly valued part of being a practicing lawyer. In law, it's called prudence. Whether pessimistic individuals are attracted to the profession of law or they develop more pessimism while practicing it, what we know is that they tend to become more attuned to how things can turn negative for themselves both at work and in their personal lives. For instance, lawyers are less likely than others to believe they will make partner or that their occupation is even legitimate, and they're more likely to believe that their spouse is unfaithful and that the economy is headed for disaster.

The Nature of Optimism

Optimism's relationship to time is dynamic and constantly shifting. Whereas confidence shows up in the *moment*—providing a foundation of belief or knowledge that we can execute the behavior or task that is

required of us—optimism is more about what happens *on either side of the moment: in the future* and *in the past.* You can think of optimism as made up of two parts: *expectations* and *explanations.* Our *expectations* refer to how we think the future will go; our *explanations* refer to how we think (and how we explain the way) a past event went.

If we *expect* good things will happen to us in the future, we are considered optimistic (if we expect bad things will happen to us, we are considered pessimistic). This difference in expectations has a significant consequence for how we will handle the pressure we are facing in the moment. If we are more optimistic, we feel less anxiety and dread, and more excitement. We are willing to take more risks and work harder. This all acts to help us perform closer to our capability in a pressure moment.

The second part of optimism occurs after an event has taken place. To make sense of the setbacks and successes we experience, we attempt to understand them by creating an *explanation* of them. If we come up with a more optimistic explanation of a success or failure, we tend to remain persistent and not give up as we face pressure in the future—and thus we are more successful. If we fall back on a more pessimistic explanation, we tend to become more discouraged and give up much sooner.

Expectations

Having positive expectations or predictions of the future helps us because it encourages us to go where the future is uncertain, where we are uncomfortable, where there is pressure, whether it be during the upheaval of a change at work or in the midst of challenges we face at home.

In order to help us take risks and work hard, we evolved a frontal lobe and specifically the prefrontal cortex (found above the eyes and behind the forehead), or PFC. It is the prefrontal cortex that allows us to *predict and plan for the future.*

In effect, the PFC acts as a *prediction or planning center* where our expectations exist. It allows us to see *beyond* the immediate barrier, challenge, or difficulty that we face and predict whether or not we should take the risk in order to move our life forward.

How Positive Expectations Help Us

Expectations about the future affect us in two ways: They change how we *feel* about a situation (our subjective feelings), and they affect *how we act in the moment*. Both of these are critical to performing under pressure.

When we face a high-pressure situation, we will feel a mixture of excitement, eagerness, anxiety, and dread. What we experience in such moments is directly influenced by our level of optimism or pessimism. If we are more optimistic and hold a positive expectation of the future, then we will feel more excitement and enthusiasm, while a pessimist will feel more dread and anxiety when facing the same challenging situation.

Optimism helps manage this dread and anxiety, which enables us to perform closer to our capability in a pressure moment. Anything that diminishes this pessimistic physical and emotional response, as optimism does, helps us.

An interesting study using individuals who were extremely allergic to poison ivy offers an important insight. In the study, thirteen people were rubbed on the arm with a harmless leaf while being told it was poison ivy; at the same time, they were touched on *their other arm* with real poison ivy but were told it was harmless. On the arm contacted by the harmless leaf (which they were told was poison ivy), *all thirteen* broke out in a rash. On the side contacted with the *real poison ivy* (which they were told was harmless), *only two* broke out in a rash. How is that possible?

According to Dr. Marcel Kinsbourne, a neuroscientist at the New School for Social Research in New York, the answer lies in the fact that the brain generates two kinds of activation patterns (networks of neurons firing together) when an event takes place. One type is termed *outside-in*, which is set in motion by information flowing *into* the brain from the outside world—smells, tastes, visual images, sounds. At the same time, another pattern of activation occurs, *inside-out*, which is initiated in our prediction center in the frontal cortex and draws on memories and feelings about what is *expected to happen*.

These two patterns intersect to inform an individual about what is

occurring in his or her environment. One of the fascinating aspects of new neuroimaging studies is the revelation that in most situations, activation of cells derived from our expectation about a situation, which is *internally generated*, fires *before* we receive the outside data.

These very fast, internally generated brain states are every bit as real, neurologically and neurochemically speaking, as anything resulting from the outside world, and they can significantly drive how our bodies and minds react to an external event. In a very real way, they change the internal chemistry of our brain and body. Dozens of new studies have found that a placebo effect occurs because of this way our expectations affect our internal chemistry. Hence the absence of any rash occurring on the arm contacted by real poison ivy, even in people who were *highly allergic* to poison ivy.

Another study, by Francis Brennan and Carl Charnetski, focused on immunoglobulin A and colds and found a similar phenomenon. Immunoglobulin A (IgA) is one of the strongest antibodies in our bodies. The more IgA you have in your system in cold season, the fewer colds you will get. In a study of 112 undergraduates from Northeastern Pennsylvania University, samples to measure IgA were collected from each student. The participants also completed an optimism measurement. The results of the study found that pessimistic thinking impaired immune system functioning. Like the poison ivy study, the research found that what goes on in our minds—in this case pessimistic thinking—directly affects the body's internal chemistry.

Importantly, optimistic thoughts go beyond our chemistry; they motivate behavior that helps fulfill our positive expectations. People who have a more positive belief about the future *exert more continuing effort* as they face a pressure situation. People who have a negative belief about the future do the opposite: engage in distraction, avoidance, or wishful thinking. Glen Nelson, a professional writer, told us a personal story that reinforces the idea that optimism goes beyond thinking to become an important driver of behavior. His daughter, Kate, at the age of four developed what every parent might fear the most: a large-sized brain tumor.

Over a period of time, Kate exhibited symptoms that worried her parents. Her balance was often unpredictable, and she sometimes

tipped over while standing still. She experienced headaches as well; then after vomiting, she felt completely fine. Her parents took her repeatedly to their pediatrician, who discounted the symptoms and said the family was making much ado about nothing. But as the severity and frequency of the symptoms increased, the parents insisted on a referral to see a neurologist.

"Within minutes, the neurologist diagnosed a massive brain tumor, and after seeing an MRI scan, an emergency marathon surgery was performed a few hours later. It was the scariest day of my life," Glen said. Afterward, the surgeons told the terrified parents that their daughter would have survived only another day or two without the surgery.

Regarding the ordeal, Glen talked about optimism and its power. "We felt both helpless and optimistic," he explained. "It was horrible pressure, a true do-or-die moment. But the thing about facing potential tragedy is that you realize that pressure at such an intensity is unsustainable. It will be resolved, one way or another, and soon. We became confident that whatever happened next, we would be able to face it as a family. That tiny ray of hope relieved the burden of pressure."

Their daughter bounced back with extraordinary speed. She was released from the hospital a few days later. Three years later, she had follow-up surgery to remove additional tumor material, and she has now been cancer-free for ten years. Glen and his wife maintained their sense of positivity throughout. "It was our family's defining moment," Glen says, "and it left scars in every way, on all of us. It weakened us in the sense that we realized how vulnerable each of us is to tragedy, and it strengthened us because we are so much more attuned to the needs of others now. It's like receiving superpowers of empathy. For us, keeping positive was a decision of empowerment. But there was nothing passive about it. We didn't just sit there and think positive thoughts. We worked extraordinarily hard to learn everything we could about her ailment and did everything in our power to help, including getting that all-important neurologist referral. It meant that we acknowledged an unknown future and accepted a responsibility to shape it and deal with whatever comes. We have—knock wood—been very, very blessed since then."

Glen and his family's story highlights that optimism is not a Polly-annaish "be positive and everything will work out" mind-set—it helps us mainly because it spurs action. We don't engage in wishful thinking; we engage in hard work to find a resolution to the situation. When you consider the number of setbacks we face over the course of a day or week, especially in pressure situations, it's easy to see that the ability to stay positive and move forward makes a big difference.

Expectations and Others

Where do our expectations come from? One of the sources of the expectations individuals hold and the resulting behavior is not surprisingly expectations that *others* have for them. A growing literature is finding that in several different environments—workplaces, courtrooms, doctors' offices, military bases, family homes, locker rooms, and psychotherapists' offices, to name a few—the expectations *others* have is one of the most important influences of an individual's own expectations and behavior.

The first study that observed and documented the role of others' expectations in influencing the attitudes and behavior of individuals was one examining the relationships between teachers and student achievement. It was conducted by Robert Rosenthal of Harvard and Lenore Jacobson, a school principal in an elementary school in the South San Francisco Unified School District. Rosenthal and Jacobson ran the study at Oak School, a somewhat run-down institution at the time, in Thousand Oaks, California. To start, they gave a group of children an IQ test at the beginning of the school year. The teachers were informed that the test was not an IQ test but something called "the Harvard Test of Inflected Acquisition," a made-up name. The teachers were led to believe that the test would measure academic "blooming," but it did not. There was no test for blooming; nor were there any predictions that the test could or would make. The IQ test was used instead as a benchmark for the students' progress over the year.

Rosenthal and Jacobson informed eighteen teachers at the school that some of the students in their classes had scored in the top 20 percent of this "blooming test." The teachers were told that these

high-potential students, as measured by their test scores, were entering a year of high achievement. What the teachers did not know was that this was all part of the experimental setup: Students were put on these lists *randomly*, not based on any qualities that predicted who would bloom and who would not. There was no difference between the students on the lists and the students not on the lists. At the end of the school year, all the students were tested again for IQ. What did the researchers find?

There was a marked difference in IQ test score gains. Students who had been put on the lists as "ready to bloom" improved *more than those who had not* been labeled in this way. Rosenthal and Jacobson's study demonstrated the power of expectations and self-fulfilling prophecy. Teachers treated these students differently, and these students, in turn, behaved differently—they performed according to the expectations their teachers had for them. They worked harder and achieved more than the students who were *not* randomly put on the lists.

Remember, these students were never told that any lists existed or whether they were placed on one list or the other. Rosenthal subsequently found in later studies that when teachers or managers or parents have higher expectations, they provide students or direct reports or children with more critical feedback and more difficult material because they believe they can handle it. They also give them more opportunities to "show their stuff," for example, by waiting longer for an answer before moving on to the next student. Teachers create a warmer, more supportive, and more encouraging interpersonal environment for the special students *than for the students on the "other" list.*

The point is that the expectations a student—or anyone—holds and their behavior are not created independently. They are influenced by the expectations that the people around them have and by the social environment they are in.

Think about this for yourself. We would suggest you look clear-eyed at your work environment and, especially, at your relationship with your boss (because of the outsized influence of the person in that position), and ask yourself if this environment is setting you up to be successful or not. Do you feel that your manager (or your spouse or

partner, for that matter) has a positive expectation for you to excel? Is this an environment that is conducive to you being your best?

If you are an influencer of others, are you aware of the expectations you have for the people around you? Ask yourself the question: Are my expectations (of my children or direct reports) helping them flourish and be optimistic or are they acting as a barrier?

To be clear, make sure you see the difference between having healthy high expectations and crossing the line into the unrealistic expectations zone. This can sometimes happen when we have different children who have different strengths yet we hold each of them to the same expectations, even if they are unreachable for one of them. This is not healthy and does not help a young person. A coach JP worked with over three Olympics, Hernan Humana, had a wonderful way of communicating expectations without crossing the line. He would communicate them in a way that made each athlete feel like he was the most important person in the world. Hernan invariably had higher expectations of the athlete than the athlete had of himself, and this would rub off on the athlete. Hernan had the ability to be demanding (and not put up with lame excuses) yet also be caring. You could not help but be infected with his optimism about what was possible after spending time with him. What Hernan never did, however, was set expectations so unrealistic that they simply increased pressure and thus diminished performance.

The second part of optimism has to do with what happens *after* a pressure moment—how you *explain* the events, both good and bad, that happen to you.

Explanatory Style

"It was my first job," says Debra, a twenty-seven-year-old and one of our most memorable workshop participants. "I'd just received my master's degree in emergency medicine. It was an intense experience, a lot of pressure, having to make critical decisions in a second, and I handled it all. It was actually a great experience, and I felt great. I was very excited. All the hard work I had put in allowed me to get a choice job in a large ER, the same hospital that my boyfriend was doing his residency

at. Hard work pays off. There was also the bonus that my parents lived within twenty minutes. The stars seemed to be aligned. My happy future had arrived. *I did it!* Well, you know, what's the expression . . . the best laid plans? Just like that, in the blink of an eye, my life changed.

"When I woke up [from the accident], my parents were at my side. Even through groggy eyes, I could see their grief. My mother's eyes were red and her sobbing made the room noisy. My father was seemingly still except when he readjusted his grip on my mother. I fell asleep for what seemed minutes, but in real time was six hours. With clearer eyes, I saw my folks were still at my side, and I felt more soreness than pain. Flowers, sent by Ted [my boyfriend], were next to my bed. My mom wanted to read the card but I didn't want to hear it. I knew his schedule and immediately thought he was doing his job.

"My thoughts were becoming clearer. I remembered the little sports car coming into sight and feeling an earthquake hit my car. Later in the day, the doctor confronted me with my new reality. I had a lot of broken bones but no nerve damage, and that gave me hope, and that helped me put on a happy face. Rehab flashed through my mind; I was in for a lot of hard work, but hey, I'm a hard worker so not a problem.

"About a month later, I was out of the hospital, back in my old room. I had no pain, and I believed it was only a matter of time before I started to regain some real strength [and was able to walk again]. My parents were wonderful, and Ted came over every day to fill my head with uplifting thoughts; to tell you the truth, I was doing OK. About two weeks after I was home, we got a visit from the insurance company. The man, I remember him, was very nice. He filled me in on the details of how the police explained the accident. He told me what I'd already guessed—it wasn't my fault. . . . [The other driver] was drunk. It was just one of those things—wrong place, wrong time. I was victimized, like millions of others, by alcohol. The driver was only twenty, a sophomore at college home for the holidays. Apparently, he had left a party intoxicated, run a light, and boom! [The insurance agent] told me that my car was a total wreck, as if I cared. Then I heard the tragic news. The young man was killed almost immediately. I cried when I heard that. He was the youngest son of a local family. The police said he wasn't wearing a seat belt. I thought about all the times I had been

preached to by family and teachers to be safe and careful and how my dad also told me to drive safely. I was, and it saved my life. I will always remember what [the agent] said to me when our visit concluded: 'Frankly, Debra, I'm astonished that you are alive.'

"During the next few months, and even now, I think about what he said. I'm lucky to be alive! I remember how early visitors told me how unlucky I was—not true, I retorted. I told them far from being unlucky, I was very lucky! I could have been the one killed; it could have been my parents mourning for the rest of their lives. And while it was true that I was an innocent victim, I knew there were countless other innocents who suffered far worse. I was lucky. . . . I told myself *that I would* still accomplish my professional goals, lead a productive life. I did not want Ted to feel obligated even though he insisted that he loved me. Still, I told him I needed to be on my own for a while and we would see what the future brings. It was an emotional talk, but it was needed and I knew he would be fine.

"As for me, my world got sunnier. I couldn't work on the ER floor, but the hospital created other opportunities for me in administration and outpatient services. I still want to get back to the ER—I will. That was two years ago. Now I'm showing noticeable strength improvements in my lower body. Now I use crutches a few hours a day. . . . I'm grateful for all that I have."

This is more than a "feel good" inspirational story; it is the story of a young woman who has an *optimistic explanatory style.*

Explaining Life

Explanatory style has its roots in the social psychology of *attribution*—the process of inferring the causes of events and behaviors. We do this every day with our own behavior and biases, as well as those of the people around us—usually without any awareness that we are doing it. Interpersonal attribution is an example: When telling a story to your friends or colleagues, you are likely to tell the story in a way that places you in the best possible light.

We tend to attribute things in ways that allow us to use what

happened in the past to make future predictions. If you were robbed in a particular area, you will most likely avoid that area in the future in order to avoid danger. Similarly, if you underperform in a particular sales call, you might avoid similar sales calls in the future to avoid further embarrassment. In short, what we attribute a past success or failure to becomes an important influence on what we feel, what we think, and how we behave in the future.

The way in which we tend to attribute causes to things is called our *explanatory style*. It's the way an individual "explains" setbacks and successes. We form these explanations by the way we perceive, determine the importance of, and explain past life experiences. It was an explanatory style that helped Debra understand and make sense of her setback.

Every day we try to make sense of life by explaining the events to ourselves, whether it be a marital breakup, not getting into the college of our choice, or failing to get the job after an interview. Sales jobs are among the more pressure filled in organizations and provide an example of how explanatory style exerts its influence.

In sales, you have to hit your goals, or "make plan," or you lose some part of your pay. That's pressure. It can be distressing to be turned down over and over and over again. It can be hard getting up on a Monday morning—or any morning—knowing you will face more rejection than success.

One of the most famous studies on optimism and performing under pressure was done at Metropolitan Life. MetLife, based in the United States, is a provider of insurance and other financial services. At its peak, Metropolitan Life was hiring five thousand salespeople a year and training them at a cost of more than $30,000 apiece over two years. Of these salespeople, half quit the first year, and four out of five quit within four years. In light of such high turnover and costs, MetLife wanted to identify a better process to select and train their salespeople.

They recognized that in order to be successful, people in sales needed to be effective at handling frustration, bouncing back from setbacks, finding solutions, and following through. The problem of

finding good salespeople who didn't quit when the going got tough was so significant that the CEO of MetLife got involved in the process. He approached psychologist Martin Seligman and invited him to employ his innovative approach using optimism to select and train the company's salespeople.

To start, Seligman devised a study. All qualified candidates for a position in sales took both the company's regular screening exam and Seligman's attribution style questionnaire (or ASQ), which was designed to measure an individual's explanatory style. The idea was to follow each group and see which test was better at predicting success.

Initially, candidates were hired based on the customary selection criteria. The results of Seligman's test were used strictly for study purposes. However, MetLife experienced a shortage of agents that year and had to hire an additional 129. Unfortunately, there were no additional candidates who passed the MetLife test, so, on Seligman's urging, the company hired candidates who had scored in the top half of the optimism test, the ASQ he had designed, but had failed MetLife's entrance exam.

Over the next two years, Seligman and his team tracked the performance of more than fifteen thousand new MetLife sales representatives. When optimism scores were matched to actual sales records, it turned out that agents who scored in the top half for optimism sold 37 *percent more* insurance over the two years than those in the pessimistic bottom half. Even more interesting, agents who scored in the top 10 percent for optimism *sold 88 percent* more than those ranked in the most pessimistic 10 percent. Optimism was a better predictor for sales success than the MetLife exam scores.

The "secret sauce" that Seligman found to be so important in this success under pressure was made up of two factors of explanatory style: permanence and pervasiveness. To understand what permanence and pervasiveness mean, let's go back to Deb's story and see how her explanatory style helped her deal with her challenging setback. (In the original research, there was a third type of explanatory style identified: personalization—when we blame ourselves for what happened. But as more research accumulated, that proved to be less relevant than permanence and pervasiveness in predicting success, and researchers now doubt its importance.)

Permanence—Always

Most physicians, therapists, and coaches will tell you about the many people they have seen who suffered a life-altering bad break like Debra and respond with depression, anger, and bitterness. They feel that they have been victimized, fueled by their perception that their condition is permanent, that it will never change. It will *always* be this way. If you look at Debra's story, you'll note that she *believed her condition was temporary*, that she would improve to resume a productive life.

Permanence here refers to your perception of the *stability* of an event or condition—how long it will last, how frequently it will occur, whether it is permanent or temporary. When is it in your best interest to think of a condition as permanent, and when is it best to think of it as temporary?

Optimists believe that good times will persist, and that *bad times* are only a *temporary* condition. Because of this belief, optimists are more likely to try harder in difficult times; their past successes allow them to *expect* that they can repeat their success. Believing that bad times are temporary makes it easy for optimists to bounce back from setbacks, to fight through difficult times—they believe there is light at the end of the tunnel. In other words, they are resilient.

With a pessimistic explanatory style, bad times are thought to be long-lasting or permanent. As a result, the individual gives up more easily and often develops feelings of helplessness. In extreme cases, he or she becomes clinically depressed.

Pervasiveness—Everything

Pervasiveness in this context refers to the degree that people allow setbacks—an injury, the loss of a loved one, a poor sales call—to affect *other parts of their lives*. A pessimistic explanatory style leads to the conclusion that the setback will affect *everything* that person does.

For instance, a parent with a pessimistic explanatory style would attribute a daughter's unhappiness to: "I'm a poor parent." People who make universal explanations for their failures become easily discouraged and tend to give up on things when they fail. People who make

specific explanations may feel inept in a particular area, but that feeling *does not generalize* to other aspects of their lives, where optimism still prevails.

When pessimists experience success, on the other hand, they tend to attribute it to a *specific reason*—"I have good computer skills." Or they attribute their success to luck and think their success is fleeting and transitory. Those with an optimistic explanatory style attribute success to their global attributes—"I'm smart, I'm a hard worker"—and believe these attributes are pervasive in all aspects of their life. Global attributions that account for success enhance one's self-confidence and reinforce an optimistic explanatory style.

For some, being the victim of a drunk driver and losing the use of their legs would be an example of the pervasiveness of their bad luck. Not for Debra. If you look back to her story, you'll recall that she used a specific explanation. She attributed her accident to a specific cause, and while it affected some parts of her life, it did not derail her from enjoying her family and friends and pursuing her professional dreams.

Balancing Optimism

Having positive expectations for the future and positive explanations of the past is undoubtedly a strength. Optimism, though, like overconfidence, can also be a danger to our ability to perform to our capability in a pressure moment, mainly by leading us to take too many risks and miss important information. We can *overestimate the likelihood of experiencing positive events in our lives and underestimate the likelihood of experiencing negative events*. For instance, we may *underestimate* the likelihood of our being diagnosed with cancer, or being in a car accident, and *overestimate* our likely longevity and career prospects.

In short, we can become more optimistic than reality warrants. A good example is marriage, where 40 percent of couples divorce yet most people say at the time of their marriage that there is 0 percent chance they will divorce.

Being overly optimistic can act like other cognitive biases, such as confirmation bias, in which we seek information to confirm our beliefs

and ignore data that doesn't, and thus it can undermine our decision-making and thinking. But in a twist, of all the biases and illusions we experience in life, optimism is the *one outlier* of the group. Ryan McKay and Daniel Dennett, who did an exhaustive analysis of cognitive biases, found that being optimistic, while a bias, actually helps us. Researchers Dominic Johnson and James Fowler went further and built a computational model that found that *overestimating* one's probability of success is advantageous in a world of uncertainty, competition, and pressure. For instance, individuals who underestimated their probability of success shied away from many *conflicts they could have won.*

What we need today, then, is to blend optimism with a healthy dose of realism—what we call optimistic realism. You can see the need for this balance between optimism and realism in the world of a start-up business like Honest Tea.

Cofounders Seth Goldman and Barry Nalebuff, like many entrepreneurs, were hopeful that their idea would be a hit in the marketplace. But they were also aware that the odds were not in their favor, as they relate in their nonfiction graphic book, *Mission in a Bottle.* The majority of new businesses, after all, fail.

Seth was a graduate student at Yale School of Management and Barry was his professor. At the time, Seth, a runner, was always in need of a thirst-quenching drink after a run or a workout. He could not seem to find anything that satiated him, as most drinks he tried were too sweet. Barry taught an entrepreneurial class at Yale, and during a class discussion on the famous Coke versus Pepsi case study, he found that he and Seth shared a passion for the idea of a less sweet but still flavorful beverage. They both felt that there was a category missing in what Coke and Pepsi and other soft drink companies were offering.

Seth graduated from Yale in 1994, and like many good business school graduates at the time, he joined a financial services company. A few years later, Seth went for a run in New York City with a college friend who used to concoct juice drinks with him after class. Just like at Yale, they found themselves mixing drinks to find something flavorful but less sweet. It occurred to Seth that they must not be the only ones who wanted a less sweet beverage alternative. He decided then

and there that he was going to create the drink himself. He e-mailed Barry to see if he was still excited about pursuing the idea.

Barry had just returned from a trip to India, where he had spent considerable time studying the tea industry. What startled him was that, in comparing Indian teas to American, he found that most of the American tea companies didn't use whole tea leaves in their brewing process. It occurred to Barry that there were much better options available that might cost a little more but would deliver higher-quality tea. He came up with a name to describe tea made with real tea leaves—*Honest Tea*. When Seth heard the name, he knew they were on to something. He knew that to be successful they needed a great product that was differentiated from other offerings and a strong brand as well. Honest Tea was it.

Energized by the future promise of Honest Tea, Seth did the unthinkable and quit his high-paying job at Calvert Investments and started brewing batches of tea in his kitchen. Only five weeks after taking the entrepreneurial plunge, he brought five thermoses of tea in recycled Snapple bottles with a mock-up label to Whole Foods Markets. After sampling the tea, the buyer said: "Not bad. I'll take fifteen thousand bottles."

Seth was over the moon. "The guy liked it! He really liked it!" This was the first sales call Seth had ever made; clearly there was interest for their less-sugary drink. The buyer said something else that Seth missed the first time around: *"And I would like you to give me those orders for free. If they sell, I will pay you on the next order."* Seth was a little less excited when he finally heard this, as, obviously, he and Barry did not have fifteen thousand bottles of tea waiting to be shipped. In fact, they had no bottles ready to ship. Their entire inventory—five thermoses' worth—was sitting on the buyer's desk.

Seth hesitated, gulped, and, being honest, said: "This is great. We are so excited to be able to work with you, and we think this will be a wonderful partnership, but we can't give this order for free." The buyer looked at Seth for a moment and, to Whole Foods' credit, agreed to pay for the order before, as opposed to after, the tea sold. Seth and Barry were in business.

The creation of Honest Tea was, essentially, optimism in a bottle. It required positive expectations to begin. It simply could not have happened unless Seth and Barry were optimistic enough to believe that they could make their company successful. Seth had to believe enough in the idea, in himself, and in the future to take the courageous risk of quitting his job and taking the plunge to start brewing tea in his kitchen. But this wasn't the end of the story: There was trouble brewing at Honest Tea.

Fast-forward three years, to 2001. Seth and Barry realized that if they were going to scale their business, they would need to get some outside investors. They didn't have sufficient invested capital to grow their bottling capacity or distribution channels.

One of the investors they contacted thought the company's valuation was a bit rich—the value Seth and Barry placed on the company was more than it was worth based on its size and the amount of sales they had. Seth replied that if they hit their sales goals that year, the valuation wouldn't be too high. The investor replied: "OK, that's reasonable. Can you guarantee it?"

Seth recalled the situation: "This was a pressure moment for us. We needed the money and we believed we could make those sales targets. When we asked our lawyer what he thought, he said he believed we were being overly optimistic, that this was a risk that might *not* be worth taking. We didn't listen to him. So we took the investment and made the guarantee. We didn't make it. 9/11 hit a few months later and the economy and our sales took a big hit."

What Seth and Barry missed in their calculations was not 9/11 specifically, but an awareness that some setbacks in a start-up business are unpredictable. "You think you have it figured out in your business plan, but you don't. You can't. We had to raise money, but it turned out to be the wrong time to raise money in 2001. We were unlucky, but no more unlucky than anyone else."

This pressure moment revealed Seth and Barry's overly inflated level of optimism. They made a decision lots of high optimists would make. They didn't realize where they sat on the optimism range, and it put them at risk.

Optimism Range

The Optimism Range denotes the scale or spectrum of optimism and pessimism along which people lie. On one end of the scale are the high optimists, and at the other side there are the high pessimists. Each of us exists somewhere on this spectrum, or on this range. According to Barry, this 2001 pressure moment revealed Seth and his level of optimism (especially as a team)—they were high optimists—which helped them in some decisions, such as taking the risk to start the business, but put them at risk for other decisions, such as guaranteeing the investment to grow the business. This story illustrates the challenge that we all face: to balance optimism so that we take enough risks and move forward in pressure moments, even when we feel the dread and anxiety, but we don't go too far and take irrational risks.

To help you assess where you roam on the optimistic range, we have developed an assessment tool, PressureBook.com.

If your score is in the optimistic part of the range, you are more apt to view the situation optimistically, making you more likely to follow through on your plan and giving you confidence that the decisions you make, while risky, have a good chance to create success.

If your score is in the pessimistic part of the range, you are more apt to view situations pessimistically, making you more likely to avoid the pressure situations you might find yourself in and thus curtail your success. Think of a recent pressure moment you faced: What did you do? Did you avoid it? Not take the risk in the first place? Quit early on? If it was a difficult, high-pressure conversation, did you get your voice heard? Did you walk away from the conversation feeling like you didn't say everything that you wanted to say? This is characteristic of a more pessimistic view of the future.

Because optimism is associated with positive feeling and pessimism with distressful feeling, continually being tuned to your level of optimism provides you with important insight; whenever you experience the physical manifestations of pressure and anxiety, chances are that you are thinking pessimistically, and it is time to use a pressure solution that minimizes anxiety and distress. In other words, use your feelings *before* a pressure moment to gauge whether you are using a

more optimistic or pessimistic thinking style; then use a pressure solution where appropriate.

A useful procedure to help assess whether your optimism is "realistic" is to have another "board meeting." Just as your personal board of directors can help you build self-confidence, it can also help you develop a sense of realistic optimism that will allow you to effectively navigate your future.

The Next Meeting of Your Board of Directors

Research reveals a curious and little known characteristic of optimism: We are optimistically biased *only* toward ourselves and our family, *not toward other people*. As optimism researcher Tali Sharot puts it: "We're optimistic about ourselves, we're optimistic about our kids, we're optimistic about our families, *but we're not so optimistic about the guy sitting next to us.*"

This conundrum—that people hold optimistic expectations about their own future but not the future of others—has an evolutionary purpose: to increase feelings of superiority that make one more confident in competitive situations—a handy attitude when it is survival of the fittest. Today, though, that can translate into arrogance, an attribute that derails success. Realistic optimism advances your career, so it's smart to take advantage of the well-documented fact that the viewpoints of *other people* often help us appraise events more realistically and thus stay grounded and not take unnecessary or ill-advised risks. A good friend who will be honest with us, or an advisor or a colleague, can see what we are blind to. About us, these people are *not* prone to the potential excesses of being biased optimistically, as we are. In so being, they can help to show us where we stand on the Optimism Range, and help us make better decisions. (This is one of the reasons why teams and collaboration are so important to decision-making in organizations today: They can mitigate the risk of pressure situations, be they making yearly budgeting decisions, assessing merger or acquisition opportunities, or choosing investment options. As an old Japanese proverb states: *All of us are smarter than any one of us.*)

To best use your board of directors, present the facts of your

pressure situation to your trusted advisors as best you can and describe how you plan to handle the situation. For instance, maybe you have the opportunity to take on a new high-profile project. Ask your board to rate, on a scale from one to ten, what they believe your realistic chances are for success. Come up with a rating for yourself. If their rating matches yours, chances are you are perceiving the situation accurately and realistically assessing your likelihood of success. However, if there is a wide discrepancy between your rating and those of others, depending on the direction, you might be overly optimistic or needlessly pessimistic—both perceptions that will hinder you. You need to investigate further.

Thus there is a discrepancy; the key is to not get defensive (manage your arousal and slow down your response). Instead use the thinking discrepancy as a learning opportunity and dig into how your board formulated their rating. You can assess their rationale, and in all likelihood, their input will provide you with some insight that you can use to your advantage. Incorporating these insights into your plan of action will increase the chances that you will achieve your goal and in the process fortify your optimism.

It is also smart to explain how you formulated your assessment; perhaps they have overlooked important information. Your fuller picture of the situation may in fact cause them to reassess the situation and validate your optimistic outlook.

Accurately assessing where you are on the scale or range of optimism and pessimism is a useful tool. Pressure can be instructive in building this awareness because pressure makes *visible* where we sit on the continuum of optimism. When we are under the gun—facing a critical decision or hitting a setback in a sale or a conflict with our spouse or partner—our natural levels of optimism and pessimism reveal themselves. Pressure certainly did this for Seth and Barry. It became clear that they had put themselves at risk by first not knowing their level of optimism and then not hedging against it (by paying attention to their lawyer's advice). Fortunately, optimism came to save the day for them, helping them to *persist in the face of setbacks* and not give up after they had the made the fateful investment decision and

9/11 hit. They course-corrected before it proved fatal, selling an asset (a bottling plant) to help them survive.

As Barry put it, "What you need when you hit bad luck are two things: optimism and a real belief in your product. Seth is the world's most wonderful optimist. He always believes that things will turn out for the best and the right. The second is a real belief in your product. We had real reason for being passionate. We really believed that every bottle of tea that we sold was improving the American diet and helping people become healthier. We passionately believed that every bottle of tea we sold was going to make a difference. Our customers were telling us that. We knew we had the big picture right. All we needed to do was not mess up and we would be fine."

The story ended well for Seth and Barry. They were able to overcome many challenges and sleepless nights at Honest Tea, no doubt partly because of their optimism. In 2008, the Coca-Cola Company invested in the tea, purchasing 40 percent of the company's equity and helping them expand the distribution of their beverages. In March 2011, Coke purchased Honest Tea outright for $100 million. Today, Honest Tea is run as an independent business unit of Coca-Cola and can be found in more than one hundred thousand stores across the United States. The dream that took root in Seth's kitchen in 1998 became a company that just celebrated its fifteenth anniversary. Seth continues to run the business as Honest Tea's "TeaEO," with the same passion toward health, the environment, and social responsibility.

You don't have to be an entrepreneur to benefit from having positive expectations of the future and positive explanations of the past the way Seth and Barry did. In fact, you move forward in life only if you take some risk as you face pressure moments and/or find that life doesn't always go perfectly as planned. Positive expectations and predictions about our future are *absolutely essential* to our long-term happiness and success. The key is to know where you are on the spectrum and do your best to temper your Optimism Range so that you can use the *evolutionary advantage* that optimism confers while mitigating its risks.

Instilling Optimism in Yourself

Numerous studies in clinical and positive psychology demonstrate that our thinking styles and mental habits can be changed. The following strategies will help you instill an optimistic perspective into your life. The caveat, of course, is that you have to practice the strategies with an optimistic mind-set in order for them to work: "If I do them, they will work."

How to do so?

Develop an Optimistic Vocabulary

One reason optimists accomplish so much and distinguish themselves from others is that they do not engage in statements about themselves that limit or rein in their expectations, cap their desire, or discourage them from believing that better is achievable. The transcripts of pessimists are filled with statements such as "I can't," "I should have," "it will never happen," "it will never change," all fueled by belief in permanence plus global, negative internal attributions. These self-statements hold an individual back because they are inherently limiting. Positive psychology, or optimism, increases opportunities for growth. Thus:

+ Use your increasing self-awareness to edit out phrases such as "I can't," "I should have," "there's nothing I can do about it."

+ Introduce optimistic language into your vocabulary: "I can," "I will," "I could," "When [not if] . . ." These phrases focus your attention on your options and increase an optimistic outlook. Pressure solution #8, "Use Your Positive GPS System," can help you do this in the moment.

Adopt the Belief That the World Is Fair

Accept and embrace the notion that, all in all, the world is fair. Optimistic people tend to believe the world is fair and that, as a result, hard work will pay off. They believe the environment will yield to their efforts, and this belief makes individuals try harder. Students, for example, who

believe in a just world give more effort because they believe they will be graded fairly. Belief in a just world helps us see that life is a series of exciting and interesting challenges to master rather than a precarious environment where we are constantly in peril. This positive perception reduces stress on many fronts in addition to helping us do our best when it matters most.

To help develop the habit of believing in a just world:

+ Make a list of the truly bad breaks you have experienced. Now make a list of the good breaks that have come your way. This should remind you that, all in all, life is pretty fair.

+ Every time something bad happens to you, immediately think of something good that has recently happened to you.

+ Be aware of how your motivation and practice impact your results.

The goal of these techniques is to help you keep in perspective that life is positive and challenging, and that hard work is the key to success.

Belief in a just world will prompt other responses that keep you optimistic and prevent you from engaging in pessimistic and counter-productive behaviors. Few optimists are constant whiners, but among pessimists, there are complainers galore.

Appreciate the World Around You

Feeling appreciation means you do not take people, events, and every-day experiences for granted, and it is looked upon as giving meaning to a person's life. If we can enjoy the life we have, adversity will be less stressful when it occurs.

Take five minutes a day to think about the positives in your life. The more you do, the more apt you will be to begin to perceive your glass as more full than empty, a perception that will make you *feel good* and push you to more optimistic thinking and resilience. Studies with physically handicapped seniors and clinically depressed individuals show that spending time focusing on the positives in one's life creates positive feelings and optimistic thoughts. Appreciation is a pretty powerful strategy for becoming more optimistic. Debra saw her glass

as half full; she was grateful to have her loved ones, interesting work, and a promising future.

Explain Your Life Optimistically

Start explaining your life as an optimist would, so you can reap the benefits. An exercise to practice: Take a half hour and write your life story as a pessimist. Then rewrite it as an optimist. Reflect on the difference and you will gain self-awareness on how you interpret and have interpreted your significant life events. Note how each story makes you feel and you will see the benefits of an optimistic explanatory style.

Step back and note how optimism works. Those with an optimistic mind-set wake up believing the day will be positive. And *positive expectations create positive feelings,* which can translate into being more pleasant and cooperative with others. When a *positive event occurs*—praise from the boss, or finding a parking space in a crowded mall—optimists *attribute it to hard work and experience.* If a glitch or *setback occurs,* optimists remember that it is only *temporary,* a *challenge* that they can handle. It reaffirms their ability to be *realistically optimistic* when encountering the next challenge. Throughout the day, be *aware and grateful* for the quality of life you enjoy. You'll go to sleep believing that when the sun comes up tomorrow, it will be the dawn of another great day.

Without tenacity our long-term survival would be impossible. With the boldness of that statement in mind, it would be advantageous for all of us to have the tenacity of the tardigrade, one of the most complex of all known organisms, which can thrive in a physically or geochemically extreme condition that would be detrimental to most life on Earth.

Commonly known as water bears, these water-dwelling micro eight-legged animals can tolerate extreme temperatures ranging from absolute zero to well above the boiling point of water, are able to adapt to pressure that is six times more forceful than pressure found in the deepest ocean depths, and can withstand bombarding ionizing radiation at doses hundreds of times higher than the lethal dose for a human being.

If there is no food or water, they are tenacious enough to hang on for at least a decade; if floating in outer space with limited air and unable to signal for help, well, Houston, it's no problem. In May 2011, the tardigrade became the first known animal to survive in space. Italian scientists booked tardigrades on a space flight, sending them on STS134, the final flight of space shuttle *Endeavour*. The scientists' conclusion was that microgravity and cosmic radiation "did not significantly affect survival of tardigrades in flight, confirming that tardigrades represent a useful animal for space research." Tardigrades are tenacious enough to have been around for 530 million years. That is tenacity.

The 2006 movie *Akeelah and the Bee* follows the inspirational story of Akeelah Anderson, who has a knack for spelling and can do it better than anyone else in her school. Growing up on the wrong side of the

tracks in Los Angeles, Akeelah is openly mocked by her classmates for being a "brainiac"; even her mother views the spelling bee as a silly pursuit, and tells her to just focus on schoolwork.

Despite an initial "lack of encouragement," Akeelah practices tenaciously in secret. After winning local, state, and regional spelling bee competitions, she goes on to earn an all-expenses-paid trip to compete in the National Spelling Bee in Washington, DC. Akeelah, of course, is a fictional character, but Angela Duckworth, a professor of Psychology at the University of Pennsylvania, has studied 190 "Akeelahs"—students who successfully qualified for the Scripps National Spelling Bee in Washington, and her results provide an important insight about what is required to perform closer to our capability in pressure moments and to be successful in life.

Professor Duckworth investigated what makes these successful spellers so successful. Did they have photographic memories, or did they score especially high on verbal IQ tests? In this incredibly high-pressure competition, what was behind their success?

Duckworth and her colleagues found that far more important than talent—in this case spelling ability—was that these spellers were able to consistently engage in "effortful activities that are designed to optimize improvement." In essence, she would say that these students, like the tardigrade, were tenacious.

Take a look around and you can see the results of tenacity in human civilization. Artistic, scientific, and physical achievement are all rooted in tenacity. The successful real estate agent, lawyer, and student have all achieved their success because of tenacity.

Duckworth's research adds another important ingredient to being able to perform under pressure: You can't just show up to a high-pressure situation and expect to perform well. You need to be tenacious—to *put the work in*. People who find it difficult to perform often discount the need for preparation and hard work. It's easier to believe in the myth of the clutch player, the leader-hero, or the prodigy. Without hard work, without tenacity, your chances of performing well under pressure are not high. We need to learn to work hard and *stay at it*. This is one of the reasons *tenacity is such a key component of performing under pressure*. Tenacity helps us persevere when we hit inevitable setbacks. We've all

encountered tenacious people in our lives, and at times, we've all acted tenaciously. Let's first define "tenacity" before turning our attention to our chief goal, adding Tenacity to your COTE of Armor.

The Jingle/Jangle of Tenacity

School engagement researchers Amy Reschly and Sandra Christenson, University of Georgia psychologists, described a phenomenon in psychology called the "Jingle/Jangle" Problem—"jingle" occurs when the same term is used to refer to different concepts, and "jangle" occurs when different terms are used for the same concept. When it comes to defining and conceptualizing "tenacity," there is a lot of jingle and jangle.

An educator, for example, is likely to use "grit" to describe those students *who are able to strenuously work toward challenges, maintaining their effort and interest over years despite failure, adversity, and plateaus in progress reaching their goal.* A clinical psychologist describes the patient who does these things as having great *resiliency.* Research psychologists frequently study *persistence* and *perseverance,* which they describe as *a continuation of a goal-directed action in spite of obstacles, difficulties, or discouragement.* A sports psychologist talks about *mental toughness* and defines it as having *the natural or developed psychological edge that enables you to, generally, cope better than your opponents with the many demands (competition, training, lifestyle) that sports places on a performer and specifically be more consistent and better than your opponents in remaining determined, focused, confident, and in control under pressure.*

Stanford psychologist Carol Dweck's characterization of an academically tenacious student (you can substitute employee, salesperson, executive, athlete) brings together a lot of the jingle/jangle that contributes to tenacity:

First, tenacious students *believe* that they belong in school academically and socially. . . . Second, they are *engaged* in learning, view effort *positively,* and are willing to forgo immediate pleasures for the sake of schoolwork. . . . Third, difficulty, be it intellectual or social, does not derail them. They see a *setback* as an opportunity for learning or a problem to be solved rather than as a humiliation, a condemnation

of their ability or worth, a symbol of future failure, or a confirmation that they do not belong. Tenacious students know how to remain engaged over the long haul and to *deploy new strategies* for moving forward effectively.

For sure, resiliency is part of the equation, but so is perseverance—it seems almost impossible to bounce back from setbacks and to persevere if you are not mentally tough. Coming up with new strategies to achieve your goal is part of what makes you tenacious.

We believe a more accurate and useful way to understand tenacity is by examining the factors that *create and reinforce* the terms that constitute the jingle/jangle surrounding the concept. These are the factors we want to help you leverage so that you become resilient, mentally tough, persistent, and able to cope with adversity and to generate pathways to success. That's tenacity—maybe not to the point of being able to survive in a gravity void, but certainly to the point of helping scientists and engineers build a vehicle to get you there.

Talent Is Never Enough

Gaining entry into a gifted program in school, achieving admission to college based on SAT scores, winning a competitive job with a prestigious company right out of college, getting fast-tracked for promotion—for all of these milestones, we overemphasize talent as a predictor of success. Organizations in a competitive landscape do their best to reinforce this misinterpretation, as it helps their brand. One of the competitive advantages of an institution like Harvard, Stanford, McKinsey, or Goldman Sachs is exclusivity. People are attracted to gaining entrance to the most selective school or organization, the best of the best. These organizations are only too happy to foster the myth of talent. The problem is not that talent does not matter; it is that on its own, it is simply not enough. What is often missed in the equation are the qualities that "unleash talent," that end up *counting for far more than talent*. A good example of the limitations of assessing based on talent is the annual NFL Combine.

The Combine is an intense, four-day "job interview" for more than three hundred college football players. It is held every February, in

Indianapolis, Indiana. At this event, top executives, coaching staffs, player personnel departments, and medical personnel from all thirty-two NFL teams are on hand to evaluate the nation's top college football prospects eligible for the upcoming NFL Draft. Many athletes see it as a make-or-break audition for getting drafted and playing in the NFL.

There is only one problem with the Combine: It is useless. Research has conclusively shown that the results from the Combine do not predict who will be successful in the NFL. According to an exhaustive study by Frank Kuzmits and Arthur Adams, there is no "consistent statistical relationship between Combine tests and professional football performance." The authors investigated the correlation between National Football League Combine test results and NFL success for players drafted at three different offensive positions (quarterback, running back, and wide receiver) during a six-year period, 1999–2004. The Combine consists of a series of drills, exercises, interviews, aptitude tests, and physical exams designed to assess the skills of promising college football players and to predict their performance in the NFL. Combine measures examined in the study included ten-, twenty-, and forty-yard dashes, bench press, vertical jump, broad jump, twenty- and sixty-yard shuttles, and the three-cone drill. Performance criteria included ten variables: draft order; three years each of salary received and games played; and position-specific data. With the notable exception of sprint tests for running backs, the Combine was *not predictive* of who would be successful, based on these performance criteria, and who would not.

How is it possible that such a large-scale, annual event could be so useless? On the surface, it would seem that testing prospective athletes this way would be the perfect gauge of their professional potential. What is missing from the Combine equation? The answer has powerful implications for anyone who has ever faced a test to show off his or her abilities.

The problem with the Combine is that it does not resemble what players will face in the real world, *what they will need to be successful* in the high-pressure environment of the NFL. Of course, athletic talent matters. But beyond a certain threshold of talent, far more important is how tenacious the player will be in *unleashing* his talent.

For instance, what decisions will he make when he shows up in the intensely competitive environment of training camp, where players are playing for a paycheck? How will he handle having to learn an NFL-sized playbook? Or reviewing game tape, looking at upcoming opposing teams? Or being given critical feedback? Or dropping down the depth chart? Or getting injured? Or the times it feels like the coaches have lost belief in him? Or when the team signs a free agent in his position? And so on. The real world is about far more than how much you can bench press or vertical jump or how fast you can run a three-cone drill in the short, artificial environment of a Combine. The NFL Combine is using an incomplete criteria. What they are missing is a test for the quality that helps a player *persevere and sustain effort toward his long-term goal in spite of the setbacks he will inevitably face.* What they are lacking is a way to measure a player's tenacity.

As President Calvin Coolidge said: "Nothing in the world can take the place of persistence. Talent will not; nothing is more common than unsuccessful men with talent. Genius will not; unrewarded genius is almost a proverb. Education will not; the world is full of educated derelicts. Persistence and determination alone are omnipotent."

Tenacity's DNA

An evolutionary geneticist might sequentially code a strand of tenacity "DNA" as G-F-H-C. These four "chromosomes"—Goals, Focus, Hope, and Coping—are sequenced this way because each fuels the creation of the next.

If one of these "chromosomes" is damaged or weak, the tenacious behavior that is required to succeed is disrupted. A student or employee who lacks meaningful goals is not likely to be a focused individual and for sure will not be tenacious in achieving goals. A person with little hope is rarely tenacious, and those whose coping skills break down find perseverance to be impossible. An important point, then, is that the healthier the individual chromosomes are—the stronger they are connected to one another—the stronger the tenacity DNA strand will be.

Goals

The first goal of any organism is to survive; a good case can be made that our most basic instinct, our *survival instinct*, is the trigger for tenacious behavior. Your survival instinct is a *powerful motivator* of behavior. Few of us, for example, would crawl through a burning building to retrieve a cell phone—but all of us would make the crawl to save our lives.

The instinct to survive is hardwired into us. A newborn's sucking behavior and crying sound are prompted by its instinct to survive, as is the chirping of a baby blackbird. In fact one could argue that our survival instinct is the essential fuel propelling individual advancement. We've all heard stories of how an individual's "will to survive" helped him or her make it through traumatic and horrifying moments. On the sports field, the will to survive is manifested as the "will to win"; in the corporate world and in classrooms, it is known as the "will to succeed." It's no urban legend that many physicians describe elderly patients who die inexplicably as having "lost their will to live." It is our survival instinct that *arouses* us *to purposeful action*. In essence, the *survival* instinct is nature's way of *motivating us* to be tenacious.

It is purposeful action that helps us achieve whatever goals we have set. If you are thirsty, the action of getting up from your comfortable chair would be the purposeful action to achieve your goal of obtaining a drink to quench your thirst. On the other hand, if you are not thirsty (or hungry or otherwise motivated to action), you might continue to sit.

First, tenacity involves *working toward a goal*. A gritty student works toward getting good grades; the mentally tough athlete works toward winning the game or match or meet; the resilient patient is determined to walk again.

Second, tenacity requires *voluntary exertion*. Without effort, there is no perseverance, resiliency, or mental toughness.

Today, educators and psychologists confirm that our chances for achievement are increased when the goals we have set are *physically* and *mentally arousing*. In other words, meaningful goals initiate the

tenacity process. These are the same attributes that allow an individual to *focus*, whether on a math problem or on what the individual's partner is saying.

Focus

When man first experienced hunger, his survival instinct *aroused* him to direct his attention to the action of searching his environment for food. Arousal narrows *attention*, and in this case, our ancestors' attention became selectively tuned to their environment. Some signs or pathways were more fruitful to follow than others; in order to select the path that would lead to food, our ancestors' attention would have had to be narrowed to the smallest of details or clues—animal excrement, or a few blades of trampled grass. Those who quickly noticed these details were better able to seek out their goal. Their *focus* gave them an advantage in ultimately finding food.

Today we use the term "focus" to refer to the ability to attend to whatever helps you achieve a goal, and to ignore what doesn't. That is why focus is so crucial in a high-pressure situation. Attention and focus are like having a flashlight in a dark room—turning it on allows you to attend to the room, but you still need to focus the flashlight beam if you want to find your way out. From an evolutionary perspective, focus is a *pathfinding* mechanism. It is a crucial skill that allows you to perform the activities that are necessary to help you achieve your short-term and long-term goals. Focus, in other words, is "mental gaze control."

Numerous studies indicate that student achievement is directly related to the *ability to focus*, and that a lack of persistence and low achievement are highly correlated with low focus. Navy SEALs, surfers, successful executives, and athletes will tell you that the ability to *stay* focused during pressure moments is crucial for doing their best. And you probably know from your own experience that a loss of focus results in a subpar performance, if not worse. Lose your focus while driving on the highway, and the results can be deadly.

Here is how one mountain climber described climbing Mount Everest in the Himalayas:

*On the mountain you couldn't [let your guard down]. . . . You had
to stay focused.*

*I visualized one step at a time. Climbing a mountain is one step
at a time. You definitely want to be focused on summiting, but you
really need to focus on the day to day and that is the key to being
successful.*

While focus has always been important to our success, it plays out
differently today than it did for our ancestors. Our ancestors thought
more about *short-term goals*. Getting food was an immediate priority,
and the arousal it generated gave them the energy to sprint after prey,
or jump across a raging stream in pursuit of it. Early man had to be
quick to respond to his environment. The evolutionary demands put
upon him, like escaping a carnivorous beast, were best served by quick,
decisive responses—hesitation could be fatal. The evolutionary archi-
tecture of man's early style of thinking could be characterized as intu-
itive, impulsive, involuntary, automatic—what Nobel Prize–winning
psychologist Daniel Kahneman calls "fast thinking." Fast, or "instinc-
tual," thinking takes place in the neural circuitry of the lower brain.
Survival tasks often involve these responses.

As we evolved, and our existence became less of a matter of day-to-
day survival, our goals became more physically and mentally *distinct*.
The focus needed to build a shelter is very different from the energy
required to hunt dangerous prey. To accomplish such long-term goals,
we had to generate more psychological effort to stay motivated and fo-
cused over the long haul. As man evolved, therefore, the neocortex of
the brain grew, which allowed us to develop another thinking style to
help us adapt. This thinking style is deliberate and voluntary, and can
help us to perform feats like learning and mastering new tasks. Profes-
sor Kahneman calls it "slow thinking."

This thinking style requires *exerting effort*; the tasks that result
from slow thinking require effort to perform. Making sound decisions,
planning a strategy, identifying and anticipating obstacles, generating
strategies to overcome them, are tasks that demand deliberate, or slow,
thinking. While it takes mental energy to formulate a strategy, it takes
behavioral effort to execute it.

Individuals who generate this mental and behavioral effort for extended times have a distinct advantage in meeting their *long-term goals* because they can focus for a longer period of time.

Those individuals who are able to focus for long periods of time are seen as persistent, motivated, and, of course, tenacious. In effect, they are in a *prolonged focus state* that keeps them attending to the specific tasks needed to meet their long-term goals. Pressure solution #4, "Focus on the Mission," is a microcosm of this point.

How long any one of us can focus is dependent on a number of factors. One is hereditary, which is why genetics is thought to play a part in attention deficit disorders. Another factor is the amount of effort and arousal that we generate and sustain. Self-preservation (fear) generates instant arousal and effort. But long-term goals are rarely physically arousing, and thus they require physical and mental effort to sustain them. Eventually, our physical and mental exertion can psychologically exhaust us and lessen our concentration.

Good examples of this point are found in research done under the rubric of "decision fatigue."

Decision Fatigue

Think back to the last time you bought a car from a car dealership. Do you recall the decisions you made as you went through the process? Did you start with a specific type of vehicle in mind? Did you conduct research online? Think about all of the decisions you were required to make in advance: manufacturer, model, color, number of doors, size of engine, rustproofing or not, optional packages, how you would finance the car (cash, loan, or lease), extended warranty, service plan?

When we buy a car, these questions and other seemingly small decisions come with a "biological cost," a rarely acknowledged sticker shock. Every decision we make in the course of the day uses mental energy. And over time, that part of our brain, the prefrontal lobe, tires out, and we start to lose tenacity. When we are low on mental energy, we take shortcuts, and make decisions without full reflection on their consequences. We lose focus on our goals.

A study done at Audi found that as people go through the decision-

making process when purchasing a new car, at some point they become so fatigued that they start opting for whatever is recommended by the manufacturer, as opposed to what they might otherwise want. In effect, they begin making more impulsive choices, just to get the decisions over with.

The problem is that car manufacturers are all well aware of this phenomenon, and some unscrupulous salespeople—not Audi—use it to their advantage. They put the less expensive, more trivial decisions first to fatigue the buyer so that when they get to the more difficult and expensive decisions, like whether to get wheel rims and service packages, later in the process, buyers are less able to discern rationally what they want. They have lost sight of their goals. This is no small matter: It can cost buyers a lot when they take shortcuts and accept the recommended options as opposed to thinking through what is best for them.

Like those car buyers, we are bombarded by so much information and so many tiny options all the time that our decision-making and self-control can be depleted, and we can start to either become impulsive or give in to the status quo. This is one of the factors that can get in the way of staying tenacious that most people are not aware of. Why do we fatigue in this way?

In one study conducted in Germany, Roy Baumeister and a group of researchers gave beepers to participants and beeped them at intervals of every thirty minutes, asking them to note down what, if anything, they were resisting in that moment. They found that, on average, people spend *four hours engaging in self-control*, or resisting impulses, during the day. These fell into four categories: controlling thoughts, controlling feelings, impulse control to override a desire, and trying to stay focused on a task. All of them act to "exhaust our supply of self-control," which changes our subsequent decision-making.

The consequences of these dips in mental energy sound harmless enough, but a study looking at Israel's justice system revealed a shocking pattern of justice (and injustice) that has broad implications for us all.

Three people sat on the Israeli parole board that determined whether inmates would be granted parole. The board consisted of a judge, a social worker, and a criminologist. A story in the *New York*

Times followed the judgment pertaining to three prisoners. All had finished at least two-thirds of their sentences, but only one was granted parole.

As it turned out, the determining factor in whether the prisoners were given pardon or not had little to do with their crimes or rehabilitation. The first prisoner to appear before the board, at 8:50 a.m., was an Arab Israeli who had been imprisoned for fraud and was serving a thirty-month sentence. The second, heard at 3:10 p.m., convicted of assault, was a Jewish Israeli serving a sixteen-month sentence. The third was another Arab Israeli who, like the first, had committed fraud and was serving a thirty-month sentence. He was heard at 4:25 p.m. on another day.

Which one was granted parole and freed? You have all the information you need to make an educated guess. Did the board respond to their ethnicities, crimes, sentences, or length of time served? No, none of the above. The prisoner heard first, in the morning, was freed. A study of more than eleven hundred decisions over a year showed that, in fact, prisoners who faced parole boards earliest were most likely to receive parole. *Seventy percent* of the time, early morning appearances before the board won parole, compared to those later in the day, from which prisoners were paroled less than 10 percent of the time. The first Arab Israeli faced the best odds and, in fact, was released. And the others? They were simply in the wrong place at the wrong time.

Jonathan Levav of Stanford and Shai Danziger of Ben-Gurion University noted that there was nothing malicious going on. The results of the parole board had to do with decision fatigue. Hearing case after case simply wore the judges out. The same conditions exist—and the same poor decisions result—when referees make bad calls at the end of a game, when business executives and politicians make scandalous choices late in the evening, and when parents lose control and lash out at their kids after a long day of work. Most of us are oblivious to this decision fatigue; researchers are looking at it to understand how it occurs and what to do to counteract it.

What this intriguing study of Israeli judges and the Audi study found was that, in general, when people become fatigued, they switch to a quicker, more efficient, less energy-consuming but more fallible

form of decision-making. When we are fatigued, we lose our ability to tamp down the onslaught of information from the outside world; these thoughts and feelings are experienced more intensely when our self-control is exhausted and we are decision fatigued. When we are fatigued, we have a much more difficult time collaborating, communicating, and compromising. We are much more prone to choose the default option when we are tired, because it is harder to think through our other options.

Low Blood Sugar and Tenacity

Believe it or not, our ability to be tenacious is even affected by the amount of glucose we have in our bloodstream—the fuel for our brains. When people have low blood sugar levels, they are less able to engage in difficult decision-making or to exert self-control. This is why the Israeli judges were more likely to go with the status-quo or easier decision of not granting parole when they were low on glucose just prior to their lunch break and at the end of the day.

In one study of children at school, Baumeister gave one-half of a group of students a full breakfast, while the other half were not given breakfast. The students who were not given breakfast acted more impulsively and had more behavioral issues compared to the group of students who were given a full breakfast. They also showed less tenacious behavior, giving up earlier on the tasks they were working on.

Once the group was given breakfast later in the morning, their behavioral issues returned to the same level as the group who received breakfast early on, and they were much more able to stay focused on the tasks at hand. In other words, they miraculously became more tenacious.

Hope

Think back to the time of our ancestors. Consider the impact on a hunting party of a long and unsuccessful hunt. Exhaustion and nasty weather may have depleted the hunting party's will to go on. What would encourage them to continue? The same question applies today to a student studying for a test when he or she has only a collection of Cs and Ds

from previous tests to guide anticipation of future grades. What keeps our focus alive when others throw in the towel? The answer is hope.

Greek myth has it that Zeus was furious with Prometheus for stealing fire from the gods and giving it to mankind. To extract his revenge against humankind, Zeus fashioned a beautiful maiden named Pandora and sent her on a journey to Earth with her dowry chest in hand. In what might be one of the first examples in literature of reverse psychology, Zeus warned Pandora not to look inside her dowry chest. Of course, as Zeus expected, the first thing Pandora did upon her arrival on Earth was to open the lid and take a look, and by doing so, she released the negative forces from the dowry chest upon the people of Earth: colic, rheumatism, and gout for the body; spite and revenge for the mind. Realizing what she had done, Pandora rushed to replace the lid. All that remained was hope, stuck beneath it.

Considering the attention that hope has been given over the ages, it is safe to assume that hope, too, escaped Pandora's dowry. Those who weighed in on the subject early in our civilization frequently viewed hope as another of the awful forces that Pandora unleashed upon the world. Plato thought hope to be a "foolish counselor," and Sophocles held that human suffering was prolonged by hope. Benjamin Franklin observed that the person who lives on hope will die fasting; others have argued that hope is an illusion or that it will not last.

Science now tells us how wrong these beautiful minds were! Numerous studies show what early man figured out tens of thousands of years ago: Being hopeful yields all kinds of psychological benefits.

Adults and children who score higher in hope (1) score higher in satisfaction, self-esteem, optimism, meaning in life, and happiness; (2) cope better with injuries, diseases, and physical pain; (3) excel in academics from elementary to graduate school; and (4) perform better in sports. What is especially compelling about the last two findings is that they occurred at levels well beyond what the researchers would have predicted based on natural abilities. In other words hope predicted academic performance better than intelligence, and athletic performance more accurately than natural ability.

What makes hope spring eternal? We'd say it's because of its evolutionary function: to promote the desire for a positive outcome. The

operative word is *desire*, commonly stated as *motivation*. Early man hoped he would find food; thus motivated, he became focused on finding the pathways that would lead him to his goal. More often than not, those who were hopeful would succeed more often in this quest than those who were less hopeful.

This simple logic seems to be validated by the hope theory formulated by C. R. Snyder when he was director of Clinical Psychology at the University of Kansas (and on the dissertation committee of Dr. Weisinger). Rick, as he was called by his graduate students, considered himself to be a keen observer of the human race, and his self-perception proved accurate.

He interviewed students who participated in his research on excuse-making, looking at why and how we distance ourselves from negative outcomes. In the course of his interviews, Rick discovered a common theme, which he described as the other side of excuse-making—"the *desire to attach ourselves to positive outcomes*." He called this desire "hope."

In essence, hope theory assumes that people are generally goal-oriented; they behave in ways that will help them to accomplish something (like trying to find food and water). Two components of hope, termed *agency* and *pathway thinking*, come into play.

Agency, commonly called "willpower," is the motivational component that propels people along their chosen routes to achieve goals. Agency reflects a person's perception that he or she can work on accomplishing a given goal. It also reflects people's appraisal of their capability to *persevere* in pursuing a goal. Although motivation is always important in pursuing a goal, it becomes especially critical in times when obstacles arise. When you hear people make comments such as "I can do this" or "I will not be stopped," they are exhibiting the *capacity* of hope, or what we sometimes call "mental toughness" or "perseverance."

If agency is the willpower required to execute a given route to a goal effectively, *pathway thinking* is the ability to identify the necessary routes to achieving that goal. Finding routes to achieve desired goals is absolutely essential to success.

Pathways are mental plans or road maps that guide our actions and

thought. In some cases, pathways can be resources, such as personal contacts who can help you advance, a financial fund that helps fund your efforts, or a social network that helps you meet the right people or experts. But pathways can also be tools—a computer software program that makes it easier for you to collect sales data that can help you achieve your quota. A pathway can also be a detailed strategy that lays out how to proceed from one step to another.

The more pathways we perceive we have to our goals, the more hopeful we become, giving us increased motivation to continue pursuing the goals. It is often the case that "where there is a will there is a way," but hope theory also tells us that "where there is a way there is a will." In other words, pathways + agency = hope.

Moreover, the results of countless studies of diverse populations suggest that hopeful thinking can be increased.

In one study, a group of clinically depressed adults learned how to improve their goal-setting priorities, as well as how to increase their ability to find pathways to their goals and motivate themselves to use those pathways. Those trained in these hope-enhancing skills showed a significant lessening of their depression.

In another study, outpatients at a community mental health center were taught hope theory principles before entering their normal treatments. Those who received such training improved over the course of their treatments compared with those who didn't get the training. A third study used videotaped hopeful narratives that were shown to female survivors of childhood incest. Those who viewed one of the hopeful videotapes reported consistently higher levels of hope than those who viewed a tape of nature scenes.

Researchers from the University of Nebraska found that hope enhanced productivity. A cross-section of managers practiced work-related goals that were personally valuable and challenging, and had clear beginning and ending points. After achieving the goals, each manager received feedback from the group on how to generate additional ways to achieve them, as well as how to prepare for additional obstacles the manager could expect to encounter. These actions all increased perceptions of hope. Those who underwent the training

became more productive in reaching their goals and were rated as more productive by their managers.

Coping

It is only a matter of time before even the most hopeful among us run into barriers or obstacles that block our efforts. For some of us, such barriers can prove to be overwhelming, and we eventually give up. Those of us who are the most hopeful are able to better manage our emotions and problem-solve ways to overcome the obstacles and achieve our goals.

Problems are inherently stressful and anxiety arousing. So coping with problems involves managing stress and anxiety.

We are hardwired to avoid distress. Developing coping strategies to avoid distress can be traced back to our earliest ancestors. Those who coped with stress more effectively had an edge in terms of day-to-day survival.

Contemporary psychologists categorize many of our coping strategies as *appraisal-focused*. In other words, they are strategies we employ to modify the way we think about a challenge or fear, allowing us to cope with the situation more effectively. Students who appraise a test as a challenge instead of a threat, for example, report less anxiety and pressure and perform better; the same is true of athletes who see their next event or competition as a challenge, rather than as a test they might fail.

We have incorporated appraisal-focused strategies in many of the pressure solutions we offer in Part 2 of the book, such as #1, "Befriend the Moment." These solutions help individuals cope more effectively in high-pressure, high-anxiety situations. In addition to helping you perform at your best when under pressure, these pressure solutions will help you decrease daily anxiety and stress.

However, even the most powerful reappraisals of adversity are not enough. Early man discovered other strategies to help him cope—what psychologists would eventually call relaxation strategies, from sitting quietly in the shade, leaning against a tree, and breathing in and out slowly, to humming or singing a song to distract him from his fears

(music is an effective distraction from anxiety and other forms of emotional distress).

Psychologists describe these kinds of coping maneuvers as *emotion-focused*, and they include managing fearful feelings with meditation and relaxation techniques. The pressure solutions we offer in Part 2 are all emotion-focused, in that they help you manage the stress and anxiety that accompany the perception of pressure.

But sometimes cognitive coping strategies, too, have their limits. A husband or wife, for example, who can no longer ignore the emotional distress of a marriage or thinks of the marriage as an obstacle to happiness, will likely eventually decide, "I can't do this anymore." A lawyer, salesperson, teacher, nurse, or civil servant who no longer thinks that his or her job is challenging enough or serves as a stepping-stone for advancement, and who finds his or her daily work life stressful, will eventually decide, "I quit."

Many of us who reach this point seek the support of others — whether therapists, psychologists, or support groups. Others cope by making behavioral changes that create a new and optimistic perspective for themselves. A salesperson who realizes that her method for generating leads is ineffective can try another method that may be more successful. The same is true for a company whose marketing strategy is ineffective, or a teacher whose students are not learning the material being taught.

Psychologists describe these coping strategies as *problem-focused*, in that they emphasize dealing with the cause of the problem. They are aimed at changing or eliminating the source of the problem or stress. Problem-focused coping can lead to finding out more information about the problem and learning new skills to deal with it. This is the rationale for a number of our pressure solutions, such as #16, "Put Away Self-Consciousness."

We have found that the best way to deal with the stress and anxiety of high-pressure situations is to use a combination of the various coping methods we have suggested. They will allow you to bounce back quickly from setbacks, overcome adversity, and continue the pursuit of your goals. They will give you the tenacity and resilience to tackle any challenge.

Step back and recognize a crucial point: Tenacity is a dynamic *process*, not a personal attribute that we either possess or do not possess. We initiate that process by focusing on goals that are arousing to us, that fill us with energy and purpose. It is that sense of arousal that helps us to be tenacious over the long haul. It provides us with the focus we need to work at a task, search for solutions, or find paths to achieving our goals. Having a number of options that assist in achieving our goals helps to motivate us when obstacles appear, as they inevitably do. Instead of succumbing to failure, we adjust our thinking and/ or behavior in pursuit of our goal.

Making Yourself Tenacious

So how do you make tenacity a choice? What are the steps you can take to be more tenacious in high-pressure situations?

Step 1: Energize Yourself by Establishing Meaningful Goals

Tenacity *requires* motivation and effort, so your first step is to create a reservoir of energy to draw on.

Establish a goal that will *arouse* you, that you see as *worthy*.

How do you create a worthy goal? By combining your *interests with an optimal level of challenge*.

First, clarify your interests. When you work toward goals that are meaningfully connected to your future success, interests, and cultural values and/or topics, you are more likely to persevere when you are faced with challenges and frustrations, whether they are a result of an unreasonable boss, a lack of effort from team members, a malfunctioning computer, or being embarrassed on the sports field.

Mark Heese, an Olympic bronze-medalist beach volleyball player who JP worked with over three Olympics, said: "Setting goals has always been an important part of my program. They act as drivers or motivators for my daily training. Without them it would have been tough to bring the right level of energy and intensity to our workouts.

"My very first experience with goals came from an odd place: being

embarrassed on center court by the best team in Canada, fifteen to two in my first ever national championship. They beat us and it brought the spotlight on me, a young rookie. I was so embarrassed that I went home and wrote down my very first goal ... beat Ed Drakich [the leader of the top team]. A day did not go by without clearly thinking about that goal. ... One year later, at the National Championships, my partner and I got our revenge ... beating Drakich and his partner fifteen-four. This was a very energizing goal and helped me realize the value of goal-setting early in my career."

Be aware of a trap that recent college graduates sometimes fall into: They believe their goals must originate from some "innate passion" that they have always had. In truth, meaningful goals are not always apparent. They can take time to emerge and come from experiences that might not be obvious. For instance, Mark Heese found a set of goals that came from an unlikely place, watching others: "Another goal that stands out was one year when I found myself paying close attention to some outstanding qualities of the top players that I competed against on a weekly basis in the qualifying for the Olympics. I decided to write down the quality I most admired in several athletes, and created goals around how I could bring those qualities to my life, on and off the court. It had a clear impact on my life, and my performance on and off the court blossomed. My overall confidence skyrocketed, because I was becoming not just the type of athlete that I wanted to be, but also the kind of man I envisioned for myself. Goals helped shape my character as a beach player, and as a husband/dad/brother/son/friend, etc."

Once you know what your goal is, based on your interests, make it *challenging*. Game designers and military trainers recognize that the key to promoting optimal performance is to create situations/goals that keep individuals in the "zone"—where the individual's level of performance matches the challenge of the activity. When this occurs, the individual can experience challenges that can bring growth. Don't challenge yourself in a way that creates anxiety or boredom. Those factors can sabotage tenacity. Individuals in the zone experience what psychologist Mihaly Csikszentmihalyi calls "flow," the single-minded state of engagement where nothing else matters. Achieving flow is

immensely pleasurable; since we are motivated to seek out happiness/ pleasure, flow is a desired state that helps us to continue our pursuit of a goal.

How do you know if your goal is optimally challenging? Naturally, it depends on the goal. Try to accurately assess *what the task requires* and *the skills you bring* to the table. A student, for example, who has to take a math course will do his or her best when the class is interesting and challenging. A student who enrolls in Advanced Calculus, without the prerequisite skill, will only be frustrated.

Step 2: Practice Focusing

One effective strategy to develop long-term focus is to first practice short-term focus. A tightrope walker first has to focus on balancing atop the wire for a few seconds if he or she is to ultimately attempt a five-minute walk.

Developing your short-term focus will help you gain more control of your attention and full engagement in achieving your short-term goals. Long-term focus, on the other hand, like high beams in a car that help you see a distant sign, allows you to see your long-term goal ahead so you can continually navigate and course-adjust to your end point. Short-term focus helps you see what is immediately in front of you; long-term focus helps you see your destination. To develop your short-term focus:

+ Keep your thoughts *in the moment*. Often, a loss of focus is caused by "time travel"—you start to think about the future, perhaps the consequences of your performance, or you journey back to the past and think about previous failures. Either trip takes you away from the here and now, where your thoughts should be focused.

+ Develop your short-term "concentration muscles." Practice the following concentration exercise in your room with no distractions for two minutes, take a thirty-second break, and repeat it. Do it five times a day for a week.
 1. Choose an object, a book, or a scene and place it a comfortable distance from your eyes.

2. Sit in a chair, keeping your feet on the floor, and focus on a particular spot on the object or scene.

3. Keep your breathing at a comfortable pace; pay attention to how the air feels as you inhale and exhale.

4. Be aware when you lose focus or your breathing changes. When it does, snap your focus back to the object and your breathing.

After a week of the above, try this variation, using the same process time:

1. Put the object you've chosen on top of a TV set.

2. Sit far enough back from the TV so you can see the spot you've selected as well as the entire screen.

3. Turn on the TV with the volume low and tune it to a channel that you rarely watch.

4. Now do the initial exercise (above), focusing on your spot and breathing. Remember to snap your focus back every time that you get distracted by the TV's sound or images.

When practiced regularly over a two-week span—a month is better—these simple exercises will help you systematically develop and strengthen your concentration muscles. Soon you will discover that you begin to more quickly snap back your lost focus and increase your concentration.

To personalize your focus, block off a specific period of time, twenty minutes to an hour, and let colleagues or family know you are not to be interrupted. During this "time lock" period, choose a particular focus task, such as visualizing how you will handle a difficult client, or return your friend's tennis serve. Naturally, a task that moves you toward a goal is preferable. In the first case, the goal is to have a better client relationship. In the second case, the goal is to beat your friend. In either case, you are focusing on a task that helps you get to your goal.

Step 3: Be Adaptable—Look for Additional Pathways

An essential mind-set of tenacity is to firmly convince yourself that you will achieve your goals. To do so, you need to know how to get there, or

how to find the resources, tools, and strategies to help you get there. The more pathways you can find to get you to your goals, the more you will strengthen your belief that you will be successful.

Pathway thinking involves "anticipatory coping"—finding ways around the obstacles that you might encounter as you move toward your goals. There are always challenges and obstacles that block our paths. Being able to navigate around them allows you to be resilient in the pursuit of your goals. Having several pathways to achieve your goals will make you more *hopeful* that you will succeed, and will help you stay motivated.

Here is an effective way to develop pathway thinking:

+ Break down your goals into small, manageable steps or units.

+ Identify multiple pathways toward each goal:

 1. Make a list of paths to each of your goals.

 2. Mentally go over what you will do if you run into an obstacle.

 3. Share your pathways and obstacles with others. Studies demonstrate that sharing your goals and expected obstacles with others will generate additional pathways to help you overcome or avoid those obstacles.

 4. Incorporate the thoughts of others into your pathway thinking. Start with the *easiest* steps first, to create small successes that will help build confidence.

For example, a recent college graduate who thinks, *I've got to get a job,* is only going to make him- or herself feel anxious and pressured. In contrast, the individual who starts out with the simple task of making a list of companies and jobs that are of interest is likely to stay more motivated and confident, because he or she recognizes that there are multiple options. That graduate becomes more hopeful. In effect, breaking the task down into smaller steps gives the job seeker a feeling of being in control, a feeling that also makes the job applicant more likely to make his or her best effort in an extended job search, as well as in the high-pressure moment of a job interview.

Step 4: Reframe Obstacles into Opportunities

Tenacious people *reframe* obstacles by thinking of them as opportunities or challenges to overcome. Get into the habit of substituting positive words and phrases into your thinking so that when you encounter an obstacle, you are inspired to overcome it. If you have, as already recommended, increased your awareness of your self-statements, this word substitution will be easy and will eventually become a mind-set that says goal blockage is a temporary condition that can be overcome. In effect, reframing obstacles as opportunities exemplifies an inherent tactic for all cognitive coping strategies—it will change how you think.

Lenny, a successful restaurant owner in Norwalk, Connecticut, whom we met at a food and beverage conference, exemplifies *tenacity in the pursuit of goals*:

"Not a minute goes by that I am not thinking about my goal—running a great and profitable restaurant. You understand? Not a minute, or at least it seems that way. I am always thinking about my goals. My dad ran a restaurant, too, so I grew up in the business and loved the idea of providing good food and service to others. I felt it was part of my family heritage. Sure, I have other goals, like spending time with my family, and staying in good health, but my business goal is where I have to be the most tenacious. It is a lot of pressure to run a restaurant—a few bad days or meals and you can see a big swing in your business. And once you lose your clients, it is hard to get them back. . . . I am always thinking of how I can make it the best restaurant in the neighborhood—that's my goal. I think of all the things I can do better: having an attractive menu, silverware, salt and pepper shakers. I have mini goals that I set for food, beverages, décor—they all lead to the same goal. During a storm, I lost electricity. Now I am prepared for that. I'm constantly focused on what could go wrong. I stay close to my customers, always asking them for suggestions for improvements. I never take [criticism] as negative, even when it is. I learn from them. When business was slow, I learned not to just sit around and wait for it to get better. I innovated with new dishes, and price breaks, and these things did help. I guess it comes down to the fact that I am always thinking about ways to accomplish my goals, and how

to overcome the challenges that go with any business, especially the restaurant business."

Wouldn't you consider Lenny tenacious? He has a meaningful goal, is energized by keeping his long-term goal in high focus, has strategies to accomplish it, continually generates backup plans for anticipated and unexpected problems. Most important, his deliberate focus on his short-term and long-terms goals has become part of his *automatic thinking style*. No wonder he is currently achieving his goal.

Lenny, of course, is also highly *enthusiastic*. Numerous studies in positive psychology show the importance of enthusiasm and positive thinking, the last but certainly not the least important material in your COTE of Armor.

Alyson Podell goes to work at 7:45 a.m. each morning with the intent of *creating* enthusiasm in those she works with at an assisted living residence in Santa Monica, California. The residence is surrounded by manicured gardens and outdoor patios, about ten blocks inland from the Pacific Ocean.

A former actress and singer, Alyson starts her day by giving her "audience" of seventy-eight- to ninety-four-year-olds a songbook and asking them to take their seats. Most of her "chorus line" she knows well, but there are two who are new today. "What are some of your favorite songs?" she asks first-timer Mel, who is in his late seventies with a host of age-related ailments, and Sara, a woman in her early eighties who was recently widowed. Chitchat fills the room, which gradually grows noisier. By 8:15 Alyson formally begins, instructing the thirty people in the room to "Please open your sheet music and follow my direction." For the next forty-five minutes, she conducts them as they sing songs from *West Side Story*. Her direction is deliberate: She builds the rhythm and volume from slow and soft to fast and loud, as this catches her listeners up in the music and they become more engaged and excited. Her hand gestures focus the group's attention to the point where the singers are almost hypnotized. She alters the pitch of her voice, now high, now deep—acting techniques that create subconscious mood changes in her listeners. She now has the group on their feet, mimicking her swaying hips, her beaming face; they shake their arms, dancing in a frenzy that results in that mental dissociation we

call "flow." The festivity is over before they know it. Newcomer Sara, as she leaves, tells Alyson, "I feel pretty, oh so pretty."

At 7:45 p.m. that evening, three thousand miles away, a bevy of Duke University students wearing blue college T-shirts are filling the front marked-off section at Cameron Indoor Stadium in anticipation of a basketball game against their arch rivals, the University of North Carolina Tar Heals; they are about to engage in the same actions the senior citizens engaged in earlier that day. The students are a diverse group, but for the next few hours, they will all share a common positive identity—they are known as the Cameron Crazies. The Cameron Crazies know exactly how to *make themselves feel enthusiastic*. It starts with the noise they make—a full minute of loud *humming* that builds to a peak and erupts at the exact moment of the opening tipoff. Unlike the other fans, the group remains standing for the entire game. When a Duke player is shooting a free throw, the Crazies extend their right arms up, and when the shot is successfully made, they lower the boom with a thundering cheer. They are never silent—they just express themselves at different noise levels—sometimes a slow cheer emphasizing a word, other times a faster cheer, often when their team is behind. The noise, their movements, including high-fiving one another after an especially good play, the synchronization, all feed each other. The intensity the Crazies exhibit in the first minute of play never wanes. They remain wildly enthusiastic for the entire game. Considering Duke's phenomenal home court record, clearly the Crazies help their team play insanely well.

These scenarios tell us some basic truths about enthusiasm:

+ First, it is an *affective state*. How do you *feel* when you are enthusiastic? "Energized" is a common response. Or "excited."

+ Second, enthusiasm is a state of *heightened arousal*. Notice your physical state when you feel enthused—your breathing rate and heart rate, for example. You are likely breathing faster, and your heart rate has accelerated.

+ Third, enthusiasm is accompanied by *positive thought*. People who are enthusiastic think: *I can do this*, or *I love this*.

+ Fourth, enthusiasm is a *behavior*. Few sit still when enthused. Enthusiasm stimulates movement, be it in the arms or legs, face or eyes. How do you act when you are enthusiastic? Most people act engaged and full of energy.

+ Fifth, some enthusiastic responses are universal across cultures— a smile, clapping—and are hardwired into us. A crowd in Brazil *cheers* when their soccer team wins, just like the Cameron Crazies do when the Duke University team wins another basketball game.

+ Sixth, and most important, enthusiasm *communicates* excitement, engagement, positivity to the people around you. It is infectious. *How* it communicates this information will tell you how to *make yourself more enthusiastic*, and how to *make others enthusiastic, as well*.

The Roots of Enthusiasm

Enthusiasm comes from two Greek words—*en*, which means "in," and *theos*, which means "God"—"in God." Enthusiasm means to be inspired or possessed by God. Like confidence, optimism, and tenacity, enthusiasm has drawn attention from some highly regarded minds. Victor Hugo wrote: "Enthusiasm is the fever of reason." Pasteur claimed: "Enthusiasm is the contemplation of the inner God." Epre said: "Enthusiasm is the invisible, inward, intensity of being."

Exactly when man or woman first experienced enthusiasm is up for debate, but our evolutionary psychology approach tells us that there are at least two *natural generators* of enthusiasm: goal attainment and human attraction.

Think back to our ancestors. A small, tenacious tribe has been searching for water for days. The members of the tribe spread out, perhaps a hundred yards from each other. Finally, one of them comes across a running stream of freshwater. The tribesman who discovered the water feels a sense of excitement—he has ensured the tribe's survival. *Excited* by his find, he signals the others in the reconnaissance party, perhaps raising the volume of his voice so the other members of his tribe can hear him. Maybe he waves his arms to let them know of his success. When the others arrive, they see he is excited, and they,

too, begin to jump up and down, waving their arms and making positive, excited noises.

The same thing happens today when a software engineer solves a difficult problem that has kept the team struggling, or when a sports team scores a winning goal. *Achieving our goals* is our first natural generator of enthusiasm.

Another generator of enthusiasm occurs when two people are attracted to each other. Research in human sexuality and social psychology tells us that mutual *attraction* increases *arousal*. Because we are attracted to people (and objects) we like and/or are interested in, our arousal is experienced as *positive* and *pleasurable*. The couple's enthusiasm motivates them to approach each other. In the same way, we are enthused when we see a film or go to a restaurant that we like. In other words, our *natural attractions/interests/likes* are another generator of enthusiasm.

Among our ancestors, we see an evolutionary *function* to enthusiasm: *to motivate our desire to deepen engagement and develop interest.* To this day, there are a host of broad success attributes associated with people who feel engaged; among our early ancestors, those who were enthusiastic had a survival edge. The same is true today.

The Effect of Positive Emotions

Pressure sabotages our ability to think, make good decisions, and work effectively together. It diminishes creativity.

Some of the powerful effects of positive emotions and enthusiasm are the way they unlock creativity, build team cohesion, and develop long-term resilience. One of the researchers who have contributed the most to our understanding of how positive emotions influence us is Barbara Fredrickson, a research psychologist at the University of Michigan.

In accordance with our evolutionary approach, Fredrickson found: "The broaden-and-build theory is about the evolutionary significance of positive emotions. In some ways, it's best viewed in contrast to the way we typically understand negative emotions. The evolutionary significance of negative emotions is that they get people to act in particular ways, best known as 'fight' or 'flight.'

"But positive emotions are better observed over the long haul. Their effects accumulate and compound over time, and the adaptive benefit is evident later, when people face new challenges and new pressure.

"Positive emotions don't necessarily narrow people toward a specific action, like negative emotions do. Positive emotions seem to broaden people's repertoires of things they like to pursue. They broaden ways of thinking beyond our regular baseline, and they accumulate. And that broadening allows people to discover and learn new things. Experiencing positive emotions then allows people to transform themselves by becoming more creative, knowledgeable, resilient, and socially integrated."

Finding ways to cultivate and increase enthusiasm helps us because, at the level of the brain, it increases our working memory, which allows us to take in more information in the moment. It allows us to see more connections and possible combinations of ideas, which leads to greater creativity. Enthusiasm also deepens our level of engagement and interest—we pay more attention and are attuned to what we are doing and the situation we are facing. We are more energized. And this, in turn, influences the other people we are working with.

Barbara Fredrickson's research also found that positive emotions act to build resources that help us over the long term. "Personal resources accrued during states of positive emotions are durable—they outlast the transient emotional states that led to their acquisition. They build a wide range of different resources that, in the long run, end up functioning as reserves that help people cope and survive. It also acts to *undo* lingering negative emotions; [it] means individuals are resilient and bounce back from situations."

This strengthening and broadening phenomenon of positive emotions is particularly important when you are faced with the long, arduous process of working on a project where setbacks are common and tensions can flare.

The Power of Enthusiasm—Pixar Under Pressure

Ed Catmull was feeling "up against it" in 1998. Ed was a cofounder, along with Alvy Ray Smith, of the animation studio Pixar. Pixar started

off as a small hardware company that was struggling just to stay afloat when they seized on a groundbreaking idea: to make the first-ever computer-animated movie. Much of what you see in computer animation and graphics today began with the work of these two original PhD computer animators. They started their careers in New York, where they found they shared a love for computers and animation and a partnership was born. Many consider them the Paul McCartney and John Lennon of the digital graphics era.

But it wasn't all smooth sailing. In 1998, twelve years after its founding, Pixar faced a great deal of pressure. Catmull calls it the company's "turning point." Three years earlier, they had won an Academy Award for their first animated film, *Toy Story*. And in 1998, they released their second film, *A Bug's Life*, to critical and box office success. But the quality of their next offering, their third film, a sequel to *Toy Story*, was simply not good enough. First, they made a strategic blunder, designing *Toy Story 2* to be a direct-to-video movie. Quality expectations for a direct-to-video movie are much lower than what is expected for theatrical releases. Direct-to-video films have a much smaller budget, and their makers are usually satisfied with B- or C-level quality; *A Bug's Life*, on the other hand, as a theatrical release, was superbly made, with a budget to match. While Pixar's most talented employees—more than 200—were working on finishing *A Bug's Life*, a second team of about 150 people in the animation, lighting, and modeling departments worked on *Toy Story 2*.

A week after *A Bug's Life* debuted, the creative team at Pixar recognized the problem. They realized the folly of their strategy of having a direct-to-video sequel to a theatrical success, but the movie, in its current form, was "a shambles." It was simply not good enough to work as a theatrical release, and it was due out in nine months. In 1998, Pixar did not have the clout to move release dates around. In 2014 Pixar moved *The Good Dinosaur* from 2014 to November 25, 2015, at will. In 1998, if the contract called for a release date in nine months, it meant nine months, or the movie didn't get released.

So Ed Catmull and the leadership team at Pixar were challenged to make a difficult and courageous decision: to scrap the existing footage. "We threw it away—and we decided to remake [the film] as

a theatrical production. The problem was that nine months was not nearly long enough."

In animation, while there is a lot of pressure throughout the project, it grows in intensity as production approaches the release date. Marketing partners rely on you in order to get their own work created to match the timing of the release date. Theaters are waiting for the film. A theatrical release is a huge project that requires meticulous attention to detail, with pressure ratcheting up daily as the release date approaches.

"We restarted this project incredibly quickly and worked nonstop. It was grueling," remembers Catmull. "We put our people through the wringer. We worked day and night, with timing ticking down. One episode told me this was all too much. Two individuals on the team, who were married and who were parents to a young baby, were working so hard that one day the father came to work and forgot that in the back of his car was their baby; he forgot to drop him off in the morning at day care. He proceeded, half-asleep, from the parking lot to his office. When, later in the morning, his wife asked him how the drop-off went, he screamed and ran outside to find the baby unconscious in the back of their sweltering car. Mortified and in a panic, they took the baby to the hospital and were relieved when it was successfully revived [and is now completely healthy]. The baby almost died."

The pressure to get *Toy Story 2* successfully made was not the high pressure of a single moment, like giving a speech or competing in a musical competition or sporting event. It was an intense, long-lasting pressure that wore people down. And it came immediately following the three-year grind of making of *A Bug's Life*, which was ten times as complex as the original *Toy Story*. Story artists drew more than two thousand concept sketches; the art department created three hundred pastels and paintings to capture their vision of the movie on paper.

On such occasions, under such extreme pressure over time, something extra is needed to be successful. That something is *enthusiasm*.

The Science of Enthusiasm

The team at Pixar in 1998 were "under the cosh"—what the *Oxford English Dictionary* describes as "in a difficult situation." For Pixar to be

successful, the team had to think creatively and make an endless series of smart decisions under intense pressure.

Over the past decade Alex "Sandy" Pentland, the Toshiba Professor of Media Arts and Sciences at MIT, has worked on the executive boards of a number of technology companies. He was astonished by what he saw happen to highly talented people and teams when they are under pressure: "People were just behaving completely irrationally. These are brilliant people. They're not dumb at all. So you say, well, what's going on?"

He became interested in how individuals and teams worked and communicated as they struggled to deliver results in difficult situations. He was especially intrigued by the fact that some people were able to inspire others to take action on the basis of something that, if you looked closely at what they actually said, you would not think possible. "How can people say things that are *very* convincing when, in fact, the facts *aren't* in the words?"

So Pentland and his team tried to understand language and communication from an evolutionary perspective. While many of us think of language when we think of communication, for thousands of years, humans communicated through an intricate system of nonverbal signals. "We ignore those ancient signals at our peril," said Pentland. "Nonverbal cues can make unreasonable arguments strangely persuasive. People just believe them because *of the way* they say it. If properly recognized and harnessed, it can make group discussions much more productive."

To study these ancient signaling systems, Sandy Pentland's research group, the Human Dynamics Lab at MIT, developed a new technology known as a sociometric badge.

More commonly known among their research group as a "sociometer," it is a wearable electronic device that automatically measures the amount of our face-to-face interaction, conversational time, physical proximity to other people, and physical activity levels using social signals derived from vocal features, body motion, and relative location. Dr. Pentland's team has built several hundred sociometric badges, using them in organizations to measure individual and collective patterns of behavior, predict human behavior from unconscious social

signals, identify social affinity among individuals working in the same team, and enhance social interactions.

"We have found that on a team what matters is *one person*," said Sandy. "That is what we found predicted success. He or she listens, asks questions, and then moves on to the next person, infecting them with *enthusiasm*."

According to their research, this one person who infects his or her team with enthusiasm and positive emotion "accounts for more *than any other factor in the performance of a team*." In the *Harvard Business Review*, Dr. Pentland described how enthusiasm unlocks the performance of teams in pressure situations, from postoperative surgical wards, to call centers, to innovation teams. "Humans use many types of signals, but what [we call] 'honest signals' are unusual in that they *cause changes in the receiver* of the signal. *Honest signals* is a biological term that refers to the nonverbal cues that social species use to coordinate themselves—gestures, expressions, tone. If we're spending time together, and I'm happy and bubbly, you'll be more happy and bubbly. There are biological functions that transfer the signals. If I'm happy, it almost literally rubs off on you."

What Sandy's team measured was both the energy or enthusiasm on a team and the contagious nature of emotions. When people interact, emotions spread via neural circuits from one person's brain to another's. Emotions ranging from excitement to anxiety can be transferred from one person to another instantaneously, a phenomenon known as "emotional contagion," where emotions such as joy or anger act as a social virus, "infecting" everyone that person comes in contact with.

"Our devices measure these things, as well as how much you face the people you're talking to, how close you stand to them, and how much you let them talk. The more successful people are the more energetic. They talk more, but they also listen more. They spend more face-to-face time with others. They pick up cues from others, draw people out, and get them to be more outgoing. It's not just what they project that makes them charismatic; it's what they elicit. The more of these energetic, positive people you put on a team, the better the team's performance."

When Sandy and his team set out to document high-performing

teams in high-pressure environments, he noticed a "buzz" of enthusiasm in their interactions, even without knowing what the members were talking about. That suggested that the key to high performance had little to do with the content of a team's discussions, but more to do with the manner in which it was communicated. In teams that were in high-pressure environments, such as innovation teams, post-op ward teams in hospitals, customer-facing teams in banks, backroom operations teams, and call center teams, they collected data on individual communication behavior using the sociometers—tone of voice, body language, whom people talked to and how much. But they found that people didn't recall the content of their communication. "With remarkable consistency, we've found patterns of communication to be the most important predictor of a team's success. Not only that, but they are as significant as *all the other factors*—individual intelligence, personality, skill, and the substance of discussions—combined."

It was these patterns of communication—triggered by one enthusiastic person—that explained the variation in performance among seemingly identical teams. What was even more surprising was the importance of this communication pattern outside of formal meetings. Energy and engagement explained "one-third of the variations in dollar productivity among groups."

In high-pressure environments, it is not the intelligence, the personality, or even the substance of the discussion within a team, but the *level of enthusiasm* that occurs *outside of* meetings, triggered by one person, that makes the difference. Research has found that NBA teams with this type of chemistry achieve six more wins per year. The same holds true in pharmaceutical sales: Better teamwork elevates sales by 13 percent compared to what can be accounted for by individual talent.

The Enthusiasm Source at Pixar

If you asked most movie-loving people who is the most successful producer or director of films over the last decade or two, you might expect them to answer Steven Spielberg or Martin Scorsese or Clint Eastwood or Peter Jackson. But the correct answer is John Lasseter, the creative leader at Pixar.

When we interviewed individuals who have studied the culture of Pixar, one theme continually emerged: the enthusiasm of John Lasseter. His enthusiasm made all the difference in the success of their team. According to David Price, who wrote *The Pixar Touch*: "John exuded confidence throughout the process. He brought an infectious enthusiasm to the team. He would kid around and laugh and relax everyone. This was crucial in 1998 when the pressure was enormous. He had this belief that, yes we will get through it. There is no need to panic."

As the *New York Times* put it, "Lasseter refreshingly projects an easygoing, down-to-earth amiability ... the very same freshness, likability, and young-at-heart quality, in fact, that lie at the core of every Pixar feature. These personal qualities, above and beyond Lasseter's technical innovation and first-rate imagination, are the ones that account for his success."

Lasseter, famous for wearing his Hawaiian shirt and organizing impromptu conga lines, is an exemplar of the enthusiasm that was so critical to Pixar's team.

"When they started on the project, John and his writing team disappeared for a weekend and came back and went through the new story with the entire company," David Price wrote. "He did it in a very expressive way—a very positive way. There are some people who speak small—they use small words and small gestures. This wasn't John. He did everything big. Big gestures. Big aspirations. He had a big physical presence and he used a choice of language that was energizing. For instance, he would more likely greet you with a hug and a big hello than a handshake. But all of this was absolutely instrumental in getting people enthusiastic about the project. Remember, for animators this can be grueling work. Many long hours. If you don't believe in the movie, if you don't have an enthusiasm for the movie, it is very hard to keep at it. John thought it was going to be good—and that made all the difference for the whole team."

Ed Catmull says, "*Toy Story 2* was the defining moment for our studio. . . . People and how they work together is more important than ideas. They [other companies] could copy our technology but they couldn't copy our team."

Incredibly, Lasseter and his team delivered on their impossible

nine-month schedule. *Toy Story 2* was an immediate box office success, grossing more than $450 million; it is one of the few sequels that outshine the original. The Pixar team has gone on to create fourteen consecutive number one movies, earning fifteen Academy Awards, seven Golden Globe Awards, and eleven Grammy Awards.

This kind of sustained creativity is unheard of in Hollywood, or anywhere. And John Lasseter's enthusiasm is a big part of Pixar's *creative* success.

Creating Enthusiasm

Many people think that enthusiasm is either something that we are born with or something that is driven by the circumstances people find themselves in. While there is no question that some people have higher base levels of positive emotion than others, and some circumstances lend themselves to greater enthusiasm, we have far more control over how much enthusiasm we generate than we realize. In the pages that follow, we will suggest specific ways to increase your level of enthusiasm, in yourself and in your team, so that when you are in a pre-pressure moment or when you face long-term pressure, you can summon the kind of energy and engagement that will help propel you to perform at your best.

First and foremost, while enthusiasm is often naturally stimulated, it is a *choice*. In any moment, we can choose to appraise a situation in a positive way and be enthusiastic, or we can look at it in a negative way and be unenthusiastic or worse.

Moreover, how we show up affects and infects others. In the middle of a taxing project, we can choose to look for the positive and bring enthusiasm to the situation. We can choose to use our natural expressers of enthusiasm to keep our team focused and creative and together.

By using the strategies below, you can increase the frequency and intensity of your level of enthusiasm. The first two—purpose and connection—have a longer-term application, while the others can help you increase enthusiasm in the moment, in the short-term situations you face.

The Power of Purpose

The Buffalo Bills were down 28–3 to the Houston Oilers at halftime. The date was January 3, 1993; it was the NFL's first wild card football play-off game of the season, played at Rich Stadium in Buffalo. The winner would go on to play the Pittsburgh Steelers. The loser would be out of the play-offs. The Bills and their coaching staff shuffled into the locker room at halftime demoralized. "We were humiliated," said coach Marv Levy.

Perhaps the score shouldn't have been a surprise. In the last game of the regular season, the Oilers had beaten the Bills 27–3. This seemed like a repeat of that game. To add insult to injury, the Bills were without their star quarterback, Jim Kelly, who had been hurt in the last game of the season. The Bills had also lost their starting running back, Thurman Thomas, to an injury earlier in the game.

This story does *not* include a "Win one for the Gipper" speech by Coach Levy that starts a miracle comeback immediately following halftime. In fact, the third quarter didn't start out well for Buffalo. Bubba McDowell of the Oilers intercepted a pass and raced down the field to score another touchdown. Early in the third quarter, the Bills were trailing 35–3.

What do you do when your team at work is down thirty-two points in a pressure-packed play-off game, with eighty thousand fans in the stadium who seem to have lost all hope?

Many of us find ourselves on a team that is down in the "score," however that is quantified. It is in these situations that we need to find some reservoir of energy and enthusiasm to pull ourselves out of our funk and stay in the game.

Fortunately, the Bills had a player who was able to tap into a special source of positivity and enthusiasm that could help resuscitate the team. This player was backup quarterback Frank Reich.

When Reich was the quarterback at the University of Maryland in 1984, he faced a similar situation. He had become the starting quarterback his senior year, but was injured in the fourth game of the season. "I separated my shoulder, and in many respects I felt like this was it, my whole life was going down the tubes. The injury wasn't so

bad that I couldn't play again. The problem was the guy that took my place played so well that when I got healthy again, they didn't want to put me back in."

Late in the season, however, in a game against the University of Miami, his Maryland team was trailing 31–0 at halftime. The coach, frustrated, removed his starting quarterback and put Reich in for the second half. Frank threw three touchdown passes and ran for another, rallying his team to an improbable 42–40 win, the biggest comeback in college football history at the time.

Fast-forward nine years and Reich found himself in the same situation in Buffalo, down thirty-two points in an NFL play-off game. In the halftime dressing room, the team was down; they were being embarrassed before their home crowd. How could they possibly come back?

"Coach Marv Levy used to say that the difference between 100 percent and 98 percent is *more than 2 percent*," says Reich. In other words, it would take much more effort for the Oilers to get that last 2 percent than it took getting the first 98 percent. In Reich's mind, "we still had a chance."

Over the course of the third quarter Reich led the Bills back. After two touchdowns, the Rich Stadium crowd got behind the Bills, and the players became infected by the positive emotion of fans. Momentum is all about emotions and belief, and it had clearly switched from the Oilers to the Bills. "After those two touchdowns, it was too late. Rich Stadium was going crazy and the momentum came to our side," Reich says. With three minutes left in the game, they overtook the Oilers and ended up winning the game in overtime, 35–32. This wasn't just any come-from-behind victory. Frank Reich had just led the biggest comeback in NFL play-off history (to follow the biggest comeback in college football history). Is this simply a random occurrence or was there something about Frank Reich's approach or mindset that we can learn from? What did Reich do? What behavior did he engage in?

What happened after the game might help answer those questions. Reich says: "As I stood behind the podium, typically they just start firing questions at you, and I just said, 'Before you ask me any questions,

I want to share the lyrics to a song that have inspired me this week.'"
Reich's sister had called Frank in the week before the game and told
him about a song she had heard. "She told me it reminded her of me
and wanted me to hear it, so I listened to the song. The song was 'In
Christ Alone.' Basically, for three to four straight days, I listened to it
every free second I could," he says.

On the podium, Frank surprised everyone by reading the lyrics to
the song. "It seemed as if that song was written for that one game in
time," Reich says.

What Reich identified in that moment in the postgame media con-
ference was the importance of *purpose* in helping us be positive and
enthusiastic. Connecting to a bigger reason has a unique way of taking
us *out* of the moment. This is one of the few times when there is a ra-
tionale to actually not be "in the moment," where most approaches to
pressure (including ours) suggest you stay.

"I know football is not all that important in the whole scope of
things," Reich says. He could see that there were things of far greater
consequence than just that game. He was able to take himself out of
the moment and connect to a larger purpose, which allowed him not
to be swallowed up by the negative emotion of the situation. When we
are able to connect to a larger purpose, it allows us to see beyond the
pressure of the moment. That is what Reich did—on the biggest stage
that a quarterback can face, not once but twice.

Tapping into the "why" can be an immensely powerful way to re-
kindle enthusiasm and positive emotion because it stimulates our pri-
mal connection to and deepest drive toward what matters most to us.

A successful entrepreneur we coach who was going through a
tough financial quarter told us that this emphasis—thinking about
the bigger impact their business had, the good work their business
does—helped her get through tough times. A volunteer at a nonprofit
organization who often faces long days and late nights, and who sees
very little of the fruits of her labor, told us that as long as she can keep
connected to the difference the organization is making, she can remain
positive.

So ask yourself: Is there a bigger reason or purpose behind the work
you do? Do you feel connected to the difference your effort makes? Not

everyone is going to feel there is a larger purpose behind their work. But if you can find ways to connect your work to a bigger purpose, it will make a huge difference. You will gain a surge of enthusiasm and positive emotion that can help when you hit a tough patch.

If you are a manager or leader, think of the ways you can connect the work that the people you are leading do with the goals of the organization. Research in organizational behavior clearly demonstrates that employees want to feel that the work they are doing is connected to a larger goal, to something bigger than themselves. When people achieve a goal that is attached to a larger purpose, it acts as a natural enthusiasm generator.

Here is an exercise to help increase your sense of purpose:

1. Take out a blank sheet of paper.

2. Write at the top, "What is the reason I do the work I do?"

3. Write the first answer that pops into your head. Don't censor yourself. Just write down whatever comes to mind. There are no wrong answers.

4. Repeat step 3 until you can't think of anything else to write. Go deeper than the initial obvious reasons that come to mind. It might take you ten or fifteen minutes.

5. Next, survey the sheet(s) of paper. Look for two themes: first, the items that are in some way connected to what *other people* want you to do, whether parents or spouse or someone else. These can be some of the most toxic and unsustainable drivers of our behavior because they don't naturally inspire enthusiasm. Then look for the items that feel more meaningful to *you*. Maybe they have to do with how your work affects others or something bigger than yourself. Or maybe they have to do with values that you want to live by. Circle two or three of these.

6. Expand on these two or three items that are more meaningful to you. Write down *why* it is that they matter to you. Why do you care so much about these things? When do you find yourself working on or doing activities that better fit these themes?

7. Finally, write down a way to craft your work or activities to be more in alignment with these two or three bigger reasons. Include a way for you to hold yourself accountable to this plan.

Connection

Just do what you are told. If you don't want to do it, there is a line of people out the door who would be glad to take your place.

In two sentences this guy crushed my dream. He made me not care about the movie I was working on. He made me not care about the studio. In two sentences.

Given that he was someone whose entire life had been focused on one dream—to work in animation at the Disney studios—it is incredible to think how one individual could have had such a powerful, negative effect on John Lasseter's enthusiasm.

We are born immensely interested in the world. Unfortunately, there are things that *get in the way of our natural enthusiasm*, and we believe it is equally important to look at those things. One of the most damaging things that get in the way of enthusiasm is social exclusion, or not feeling connected. When we feel socially excluded, our enthusiasm takes a big hit.

Think about times in your life when you have felt excluded or disconnected from a group. It could have been at high school or college or at work or in your community. How did it make you feel? What was your energy level like? Were you enthusiastic and positive? Of course not. Social evaluation or judgment is a key part of pressure. Part of the reason that social exclusion is so toxic to our sense of enthusiasm is that, at heart, we each want to belong. We want to feel connected. When we feel like we are on the outside of a peer group, it significantly dampens our enthusiasm and inhibits our performance.

Lasseter's first job after graduating from the California Institute of the Arts was with the Walt Disney Company, where he worked as an animator. This had been his lifelong ambition: to work at the movie studio that put animation on the map. He could not have been more

enthusiastic when he got the job. But according to David Price, "The old guard at Disney didn't welcome young animators like John's input. They were very highly critical and had a belief that these young guns needed to put their time in to earn a place at the table."

According to Lasseter, "I was trying to make the movie better by suggesting something and this senior guy looked at me as if I didn't belong and delivered these two crushing lines."

It was John's first experience at Disney, and it had a profound impact on how he would later manage at Pixar.

According to Price, "The philosophy he put in place at Pixar was to be open to ideas wherever they might come from. All ideas were heard, no matter who said them. People felt included—this was a real team—and this brought great enthusiasm to the project. John wanted the discussion to be open to all people so they felt like they could make a contribution—that they were part of the team. Now, a decision would need to be made—this was not a democracy—and John would make the final decision, but this approach created an incredible connection on the team."

One of the most powerful ways that John Lasseter's enthusiasm inspired Pixar employees was in the feedback sessions they had.

According to Ed Catmull: "We had a review process that was unique to Pixar. Suppose in the process of making a film, you were an animator and you had to show your work to other world class animators? That's pressure. In this creative situation where you were working with very talented people, we found people wanted to hold off on showing their work until it was in a better form. It's natural—you didn't want to come across as less than talented. You didn't want to look weak. The trick is to end that behavior. So we made everybody show their work every day in its incomplete form. Every day, they would share, even if they hadn't made much progress. It changed the dynamics. When everyone shows their work every day, they get over embarrassment, they become more creative."

John would walk around and make people feel connected before and during feedback sessions, and it allowed people to be more at ease, to take the feedback not as an indictment of their work, or an indication of whether or not they were respected or belonged, but simply as a

way to make the movie better. His infectious enthusiasm and positive reinforcement allowed the team to stay connected even in the midst of tough feedback sessions.

"When we are in a state of relative safety—when there are few threats demanding intense, narrowed attention," says Barbara Fredrickson, "positive emotions allow us to pursue our long-term interests. In our ancestors, transitory states of positive emotions led to behavior that may seem pointless or extravagant from the perspective of immediate survival, but that perhaps conferred serious advantages in the long term. That is the function of positive emotion—to tell the body, now is the time—you are safe, so you can stop worrying about the day-to-day worries of the present, and go make true your dreams of the future"

To help your team achieve their goals:

1. Don't get caught in the "task trap"—where you are so focused on getting things done that you miss the importance of building relationships on your team. Getting things done is important, but if it consistently comes at the expense of connection, enthusiasm can wane.

2. Whenever you change the composition or structure of a team, keep in mind the importance of having at least one person who can bring enthusiasm and connection to it. Remember the difference MIT's Sandy Pentland discovered that one person made to the enthusiasm level and group dynamic of a team.

3. Build a plan to keep your team connected. Remember Dr. Pentland's other finding—his research team could predict success by what happened *outside of* formal team meetings. Find ways to build team morale that have nothing to do with the work you are involved in. John Lasseter organized different employee functions, such as movie screenings (they had a yearly "Pixarpalooza"), a car show, and other seemingly meaningless activities that helped to promote team connection. Clearly it worked.

4. Be mindful of the physical space that your team works in. Is your space conducive to having serendipitous interactions? Pixar was very mindful of the importance to their team of connection when they

designed the physical structure of their workspace. They placed the atrium to act as a central hub for the purpose of stimulating and encouraging employee interaction. The atrium contained employee mailboxes, restrooms, a cafeteria, a fitness center. In effect, it was really a "social hub" that created spontaneous creativity sessions, team problem-solving, and collaboration.

5. If you are a coach or manager, you will be faced with having to make a decision about who makes the starting team or who gets more playing time or gets the higher-profile jobs. Remember to pay attention to how you communicate to the people *not* chosen. Do your best to make them feel part of the team and not excluded. This can go a long way toward managing the hit on enthusiasm they will naturally feel from not being chosen.

Establishing a Positive Identity

Individuals and organizations have to earn a positive identity. But we don't need to wait for that reputation to grow organically. We can work to actively *create* a positive identity.

Think of some aspect about yourself that makes you feel enthusiastic and inspired. Is there some quality that you or other people tend to associate with you? When JP was earning his undergraduate degrees, he created an identity for himself related to determination and hard work. He told himself, "I will *not* be outworked by anyone." It was a phrase he wrote on a piece of paper and taped to the back of his door in his dorm room. Underneath it he affixed inspiring quotes with a similar theme. When the door was open, the back of the door was to the wall and no one could see JP's reminder to himself. But when JP was inside, with the door closed, he saw a constant reminder of the identity he had forged; it helped him through tough courses like Organic Chemistry and Neuroanatomy.

You can do the same: Choose an identity or theme to focus your efforts and behavior around. The phrase or behavior or identity you pick need not be of significance to anyone but to you. Feel free to comb through literature, film, music, sports, science, your personal

strengths, special friends, or family members for associations. Think of specific skills that you have, or want to acquire; fashion a nickname around that. An insurance agent we've worked with calls himself "the Closer." He says, "It makes me feel invincible. Every time I see a client, I tell myself, send in the Closer."

Next, create positive visuals around your nickname; they will intensify the enthusiastic sensations you experience and help anchor your new positive identity to your thinking and behavior.

The same holds true for establishing a positive identity for your team. Again, people want to be part of something bigger than themselves; they want to know that their work is making a difference.

It is important that you bring your team into the process of crafting an identity, because obviously they need to buy into it. Choosing an identity on your own and foisting it on the group will likely backfire and breed resentment rather than enthusiasm. Here is one way you can invite your team into the conversation:

1. Bring the team together.

2. Initiate a discussion about what people see as the purpose of the team. Why does their work matter? To whom? What is the group's or organization's larger purpose? Do you do really great work? What difference does it make? You can broaden the discussion to the values of the organization or team. Talk about how the team works together. All of this can lead to themes that your team can use to craft a larger group identity.

3. Have the team come up with a name that communicates their purpose and stimulates their connectedness and enthusiasm.

This process of creating an identity feeds into the second factor that plays into enthusiasm: connection.

In-the-Moment Enthusiasm Strategies

In the opening pages of this chapter, we saw how Alyson Podell and the Cameron Crazies helped to create enthusiasm because of their zany antics. There is a reason for this: *Actions create feelings.*

Conventional wisdom and research suggests that feelings motivate us to action; but there are numerous more recent studies that support the James Lange theory of emotion—that we induce *our feelings from the actions* we perform. We know that we feel scared because we are running; we know we are anxious by our fidgeting, nail biting, and foot tapping; we know we feel enthused because we are cheering, waving, and moving our bodies in a highly energetic way.

In one research study, a subject was told to act angry, anxious, euphoric, or depressed; the individual inevitably ended up feeling the way he or she was acting. In another study, a "confederate" (an individual who is "planted" by the researchers to act a certain way as part of the study), unbeknownst to the other subjects, was only acting out a particular emotion. The subjects in the study who interacted with the confederate began to act similarly and to feel the same emotion. The point is that simply *acting enthusiastically* will make you *feel enthusiastic.* The elderly residents in Santa Monica who are lucky enough to interact with Alyson Podell on a daily basis feel her level of enthusiasm, as do those fans at the Cameron Center on the campus of Duke University.

Before a high-pressure situation, first *gauge* your level of enthusiasm—whether you are meeting with a client or embarking on a first date. Once you have gauged your level of enthusiasm, ask yourself if you need to amp it higher. The techniques below will help you to do that.

Beforehand, Engage in Enjoyable Activities

Engaging in enjoyable activities is a natural generator of enthusiasm. Studies show that enthusiasm generated that way creates arousal long after the enjoyable activity is concluded. The "carry-over arousal" will give you a sense of heightened enthusiasm that might just make subsequent high-pressure tasks more tolerable and help you to perform them more effectively.

Another strategy is to do something fun the night before a big meeting or performance, to put yourself in a positive mood. Athletes often describe the enjoyable activities they engage in a day or two

before a championship game. Those activities create positive arousal, which helps combat the anxiety that accompanies the first pitch, tip-off, or kickoff.

Walk, Dance, Move

Surprisingly, simply moving our bodies increases our enthusiasm, arousal, and creativity. A recent study at Stanford University showed that an activity as simple as walking has a carry-over arousal effect that increases creativity.

"Many people anecdotally claim they do their best thinking when walking. We finally may be taking a step, or two, toward discovering why," Marily Oppezzo and Daniel Schwartz wrote in a study published recently in the *Journal of Experimental Psychology: Learning, Memory, and Cognition*. The overwhelming majority of the participants were found to be more creative while walking than while sitting; their creative output increased by an average of 60 percent, according to the study.

More important, the effects of walking lingered long *after the walk had ended*. Participants were tested after they had completed the sitting or walking component of the study; walking improved people's ability to generate creative ideas even when they sat down after the walk. So if you have an important meeting ahead to brainstorm ideas, go for a five- to ten-minute walk beforehand.

Show us a person who feels like he or she is "cutting a rug"—fully engaged in dancing—and we will show you an enthusiastic person. You don't need to be convinced that when you dance you feel enthused. While you might at first feel awkward at weddings and parties, once you're up, you're up! Natural enthusiasm expressions, such as celebratory movement, exciting human contact, "eye dancing," increased arousal, couched in a positive context, all combine and strengthen one another. Factor in your dance partner, and the experience, via emotional contagion, is magnified. You may feel as if you are dancing on air. To ratchet up your enthusiasm before a meeting or presentation, try adding a three-second dance routine in your office to pump yourself up.

So get active before you need to perform. If you are at the end of a weeklong meeting and you need to give a presentation and are feeling lethargic, find a set of stairs and walk them for five to ten minutes. We do this ourselves before we give presentations, and it helps us show up with more energy and enthusiasm, and hopefully results in a more powerful keynote presentation.

Play Music

Whenever a baby is born, Norwalk Hospital broadcasts a lullaby over its loudspeaker; big smiles cross the faces of the staff, and they become instantly enthused. New York Mets baseball players bring their own music to the ballpark as a way to jazz themselves up. The stadium organist plays the familiar notes that signal the home crowd to "charge" as a way to rev up the crowd's enthusiasm.

Music can be a natural mood enhancer. Studies in audiology and music physiology show that playing "simulative" music can raise our arousal levels for an hour or more. Music emotions are universal; music can inspire feelings of sadness, happiness, anger, and fear, whatever your cultural background.

Give yourself a dose of enthusiasm by listening to music that inspires and excites you.

+ Turn up the volume—use headphones if necessary.
+ Music with a fast tempo can help get you moving.
+ Songs with a strong, steady beat can help to stimulate your mind and body.
+ Singing along can give you added energy if the lyrics make you *feel* good.

Speak with Enthusiasm

Part of John Lasseter's effectiveness with the animators and production people under him was a result of the energy and enthusiasm he conveyed in speaking with them. This is something you can incorporate as well. Remember to:

- Avoid speaking in a monotone.
- Use positive, descriptive, emotional language: "You look great," "That is a brilliant sketch!"
- Speak forcefully, with energy.
- Use inflection.

Ask your staff or family or friends to let you know when you sound enthusiastic. You will learn also from your own actions and from observation of others. Start your next meeting by having each team member talk about his or her job for one minute—enthusiastically!

Laugh and Smile

Since the dawn of history, laughing has been an enthusiasm builder—it stimulates the production of endorphins that creative *positive physical arousal* or "internal jogging." When you laugh, you also tend to smile, another enthusiasm builder. You can increase the frequency of your laughter simply by paying attention to silly things you or others do, or by reliving funny experiences. We can each get very serious as adults when we face what feels like relentless pressure at work or at home. By choosing to laugh more, you will increase your level of enthusiasm and also feel better. Remember, acting a feeling helps to *create* that feeling. In a number of studies of college students, customer service reps, and surgical recovery patients, increasing the frequency and duration of their laughing and smiling resulted in those around them feeling less distressed and more energized. The people around you, whom you work with and live with, will appreciate it.

Recall Positive Events from Your Past

In effect, you are using enthusiasm from past events to foster enthusiasm in the here and now. Many marriage counselors find that getting their clients to speak of positive memories from the couple's past helps them to feel more engaged and connected with each other. List some of

your favorite memories or accomplishments on an index card; keep it on your desk to remind yourself of positive things to think about when you feel yourself dragging.

Clap

Do you recall the film *Hoosiers?* It's a story based on a small Indiana high school's basketball team that goes on to win the state championship in 1952. Academy Award–winner Gene Hackman plays the team's coach. Before each game, he gets his team in a huddle and has them clap at a feverish pace—and then lets them take the court—with great enthusiasm! Look at the halftime basketball breaks that are televised on ESPN: Every one ends with a "Hack" imitation.

Clapping is a percussive sound—one that is made by an object being struck or rubbed by hand. Next to the human voice, percussive sound is considered to be the earliest man-made sound. It is a natural enthusiasm builder that combines sound and movement to amp up your good feeling. We clap when we see a great performance or receive exciting news. Clapping (before horns) may have been used early on as a signal to communicate *success* (we don't clap when we are scared or when our team performs poorly), as sound travels pretty quickly. The more positive we feel, the faster we clap, and this physical activity heightens our positive arousal. The louder the clap, the more inspired we feel. (We rarely applaud loudly and feverishly for mediocrity.)

In high-pressure situations, enthusiasm has a vital role to play in helping us stay in the game. Our level of enthusiasm *broadens* our perspective—allowing us to see more options and better utilize our resources, helping us be more resilient and better able to bounce back from setbacks. It starts by recognizing that the level of enthusiasm we experience is a choice. We have the power to decide what we focus on every moment of every day. When we focus on our purpose, stay connected (and keep others on our team connected), and use some of the short-term enthusiasm strategies, we take charge of that choice, and we not only increase our level of energy and enthusiasm, but we directly impact all of those around us, both at work and at home.

Maintaining Your COTE of Armor

We won't be redundant by summing up key points that we have already made. Instead, we conclude by providing four simple actions we'd like you to do every day to maintain, strengthen, and polish your COTE of Armor. Taken together, the actions encapsulate the attitudes and skills we've presented. Be warned: Failure to do them daily will rust your COTE.

Affirm Your Self
Be Positive Every Day
Commit to Your Best
Celebrate

These four simple actions will give you your best possible life. You can ride with the Four Horsemen!

Over the last decade, JP's organization, the Institute for Health and Human Potential (IHHP), has conducted numerous research projects to better understand the factors that influence human behavior and performance. More than 250,000 people from more than 75 countries have participated in their various surveys and research. The institute does this so that its performance and leadership strategies are anchored in science yet still applicable and resonant to the challenges most individuals face in organizations today. The goal is to help individuals and organizations perform more effectively under pressure in order to be their *best when it matters most.*

One of the studies they have conducted over the past seven years asks the following question: Among individuals operating in high-pressure environments, what differentiates those who are better able to manage pressure and perform effectively from those who are not? The data has provided rich revelations and served as the building block for IHHP's learning program, the Science of Leadership Under Pressure, as well as being integrated into this book. We've included some general details. Those who want more complete information should contact IHHP.

The Study

Using the proprietary EI360 instrument,* a multi-rater assessment tool used in the Science of Leadership Under Pressure learning program, the team at IHHP assessed more than twelve thousand individuals (12,256).

Individuals came from a variety of IHHP's clients around the world (twenty-five countries in total), representing organizations as diverse as the US Army and Navy, HBO, Credit Suisse, Merck, New York Presbyterian Hospital, Johnson & Johnson, Marriott, and Orlando Magic, among many others.

A "360" or multi-rater tool asks people (up to sixteen) who are close to the individual being evaluated to anonymously assess that person on a number of behaviors, qualities, and competencies. Each of the 12,256 individuals in our study was assessed by his or her manager, direct reports, peers, clients, and even family and friends. In other words, people "all around" the individual (360 degrees), who interact most frequently with him or her, assessed how that person operated in difficult, pressure-filled environments. Each individual being rated also rated him- or herself using the same questions.

Data Analysis

We analyzed the behaviors of the top 10 percent and the bottom 10 percent and compared it to each group's performance. Performance criteria included a comparison to others in the individual's work environment ("when compared to others how good is the employee") as well as how effective the individual was at working on a team, developing people, and managing people or leading people.

The analysis strongly suggested clear patterns that characterized

* The reliability of the EI360 scale for both participants and managers is very high (alpha = .93 and .96 respectively). Reliability of an assessment tool is the degree to which an assessment tool produces stable and consistent results. The EI360 does this very well. Validity refers to how well a test measures what it is purported to measure, and the EI360 has been found to have high validity.

the individuals in the top 10 percent and enabled them to be more effective at managing and performing under pressure.

The Big 10

Items that were most highly correlated with performing under pressure are found below. We call them the Big 10 because they have an outsized influence on performing under pressure. Statistically, each item has high correlations with performance. Correlation between sets of data is essentially a measure of how well the two sets of data are related; the most common measure of correlation in statistics is the Pearson correlation. A Pearson correlation in the range of .405 to .519, which is what these items possess, is considered significant. In other words, these behaviors are highly correlated to performing under pressure. So there is a good chance that if you get better at these behaviors, you will get a lift in your performance under pressure. It is also true that if you increase your effectiveness in one behavior, you will improve in others. If you analyze each item, you can see its influence throughout the COTE of Armor and in the short-term pressure solutions found in Part 2.

If you would like to measure yourself using this tool, you can go to PressureBook.com to self-assess. You also have the option of getting your manager to assess you on these questions.

Big 10:

+ Does not become defensive when criticized

+ Can stay calm under pressure

+ Handles setbacks effectively

+ Manages anxiety, stress, anger, and fear in pursuit of a goal

+ Utilizes criticism and other feedback for growth

+ Is positive

+ Maintains a sense of humor

+ Tries to see things from another's perspective

+ Recognizes how his or her behavior affects others
+ Airs grievances skillfully

Career Advancement

An additional analysis that was part of this study was to look at the behaviors that were most highly correlated with career advancement in high-pressure environments. There were three items or behaviors that were found to best predict *career advancement* (most promotions over the course of a year) (correlations were in the range of .408–.456):

+ Can listen without jumping to judgment
+ Is aware of his or her emotions
+ Can freely admit to making a mistake

Again, you can go to PressureBook.com to self-assess or get your manager to assess you on these items.

Why You Want Others to Assess You

An interesting finding from this study was how poorly individuals perceive and rate their own behavior and performance. In our data, we found that an individual's self-ratings were *not* related to performance; some of those who gave themselves the *highest* ratings had the *lowest* performance as judged by their managers. For those more psychologically inclined, we found that self-assessment predicts only 2.6–4.2 percent of variance. This is a very small correlation.

The negligible correlation strongly suggests that how an individual perceives him- or herself and rates his or her behaviors is *not* related to that individual's performance. You could say that people are "blind" to the behavior they engage in and/or are not aware of the impact their behavior has on the people around them. Certainly they do not see how their behavior affects their performance. As you learned throughout the book, this makes sense: When we are under pressure, we lose working memory, become mentally rigid, and do not see the situation or our behavior in an objective way. The takeaway is to know that *you*

need others. Getting other people's feedback and using 360 assessments is critical if you want to improve your awareness and performance. This is one of the reasons we suggest in Part 3 that there is value in creating a "personal board of directors" as a means of getting important feedback and building your confidence. Only others can give you the feedback that will help you improve performance.

WEISINGER PRESSURE ASSESSMENT AND INVENTORY (WPAI)

The Weisinger Pressure Assessment and Inventory is a clinical assessment tool that is designed to increase your awareness of your "pressure experience" for the purpose of enhancing your pressure management skills. The WPAI can be used individually or as an "activity" to stimulate pressure discussions among your staff and team.

The collection of responses can give you and your organization valuable information that will help human resource professionals and those charged with organizational development and training identify the pressure needs of the organization, which can be used to formulate individual and organizational interventions for learning and applying pressure management skills.

The Inventory is also useful in learning differences and similarities in how pressure impacts various organizational operations, such as sales, marketing, advertising, and customer service.

The WPAI consists of three parts:

Part I: Pressure Revelations: *to increase your awareness of how you experience and think about pressure*
Part II: Pressure Assessment: *to increase your awareness of how pressure affects your performance*
Part III: Pressure Analysis: *to help you respond to your pressure moments more effectively*

There are no "correct" answers. The more complete and reflective you are with your responses, the more the Pressure Inventory can assist you in developing pressure management skills.

Pressure Revelations

1. Quickly list your first five associations to "pressure."

2. Reflect upon your pressure associations. What do they reveal about how you experience pressure?

3. Reflect upon the impact that pressure has had in your life. How has it impacted you? What decisions did it influence?

4. What are the differences between your personal and professional pressures?

Pressure Assessment

1. Rate each of your pressure needs from low (1) to high (9):
 * Perform better under pressure ____
 * Reduce daily pressure feelings ____
 * Overcome fear of pressure ____

2. How do you typically perform under pressure? Circle response.
 * Worse than usual
 * As usual
 * Better than usual

3. Where do you stand on the following? Would you rather:
 Minimize anxiety (1) Increase security (9)
 Avoid rejection (1) Gain acceptance (9)
 Avoid losing (1) Try to win (9)

4. Rate each situation from low pressure (1) to high pressure (9):
 * Being interviewed for a position
 * Giving a presentation
 * Taking a performance appraisal
 * Managing a group project
 * Receiving a performance appraisal
 * Sales call

+ Crucial conversation with a colleague
+ Working on your own project
+ Business dinner
+ Unexpected conference call with clients

5. Examine your pressure rankings. Do you experience more pressure in interpersonal pressure moments (performance appraisals, crucial conversations, business dinners, managing group projects) or in spotlight moments (interviews, presentations, sales calls, solo projects)?

6. Reflect upon why you feel pressure in your high-pressure moments and low-pressure moments.

Pressure Analysis

1. Describe a high-pressure moment.

2. Rate each factor's contribution to pressure intensity from low (1) to high (9):

+ Importance of consequences
+ Outcome accountability—responsibility
+ Uncertainty of outcome

3. Which factors do you need to reduce to feel less pressure?

4. Describe strategies to reduce pressure factors.

The WPAI is most effective when integrated with pressure management activities that facilitate and develop pressure management skills. For further information, contact the author.

ACKNOWLEDGMENTS

Hendrie Weisinger

The idea for a book on managing pressure was sparked thirty-nine years ago during my internship at the Brentwood VA Hospital. Since then, a lot of people have helped develop the idea into a reality, and many have helped me manage the pressure of making it a reality. First group first.

A serendipitous meeting with Dr. Kevin Elko crystallized the idea. When he told me he was a psychologist who worked with the Pittsburgh Steelers, I remember encouraging the "young fellow" to write a book and suggested a perfect title: *Nerves of Steel: Staying Focused When the Heat Is On.* Since he worked with the Steelers, it was a perfect title for him. Since then, Kevin has become one of the most prominent sports psychologists in the world—the chances are excellent that he has helped your team win a Super Bowl! If you live in Alabama or Florida, he helped your team win NCAA titles! That encounter got me thinking, though, about performing under pressure and started my academic quest to learn about the concept of "pressure" and, as a "self-help psychologist," determine the best ways to manage it. If I hadn't met Kevin, this book would not have materialized.

My curiosity in performance and pressure was fueled by my love for the New York Yankees. Now, having transferred myself from Brentwood, California, to Westport, Connecticut, I would watch Yankee games each evening. Every night I saw my team fail to produce when it counted the most. A bunch of "chokers," and I thought, "Why do people choke?"

My questions led me to and through the work of preeminent "pressure hunters"—a mix of researchers, scholars, and practitioners, all committed

to hunting down relevant factors that influence the pressure experience and the best ways to handle pressure effectively. Sian Beilock at Michigan State University and now at the University of Chicago, Roy Baumeister at Florida State University, Darrell A. Worthy and W. Todd Maddox at the University of Texas, Mark Otten at California State University, Northridge, Christopher Mesagno at Federation University, Australia, Stephanie Palmer, and Joan Vickers at the University of Calgary are some of the scholars and researchers who provided valuable knowledge and examples for this book. There are also pressure hunters in Australia, Hong Kong, and many in the UK, such as psychologists Andy Lane and Graham Jones. Collectively, their work gave me a rock-solid foundation and led me to an evolutionary clinical perspective of pressure.

Formulating ideas is part of the process for any social scientist, but so is the application of ideas. For over twenty years, Gordon and Cecile Peters and their Institute for Management Studies (IMS) have provided me the support and opportunities to express my ideas worldwide. Thanks! Also thanks to all the IMS chairmen who have invited me to their chapters numerous times. They have become my friends and thus know I expect to be invited to their home every year.

Ever since I met Dick Rutledge at LaGuardia, he has been introducing my work to the field of project management via the popular conferences he orchestrates. Even better, he has become my friend, who has come to understand the meaning of "Sweet Jayhawks."

Gratitude is expressed to the universities that have given me numerous opportunities over the years to bring my ideas to the outstanding executives and managers who attend their executive education programs, especially UCLA, Wharton, Cornell, Penn State, University of Washington, MIT, and NYU. These opportunities allowed me to crystallize my thoughts and develop important insights via the questions of the class participants.

When Alice Martel responded to my query and asked for the fullblown book proposal, I knew I had something special. What was especially gratifying was her great enthusiasm and belief in the topic. Her suggestions made it even better to the point that the end product was far, far better than what I gave her. That is a great agent!

Next up is coauthor J. P. Pawliw-Fry. I met J.P. at a conference, and after hearing him speak about his coaching experiences with elite athletes and business executives, many conversations with him convinced me that he would have many interesting examples that would illustrate the content I had developed and could help me "spread the P word." I thank him for accepting my invitation to join the project.

Every author should be lucky to have an editor who is encouraging, patient, and skillful. Roger Scholl was all three. Those close to the book know that he had a very difficult task, and he handled it admirably.

I thank all of these folks and the ones I have forgotten due to the pressure of meeting a deadline.

PERSONAL PRESSURE REDUCERS

Briana and Danny—My daily pressure reducers!

Kenny Cinnamon: Some give others chicken soup to reduce pressure; Kenny C. gives me chicken at the mart. Just like he did with my *Anger Work-Out Book*, Kenny went over every pressure solution, making sure I kept them accessible and clever, and he would not let me submit the book proposal until he deemed it acceptable to standards of creative excellence. Anytime I had a question or needed a clever phrase, he was either a text or a call away. He was my 911 pressure app.

Joyce Kaffel: A big sister and a big friend. She has reduced pressure in my life as only a sister can. As a friend, her understanding and humor are essential to my ability to handle the pressures that come my way.

Mel Kinder: From the second I told him about the "book," Mel has been onboard, adamantly telling me "This is not a foolish idea . . . this is a smart idea!" For years, Mel has listened to my thoughts and helped me find the path to take. He has continually reduced my pressure by reminding me to "step back" and see the big picture. Because of him, the Bruins are getting copies of the book.

Howard Norman: Howard was one of my first pressure reducers—he did it by making it easy for me to get opportunities at the best executive education programs in the world. It is always great to speak with him and hear his wishful Diamondbacks thinking.

Lenny Levine: The desire to win creates lots of pressure, and it is

disappointing when we fail. Lenny helps me reduce pressure by always calling me after every Kansas and Yankee loss to remind me that no team can win all the time, not even UCLA.

Alyson Podell: An advantage I have over most is that I can reduce pressure by checking in for an extended stay at Hotel Podell. Alyson makes my stay pressureless by providing family hospitality and admission to the Tanner Cabaret shows.

Ron Podell: There is no better pressure reducer than Ron. In all aspects of my life, his pressure-reduction strategies have helped me do my best when it matters most. He is my consigliere.

Lee Sachs: A longtime friend and Russian colleague, Lee reduces my pressure by keeping me in the moment and on paths that lead to my best interests.

Terry Schmidt: For two decades, Terry has helped me manage pressure by teaching me how to increase my personal power. Applying his strategic management concepts have made my projects more enjoyable and more effective. He has also been most appreciative for being taught the "art of criticism" in restaurants and traffic booths.

Kenny Shapiro: For over forty years, Kenny S. has reduced my pressure by simply being my friend—always a listener, a problem solver, and having a great sense of humor.

Kathryn Welds: She reduces my pressure with her enthusiasm, support, and always positive attitude. Kathryn is an incredible resource—a wealth of information in multiple areas of psychology—much more than my own, but I am smart enough to pick her brain. She brought pressure solution #14 to my attention way before it became mainstream in popular periodicals.

J. P. Pawliw-Fry

John Burroughs wrote, "Leap and the net will appear." In many ways, that is the starting point for this book and my expression of gratitude for those who helped with its creation. Without the profoundly secure base that I received as a child from my parents, Paul and Nettie Pawliw, I would have never been able to take the risks that led to a career and life that eventually guided me to this book. How to say thank you for something so immense? Not easy. My family, Elizabeth, Brigitte, Grace, and Wes, and my sister,

Jo-Ann, and brothers, Bob and Dan, cheered me on at each stage of the process, through some long days away from the kids writing, rewriting, and rewriting some more. Thank you for the time and space to write this book.

Without my partner in crime at the Institute for Health and Human Potential (IHHP), Bill Benjamin, I would not have been able to withstand the pressure that came with writing this book, running our business, and living this life. Half the pain, double the fun!

This is my first book, and it did not come easy. I learned a great deal about writing from a variety of people. Glen Nelson and Susan Valentine deserve special praise for providing me with clear, insightful coaching and editing that helped me find my voice. Heartfelt thanks to them and also to John Mendelsohn.

My team at IHHP was patient and supportive as I labored to make yet "another" deadline. I am sure they wondered if this was ever going to be truly done. It was only with a team this good that I could take a sabbatical from the business in order to fully focus on writing to help further IHHP's mission: helping individuals and organizations everywhere *be their best when it matters most!*

Our editor, Roger Scholl, had the unenviable task of taking two passionate people with two different voices and, at times, differing approaches, and finding a way to make it all work. This was no easy task. His reservoir of patience and thoughtfulness was inexhaustible. The degree to which this book touches on more than a business audience—who is immune to pressure after all?—and successfully delivers on the topic's vast potential can be directly attributed to Roger's steady hand and clear vision. I learned so much from Roger and feel fortunate to call him my friend.

Alice Martel's enthusiasm and support cannot be underestimated. It is easy to lose the big picture when you are caught in the details and unending iteration of the writing process. She was there to make sure we understood our ultimate goal, expertly shepherding this process to its successful completion.

Thanks is also due to the more than 12,000 people who were part of the original IHHP research study that supported the ideas in this book. Some sat for long interviews on top of the psychometric assessment we

conducted, and their stories and data made a valuable contribution to our understanding of human behavior. Likewise, our clients—both in organizations, at business schools, and from the world of sports—provided us the opportunity to refine our strategies and approaches, culminating in deepening expertise in this exciting area.

If we are creatures of our environment, I must send a special note of gratitude to the members of the Toronto Writers' Centre, who supported me in profound ways as they went about writing and working on their own projects. Their enthusiasm was infectious. In the same vein, I had a cadre of support from my dear friends who provided great emotional support through the ups and downs of this process: Martin Perelmuter, Gus Tsiapalis, Hernan Humana, Julia Douglas, Peter and Betty-Lou Fry, and Kathleen Fry.

Finally, but certainly not last, this book simply does not happen without the clear insight and deep expertise of my coauthor, Hank Weisinger. Hank identified the need in the zeitgeist as only Hank can, and duly spent years reading and researching all aspects of pressure to come up with many of the important ideas that are found in this book. I feel so grateful to be asked to partner with him on this endeavor. The old Japanese adage that "All of us are smarter than any of us" symbolized our partnership. It is with great pride that we pass this book on to you to enjoy and, hopefully, take action on.

Introduction

Page 1 **Bob Andreatta, however, is not a fictional character** Personal interview with Bob Andreatta, 2014.

Chapter 1 The Power of Pressure

Page 13 **A professor emeritus at the University of Washington, John Gottman has spent a lifetime** John Gottman, *The Seven Principles for Making Marriage Work* (New York: Three Rivers Press, 1999).

Page 17 **Heidi K. Gardner is an assistant professor of Business Administration** Heidi K. Gardner, "Performance Pressure as a Double Edge Sword: Enhancing Team Motivation While Undermining Use of Team Knowledge," Working Paper, Harvard Business Press, January 26, 2012.

Page 20 **A classic experiment by psychologists John Darley and C. Daniel Batson suggests otherwise** J. M. Darley and C. D. Batson, "From Jerusalem to Jericho: A study of Situational and Dispositional Variables in Helping Behavior," *Journal of Personality and Social Psychology* 27 (1973): 100–108.

Page 23 **David Grabiner, however, probably walked out of the theater thinking,** *Bull!* Personal interview with David Grabiner, 2014 .

Page 27 **Harvard Business School professor Teresa Amabile is in the midst of a ten-year study** Teresa M. Amabile, "Creativity and Innovation in Organizations," Harvard Business School Background Note 396-239, January 1996.

Chapter 2 The Stress of Pressure

Page 35 **We met John O'Donnell one year after he had become president and CEO of Allstate Canada** Personal interview with John O'Donnell, 2014.

Page 39 **Erinn Andrews knows something about this competition** Personal interview with Erinn Andrews, 2014.

Chapter 3 The Nature of Pressure

Page 45 **Months into the investigation, on a rainy Saturday night in June, Julie Howard** Personal interview with Julie Howard, 2014.

Chapter 4 The Anatomy of Choking

Page 59 **An entrepreneur, Kim Adams Nelson, appeared on the current hit television program** *Shark Tank* Personal interview with Kim Nelson, 2014, and Shelly Emling, *Kim Nelson Turned Shark Tank Cash into Delicious Desserts,* http://www.huffingtonpost.com/2013/01/14/kim -adams-nelson-shark-tank-daisy-cakes_n_2388103.html.

Page 67 **"The predictors of who actually gets the money are all about how you present yourself** Lakshmi Balachandra, "What Negotiators Can Learn from Improv Comedy," *Negotiation* 9, no. 1 (2006): 1–3.

Chapter 5 How Pressure Affects Our Thinking

Page 76 **We visited with some of the young new researchers who are doing cutting-edge research** Personal interview with Jeremy Jamieson.

Page 77 **In 2010, Kathryn Minshew quit her job at the Clinton Health Access Initiative** Jennifer Wang, "Inside Silicon Valley's Annual Failure Conference," *Entrepreneur,* January 23, 2013.

Chapter 6 Pressure Traps

Page 82 **Researchers Jennifer Butler and Roy Baumeister of Florida State University** Jennifer Butler and Roy Baumeister, "The Trouble with Friendly Faces: Skilled Performance with a Supportive Audience," *Journal of Personality and Social Psychology* 75, no. 5 (November 1998): 1213–1230.

Page 85 **Princeton psychologist Sam Glucksberg conducted an experiment** Sam Glucksberg, "Problem Solving: Response Competition and the Influence of Drive," *Psychological Report* 15 (1964): 939–942.

Pressure Solutions

Page 109 **After a year in which his team failed to deliver on an already lowered business plan, Jim Breach** Personal interview with Jim Breach, 2014.

Confidence

Page 160 **As Simon Tedeschi walks out onto the stage of Melbourne's darkened Hamer Hall** Personal communication with Simon Tedeschi, 2014.

Page 163 **In January 2013, Simon Tedeschi confessed to using beta-blockers** Simon Tedeschi, "Classical Music," *Limelight*, January 24, 2013, http://www.limelightmagazine.com.au/Article/329982.simon -says-i-admit-to-doping.aspx.

Page 163 **As Blair Tindall, a professional oboist and author of the book** *Mozart in the Jungle*, says Blair Tindall, "Better Playing Through Chemistry," *New York Times*, October 17, 2004, p. 14.

Page 166 **According to Roy Baumeister, a professor at Florida State University** Roy F. Baumeister, Jennifer D. Campbell, Joachim I. Krueger, and Kathleen D. Vohs, "Does High Self-Esteem Cause Better Performance, Interpersonal Success, Happiness, or Healthier Lifestyles?" *Psychological Science in the Public Interest* 4, no. 1 (May 2003).

Page 168 **On the morning of January 4, 1988, a fire erupted at the Cargill fertilizer storage facility** Personal interview with Jim Prokopanko, 2014.

Page 171 **According to research by Kahneman and others** David Brooks, *The Social Animal: The Hidden Sources of Love, Character, and Achievement* (New York: Random House, 2012).

Page 172 **Jamie Rooney, president of the NFL Houston Texans** Personal interview with Jamie Rooney, 2014.

Page 176 **Testosterone predicts which chess player will play better under pressure** Alan Booth et al., "Testosterone and Social Behavior," *Social Forces* 85, no. 1 (2006); in Po Bronson and Ashley Merryman, *Top Dog: The Science of Winning and Losing* (New York: Hachette Book Group, 2013).

Page 176 **Rather testosterone keeps emotions from interfering with our cognitive processing** Paul Cisek and John Kalaska, "Neural Correlation of Mental Rehearsal in Dorsal Premotor Cortex," *Nature* 431 (October 21, 2004): 993–996.

Page 178 **An interesting thing happened when Amy adopted this strategy.** Dana R. Carney, Amy J. C. Cuddy, and Andy J. Yap, "Power Posing: Brief Nonverbal Displays Affect Neuroendocrine Levels and Risk Tolerance," *Psychological Science* 21, no. 10 (January 2010): 1363–1368.

Page 180 **An example of someone who was able to use power posing to**

perform under pressure is slam poet Ian French Personal interview with Ian French, 2014.

Page 183 Studies have shown that when we experience a victory or what we *perceive* to be a victory John Coates, *The Hour Between Dog and Wolf: How Risk Taking Transforms Us, Body and Mind* (New York: Penguin, 2012).

Page 187 In the same study in which Teresa found that pressure leads to less creativity T. M. Amabile and S. J. Kramer, "The Power of Small Wins." *Harvard Business Review* 89, no. 5 (2011): 70–80.

Optimism

Page 197 Bill and Melinda Gates, speaking to the 2014 graduating class at Stanford Stanford Commencement Address, Bill and Melinda Gates, June 2014, http://news.stanford.edu/news/2014/january/gates-2014-commencement-012814.html.

Page 200 In order to help us take risks and work hard, we evolved a frontal lobe P. T. Schoenemann, M. J. Sheehan, and L. D. Glotzer, "Prefrontal White Matter Volume Is Disproportionately Larger in Humans than in Other Primates," *Nature Neuroscience* 8 (2005): 242–252.

Page 201 When we face a high-pressure situation, we will feel a mixture of excitement, eagerness, anxiety, and dread Charles S. Carver and Michael F. Scheier, in *The Oxford Handbook of Positive Psychology* (2nd ed.), edited by Shane J. Lopez and C. R. Snyder (Oxford, England: Oxford University Press).

Page 201 An interesting study using individuals who were extremely allergic to poison ivy Sandra Blakeslee, "Placebos Prove So Powerful Even Experts Are Surprised," *New York Times*, October 13, 1998.

Page 202 Glen Nelson, a professional writer Personal interview with Glen Nelson, 2014.

Page 204 The first study that observed and documented the role of others' expectations Robert Rosenthal, "Interpersonal Expectancy Effects: A 30 Year Perspective," *Current Directions in Psychological Science* 3, no. 6 (1994).

Page 213 Ryan McKay and Daniel Dennett, who did an exhaustive analysis of cognitive biases Ryan McKay and Daniel Dennett, "The Evolution of Misbelief," *Behavioral and Brain Sciences* 32 (2009): 493.

Page 213 Cofounders Seth Goldman and Barry Nalebuff Personal interview with Seth Goldman, 2014.

Tenacity

Page 224 **Angela Duckworth, a professor of Psychology at the University of Pennsylvania** Angela Duckworth and Christopher Peterson, "Grit: Perseverance and Passion for Long-Term Goals," *Personality Processes and Individual Differences* 92, no. 6 (2007): 1087–1101.

Page 226 **What is often missed in the equation are the qualities that "unleash talent"** F. E. Kuzmits and A. J. Adams, "The NFL Combine: Does It Predict Performance in the National Football League?" *Journal of Strength and Conditioning Research* 22, no. 6 (2008): 1721–1727.

Enthusiasm

Page 251 **One of the researchers who have contributed the most to our understanding of how positive emotions influence us is Barbara Fredrickson** Barbara Fredrickson, "The Broaden and Build Theory of Positive Emotions," *Philosophical Transactions of the Royal Society London, Biological Science* 359 (2004): 1449.

Page 255 **Over the past decade Alex "Sandy" Pentland, the Toshiba Professor of Media Arts and Sciences at MIT** Larry Hardestry, "Social Studies," *MIT Technology Review*, October 27, 2010.

Page 255 **More commonly known among their research group as a "sociometer"** Lab description of sociometers found at MIT's Human Dynamics Lab, http://web.media.mit.edu/~sandy/.

Page 256 **"We have found that on a team what matters is *one person*,"** said Alex "Sandy" Pentland, "The New Science of Building Great Teams," *Harvard Business Review*, April 2012.

Page 258 **According to David Price, who wrote *The Pixar Touch*** Personal interview with David Price, 2014.

Page 265 **According to Ed Catmull: "We had a review process that was unique to Pixar"** Ed Catmull, "How Pixar Fosters Collective Creativity," *Harvard Business Review*, September 2008.

Page 270 **"Many people anecdotally claim they do their best thinking when walking"** Marily Oppezzo and Daniel L. Schwartz, "Give Your Ideas Some Legs: The Positive Effect of Walking on Creative Thinking," *Journal of Experimental Psychology: Learning, Memory, and Cognition*, online first publication, April 21, 2014, http://dx.doi.org/10.1037/a0036577.

Ashcraft, M. H., and E. P. Kirk. "The Relationship Among Working Memory, Math Anxiety, and Performance." *Journal of Experimental Psychology, General* 130 (2001): 224–237.

Babyak, M., and J. Blumenthal. "Exercise Treatment for Major Depression Maintenance of Therapeutic Benefit of Ten Months." *Psychosomatic Medicine* 62, no. 5 (2000): 633–638.

Bahrke, S. M, and B. Hale. "Effects of Attitude on Mood Behavior and Cognitive Functioning." *Sports Medicine* 16 (1993): 97–125.

Bakker, F. C., R. R. D. Oudejans, O. Binsch, and J. Van der Kamp. "Penalty Shooting and Gaze Behavior: Unwanted Effects of the Wish Not to Miss." *International Journal of Sport Psychology* 37 (2006): 265–280.

Barrett, L., M. M. Tugade, and R. W. Engle. "Individual Differences in Working Memory Capacity and Dual Process Theories of the Mind." *Psychological Bulletin* 130 (2004): 553–573.

Baumeister, R. "Choking Under Pressure: Self-Consciousness and Paradoxical Effects of Incentives on Skillful Performance." *Journal of Personality and Social Psychology* 40, no. 3 (March 1984).

Beckman, J. "Clenching Fists." *Journal of Experimental Psychology, General* (2013).

Beilock, S. *Choke: What the Secrets of the Brain Reveal About Getting It Right When You Have To.* New York: Free Press, 2010.

Beilock, S., and T. H. Carr. "On the Fragility of Skilled Performance: What Governs Choking Under Pressure?" *Journal of Experimental Psychology, General* 130 (2001): 224–237.

Beilock, S. L., and T. H. Carr. "When High Powered People Fail:

Working Memory and 'Choking Under Pressure' in Math." *Psychological Science* 16 (2005): 101–105.

Beilock, S. L., and M. S. Declare. "From Poor Performance to Success Under Stress: Working Memory, Strategy Selection, and Mathematical Problem Solving Under Pressure." *Journal of Experimental Psychology: Learning, Memory and Cognition* 33 (2007): 983–998.

Bracco, F., and R. Gianatti. *Cognitive Resilience in Emergency Room Operation: A Theoretical Framework.* Genova, Italy: Department of Anthropological Studies, Unit of Psychology, University of Genova. Bracco@disa.unige.it.

Breenan, F. X. "Explanatory Style and Immunoglobulin A." *Integrative Physiological and Behavioral Science* 35, no. 4 (2000): 251–254.

Briones, I. "Young Archer Coaching His Way to Success." *In the News, Eastern Foundations*, May 22, 2013.

Bull, S., and C. Shambrock. "Towards an Understanding of Mental Toughness in Elite English Cricketers." *Journal of Applied Sports Psychology* 17 (2005): 209–227.

Burke, S., and T. Orlick. "Mental Strategies of Elite Mount Everest Climbers." *Journal of Excellence*, no. 8 (2003): 42–58.

Butler, J. L., and R. F. Baumeister. "The Trouble with Friendly Faces: Skilled Performance with a Supportive Audience." *Journal of Personality and Social Psychology* 68 (1995): 649–652.

Byrne, M., and S. Boviar. "A Working Memory Model of a Common Procedural Error." *Cognitive Science* 21, no. 1 (1997): 31–69.

Cadinu, M., A. Moss, A. Rosabianca, and J. Kiesner. "Why Do Women Underperform Under Stereotype Threat?" *Psychological Science* 16 (2005): 572–578.

Carver, C. S., and M. F. Scheier. "Assessing Coping Strategies: A Theoretical Based Approach." *Journal of Personality and Social Psychology* 56 (1989): 267–283.

Darley, J., and C. Batson. "From Jerusalem to Jericho: A Study of Situational and Dispositional Variables in Helping Behavior." *Journal of Personality and Social Psychology* 27, no. 1 (July 1973): 100–108.

Davidson, K., and K. Prkachin. "Optimism and Unrealistic Optimism Have an Interacting Impact on Health Promoting Behavior and Knowledge Changes." *Personality and Social Psychology Bulletin* 23, no. 6 (June 1997): 617–625.

Dewberry, C., and S. Richardson. "Effect of Anxiety on Optimism." *Journal of Social Psychology* 130, no. 6 (1990): 731–738.

Emerson, R. "Mount Everest: A Case Study of Communication, Feedback and Sustained Group Striving." *Sociometry* 14 (1996): 213–227.

Fitzgerald, T. E., and H. Tennen. "The Relative Importance of Dispositional Optimism and Control Appraisals in Quality of Life After Coronary Bypass Surgery." *Journal of Behavioral Medicine* 16, no. 1 (1993): 25–43.

Gardner, H. "Coming Through When It Matters Most." *Harvard Business Review* 90, no. 4 (April 2012).

"Getting Inside Their Heads." *Chicago Tribune*, February 20, 2008.

Gillham, J. E., and M. Seligman. "Footsteps on the Road to a Positive Psychology." *Behavior Research and Therapy* 37 (1999): 163–173.

Glucksberg, S. "The Influence of Strength and Drive on Functional Fixedness and Perceptual Recognition." *Journal of Experimental Psychology* 63, no. 1 (January 1962): 36–41.

Goodman, R. *Performance Under Pressure: Examination of Relevant Neurobiological and Genetic Influence.* Dissertation, University of Maryland, April 2008.

Gopher, D., M. Weil, and T. Bareket. "Transfer of Skill from a Computer Game Trainer to Flight," *Human Factors* 36 (1994): 1–19.

Gray, W. D. "The Nature and Processing of Errors in Interactive Behavior." *Cognitive Science* 24, no. 2 (2000): 205–248.

Grimming, D., P. Huguet, J. Caverni, and F. Cary. "Choking Under Pressure and Working Memory Capacity: When Performance Pressure Reduces Fluid Intelligence." *Psychonomic Bulletin and Review* 13 (2005): 101–105.

Gucciardi, D. F., and J. A. Dimmock. "Choking Under Pressure in Sensorimotor Skills: Conscious Processing or Depleted Attentional Resources?" *Psychology of Sport and Exercise* 9, no. 1 (2008): 45–59.

Hayes, S., C. Hirsh, and A. Mathews. "Restriction of Working Memory Capacity During Worry." *Journal of Abnormal Psychology* 17 (2008): 712–717.

Helsen, W. F., and J. L. Starkes. "A Multidimensional Approach to Skilled Perception and Performance in Sport." *Applied Cognitive Psychology* 13 (1999): 1–27.

Hembree, R. "The Nature, Effects, and Relief of Mathematics' Anxiety," *Journal for Research in Mathematics Education* 21 (1990): 33–46.

Herrera, N. "The Chicago Cubs and the Curse of a Stereotype." *Personality and Social Interaction* (blog), October 26, 2009. www.psychologytoday.com/blog/personality.

Jones, G., S. Hanton, and D. Connaughton. "A Framework of Mental Toughness in the World's Best Performers." *The Sport Psychologist* 21, no. 2 (2007): 243–264.

Jordet, G. "When Superstars Flop: Public Status and Choking Under Pressure in International Soccer Penalty Shootouts." *Journal of Applied Sport Psychology* 21 (2009): 125–130.

Kaufman, C. "Positive Psychology: The Science at the Heart of Coaching." In D. Stober and A. Grant (eds.), *Evidence-based Coaching Handbook: Putting Best Practices to Work for Your Clients* (pp. 219–253). Hoboken, NJ: Wiley, 2006.

Kay, M. Interview with Eli Manning. *Michael Kay Show*. ESPN New York Sports Radio, 2011.

Keith, K.D., and R. L. Schalock. "The Measurement of Quality of Student Life Questionnaire." *American Journal of Family Therapy* 22 (1994): 83–87.

Kolker, R. "Cheating Upwards." *New York*, September 16, 2012.

Kowalski-Trakofler, C. Vaught, and T. Scharf. "Judgment and Decision Making Under Stress: An Overview for Emergency Managers." *International Journal of Emergency Management* 1, no. 1 (2003): 278–289.

Kyle, T. "Preventing Choking and Raising Performance Under Pressure." *Kin* 365 (2009): 2–10.

Lam, W. K., J. Maxwell, and R. Masters. "Analogy Learning and Performance of Motor Skills Under Pressure." *Journal of Sport and Exercise Psychology* 31 (2009): 337–357.

Landsburg, S. "Women Are Chokers: Studies Show They Cave Under Pressure. Why?" *Slate*, February 9, 2007.

Lazarus, R. S. *Passion and Reason: Making Sense of Our Emotions*. New York: Oxford University Press, 1995.

Luthans, F., and J. Avery. "The Development and Resulting Performance Impact of Positive Psychological Capital." *Human Resource Development Quarterly* 21, no. 1 (Spring 2010): 41–67.

McKinney, E. H., and K. J. Davis, "Effects of Deliberate Practice on Crisis Decision Performance." *Human Factors* 45 (2003): 436–444.

Mesagno, C. "Alleviating Choking: The Sounds of Distraction." *Journal of Applied Sport Psychology* 21 (2009): 131–147.

Milton, J., A. Solodkin, P. Hlustik, and S. L. Small. "The Mind of Expert Motor Performance Is Cool and Focused." *Neuroimage* 35 (2007): 804–813.

Ochsner, K., and J. Gross. "Cognitive Emotion Regulation: Insights from Social Cognitive and Affective Neuroscience." *Current Directions in Psychological Science* 17 (2008): 153–158.

Orlich, T. "Interview with Curt Tribble, Elite Surgeon." *Journal of Excellence*, no. 5 (September 2001): 117–125.

Otten, Mark. "Choking Vs. Clutch Performance: A Study of Sports Performance Under Pressure." *Journal of Sport and Exercise Psychology* (2009): 583–601.

Oudejans, R. D. "Reality Based Practice Under Pressure Improves Handgun Shooting Performances of Police Officers." *Ergonomics* 51 (2008): 261–273.

Patrick, T. D., and D. Hrycaiko. "Effects of a Mental Training Package on an Endurance Performance." *The Sport Psychologist* 12, no. 3 (1998): 283–299.

Peterson, C., and L. Bossio. *Health and Optimism*. New York: Free Press, 1991.

Praca, C. "World Champion Highlights Round 1 Winners at 2009 Wrangler National Finals Rodeo." *Praca Events Report*, February 4, 2009.

Ramirez, G., and S. L. Beilock. "The 'Writing Cure' as a Solution to Choking Under Pressure in Math." Poster presented at the annual meeting of the Psychonomics Society, Chicago. November 2008.

Reschly, A. L., and S. L. Christenson. "Jingle, Jangle, and Conceptual Haziness: Evolution and Future Directions of the Engagement Construct." In S. L. Christenson, A. L. Reschly, and C. Wylie (eds.), *Handbook of Research on Student Engagement*. New York: Springer, 2012.

Rubin, Z., and L. A. Peplau. "Who Believes in a Just World?" *Journal of Social Issues* 31, no. 3 (1975): 65–79.

Ryn, Z. "Psychopathology in Mountaineering: Mental Disturbances Under High Altitude Stress." *International Journal of Sports Medicine* 9 (1988): 163–169.

Schlenker, B. R. "Championship Pressures: Choking or Triumphing

in One's Own Territory?" *Journal of Personality and Social Psychology* 68 (1995): 644–648.

Schmalstieg, F. C., and A. S. Goldman. "Ilya Ilich Metchnikoff (1845–1915) and Paul Ehrlich (1854–1915): The Centennial of the 1908 Nobel Prize in Physiology or Medicine." *Journal of Medical Biography* (England) 16, no. 2 (May 2008): 96–103.

Schomer, H. "Mental Strategies and the Perception of Marathon Runners." *International Journal of Sports Medicine* 9: 163–169.

Scioli, A., C. M. Chamberlin, et al. "A Prospective Study of Hope, Optimism, and Health." *Psychological Reports* 81, no. 3 (1997): 723–733.

Seligman, M. *Learned Optimism.* New York: Random House, 1991.

Shectman, N., A. DeBarger, and C. Dornsife. *Promoting Grit, Tenacity and Perseverance: Critical Factors for Success in the 21st Century.* U.S. Department of Education, Office of Educational Technology, SRI International, February 13, 2014.

Shohan, A., M. G. Rose, and R. L. Kahle. "Practitioners of Risky Sports: A Quantitative Examination." *Journal of Business Research* 47 (1986): 237–251.

Simon, A. "Perception in Chess." *Cognitive Psychology* 4 (1973): 55–81.

"Sniffing for Bombs: Meet America's Most Elite Dogs." *60 Minutes,* April 11, 2013.

Snyder, C. R. "Hope Theory: Rainbows in the Mind." *Psychological Inquiry* 13, no. 4 (2002): 249–275.

Snyder, C. R., and D. McDermott. *Hope for the Journey: Helping Children Through Good and Bad Times.* Boulder, CO: Westview Press, 2001.

Spencer, S. J., C. M. Steele, and D. M. Quinn. "Stereotype Threat and Women's Math Performance." *Journal of Experimental Social Psychology* 35 (1999): 4–28.

Staal, M. *Stress, Cognition, Human Performance.* Available from NASA Center for Aerospace Information, 7121 Standard Drive, Hanover, MD 21076-1320.

Steele, C. M. "A Threat in the Air: How Stereotypes Shape Intellectual Identity and Performance." *American Psychologist* 6 (1997): 613–629.

Steele, C. M., and J. Aronson. "Stereotype Threat and the Intellectual Test Performance of African-Americans." *Journal of Personality and Social Psychology* 69 (1995): 797–811.

Understanding Pressure: Stop the Choking. Winning Edge Psychological Services, LLC.

Ungerleider, S., and M. J. Golding. "Mental Practice Among Olympic Athletes." *Perceptual and Motor Skills* 72: 1007–1017.

Vickers, J. *Perception, Cognition, and Decision Training: The Quiet Eye in Action.* Champaign, IL: Human Kinetics, 2007.

Wan, C. Y., and G. F. Huon. "Performance Degradation Under Pressure in Music: An Examination of Attention Processes." *Psychology of Music* 33 (2005): 155–172.

Wang, J., D. Marchant, and T. Morris. "Coping Style and Susceptibility to Choking." *Journal of Sport Behavior* 3 (2004).

Wegner, D. M. "How to Think, Say, or Do Precisely the Worst Thing for Any Occasion." *Science* 325 (2009): 48–51.

Weisinger, H. *Dr. Weisinger's Anger Workout Book.* New York: William Morrow, 1985.

Weisinger, H. *Emotional Intelligence at Work.* San Francisco: Jossey-Bass, 2000.

Weisinger, H. *The Genius of Instinct.* Saddle River, NJ: FT Press, 2009.

Weisinger, H. *The Power of Positive Criticism.* New York: AMACOM, 2000.

Wiley, J. "Expertise as Mental Set: The Effects of Domain Knowledge in Creative Problem Solving." *Memory and Cognition* 26, no. 4 (1998): 716–730.

Worthy, D. A., A. B. Markman, and W. T. Maddox. "Choking and Excelling at the Free Throw Line." *International Journal of Creativity and Problem Solving* 19 (2009): 53–58.

Yarrow, K., P. Brown, and J. W. Krakauer. "Inside the Brain of an Elite Athlete: The Neural Processes That Support High Achievement in Sports." *Nature Reviews, Neuroscience* 10 (August 2009): 585–596.